Praise

"Mike Sager writes with uncommon grace and, always, with respect for those who give him their time. His stories cut to the bone of our common humanity."
> —Paul Hendrickson, author, *Hemingway's Boat* and *Sons of Mississippi,* on *The Someone You're Not.*

"You know those engrossing books that keep you up all night? Don't pick this one up if you have somewhere to be the next morning."
> —*E Online.com* on *Scary Monsters and Super Freaks*

"Like his journalistic precursors Tom Wolfe and Hunter S. Thompson, Sager writes frenetic, off-kilter pop-sociological profiles of Americans in all their vulgarity and vitality. He writes with flair, but only in the service of an omnivorous curiosity. He defies expectations in pieces that lesser writers would play for satire or sensationalism... a Whitmanesque ode to teeming humanity's mystical unity."
> —*The New York Times Book Review* on *Revenge of the Donut Boys*

"I can recognize the truth in these stories—tales about the darkest possible side of wretched humanity."
> —Hunter S. Thompson, author, on *Scary Monsters and Super Freaks*

"This collection of pieces by Mike Sager is just brilliant— brave, written with soul and beauty, and unflinching in the depiction of a real America that needs to be revealed. Bravo to Sager for being one of the few writers left willing to do it."
> —Buzz Bissinger, author, *Friday Night Lights,* on *Wounded Warriors*

THE SOMEONE YOU'RE NOT

TRUE STORIES OF SPORTS, CELEBRITY, POLITICS AND PORNOGRAPHY

By Mike Sager

THE SAGER GROUP

Artifex Te Adiuva

Cataloging-in-Publication data for this book is available from the Library of Congress.
ISBN-13: 978-1481003087
ISBN-10: 1481003089

Cover Designed by: Siori Kitajima, SF AppWorks LLC. www.sfappworks.com
Formatting by Siori Kitajima and Ovidiu Vlad for SF AppWorks LLC
E-Book Formatted by: Smashwords
E-book published by The Sager Group at Smashwords.
info@TheSagerGroup.net
info@MikeSager.com

Always for Miles.

Dear Mike:

You courteously wrote me two letters during the latter part of last year, asking if I'd blurb your forthcoming collection; and I said I would. I have not received the work from your publisher, however; and now, unfortunately, I am leaving New York for the better part of two months, and fear that during my absense (sic) there will be phone calls (and more calls) from your publisher's publicity dept. wondering why I'm not returning their calls regarding the deadline for the blurb being usable for the pre-publication notice to the sales department, etc. I'm sorry about this; it was not for lack of willingness on my part.

PS—Wishing you great luck, nonetheless.

—Gay Talese, via post card, 2/12/2007

"Nothing can bring you peace but yourself."

—Ralph Waldo Emerson,
Self-Reliance and Other Essays

Contents

❶

Todd Marinovich was once known as RoboQuarterback, engineered from birth by his father to be the greatest of all time. But his career never happened; twenty years later, he's a recovering junkie. A cautionary tale of fathers, sons and sports, this is the thirty-thousand word "nonvella" version of the 2010 ASME award winner for best profile, the inspiration for ESPN's award-winning documentary "The Marinovich Project."

Warren Durso is the kind of guy you have to know to love, a five-foot-seven-inch, 175-pound, Italian sausage sub from upstate New York. He has a big cement-block head; his neck is reminiscent of a bullfrog's; life has not always been kind. But somehow, when he looks in the mirror, he sees a man who is six-foot-four with ripped abs. The soul of us all uncovered, the naked underneath.

Love her or hate her, but do you really know her? In real life, for instance, her squeaky voice is low and sultry. Spend three intimate days and nights with Paris Hilton and her menagerie, including Tinkerbell, Princess Pigelette, her boyfriend, her PR person and the rest. The most publicized Hilton since Uncle Nicky, she may yet become the most successful since her great-grandfather, the hotelier Conrad.

by a white supremacist determined to kill some "A-rabs" for revenge. Ten years later, after a harrowing recovery, Bhuiyan mounted an international crusade against hate. His first cause: attempting to win a stay of execution for the man who'd attacked him.

The Zen of Big Balls Pete / 189

As unlikely as it seems, Pete Carroll is one of the winningest coaches in college football history—a Grateful Dead-loving, former undersized D-back from hippified Marin County who believes in Zen philosophy, tweets nonstop, and jogs everywhere he goes, even to the bathroom. Can he make it as a coach in the NFL?

The Demographic Man / 207

Kenyatte Nelson is thirty-one years old—six foot two, two hundred pounds, with high cheekbones and a chiseled jaw that tapers into a sexy cleft chin. He is all of us and he is nobody at all—like the guys in the advertisements he inspects so carefully, he is a picture of who we're supposed to be, the iconic upscale consumer. Take a stroll in the designer shoes of the winner of *Esquire's* Best Dressed Real Man contest.

The Porn Identity / 223

When his wife decamps from the household, leaving his life and his bank account in tatters, our hero takes a much needed assignment traveling the country in search of...retired porn starlets. From Nina Hartley's toy-filled dungeon, to Kay Taylor Parker's spirit-filled studio, to Asia Carrera's split-level hideaway in the mountains north of Las Vegas... How one man got his mojo back.

Introduction

Suspending Disbelief

I'm proud to welcome you to my fourth collection. The pub date coincides roughly with the anniversary of the evening, thirty-three years ago, when Watergate investigator Bob Woodward summoned me to his fishbowl of a glass office in the newsroom of the *Washington Post*. Forgive me if I reminisce.

For just under a year I'd been working full time on the graveyard shift as a copy boy, doing my best to cadge freelance assignments during the days. I'd come to Washington from Atlanta for an abortive, three week stint in law school, an unwitting stow-away on the bandwagon carrying President Jimmy Carter's peanut mafia into town. Previously I'd majored in history with a minor in creative writing, spent two years editing college publications and served a transformative internship at the pioneering alt-weekly *Creative Loafing*. (How clever it felt to be able to say I'd actually worked at a place called *Creative Loafing*—until the afternoon the legendary executive editor of the *Post*, Ben Bradlee, bid me to recite my *curriculum vitae*.)

Now I was perched on the seat-edge of one of the egg-shaped chairs that populated the acre-square newsroom, in the office of this living historical figure. He'd taken down a crooked president and inspired a generation of boomer kids to become reporters. This was the late seventies, an era when journalism felt more like Hemingway than *TMZ*, a calling at once macho and noble. Following his investigative triumphs, Woodward was trying his hand at management. As assistant managing editor of the Metro section, he was being groomed for Bradlee's job.

As you may remember, Woodward was played in the movie version of his book, *All the President's Men*, by the actor Robert Redford. One afternoon the matinee idol would come to visit Woodward in his fishbowl. As it happened there was a copy machine right behind it. The line of female employees—from all floors of the building—waiting to make copies snaked past the National desk and all the way back to Business. The real-life Woodward has a broad forehead and a broad Midwestern accent normally associated with a rube. In person (unless you're being interrogated, as I would be a few years later, in connection with Janet Cooke's Pulitzer scandal—see "Janet's World" in *Scary Monsters and Super Freaks*) there is no hint of his relentless killer instinct. He chewed gum and walked slew-footed, with his head thrown back, like a guy exhaling smoke from an expensive cigar. On his strolls through the rows of desks in his Metro fiefdom, he'd stop at your chair and mug for several full seconds. "Hihowareya?" he'd say, sounding like the church lady's husband. Sometimes he'd ask the same personal question two days in a row—which mattered not a bit, because you were talking to Bob-*frickin*-Woodward! He even showed up some Sunday mornings to play co-ed touch football in the field just north of the Washington Monument, which all of us junior media titans enjoyed calling the Stone Bone. When my parents came to visit, Woodward even autographed a book for them, easing to some degree the pain of my law school debacle, I am sure.

On this evening in the late summer of 1978—right around deadline on Wednesday, September 12 to be exact—I was running on fumes. I'd been up most of the night working my shift on the city desk—answering phones, logging tips, fetching food and coffee, taking modest dictation, running copies of corrections lists around the building. (My favorite stop was the typesetters on four. Most of them were deaf; their furious and animated signing amid the din of the machines and conveyor belts and Orwell-like pneumatic tubes carrying copy in plastic capsules from the newsroom was like a cacophonous silent dance of hands and animated faces. I still have on my desk the two lines of lead type that spell out my *Post* byline, gifted by a fourth floor friend.)

Since the moment I'd entered the *Post's* employ—denied a job at first for my failure to pass the spelling and typing tests administered upstairs in human resources—I'd waged a relentless, if well-mannered, campaign to get myself promoted to reporter. I did everything I was asked and always more—I stayed late, volunteered for scut work, ran errands at actual double time, offered a suggestion where needed, took initiative, sometimes too much. If there was a job posted, I applied—religion news aide, assistant city editor, Moscow bureau chief: the *Post* was a union shop, they were required to interview any union member who signed up. If there was a section that used string-ers, I went to see the editor with a list of ideas. I even wrote a whole (awful) story for the *Post* magazine on spec about "handicapped peo-ple," having been inspired by the courage of my blind cousin. If some of the older editors asked me along after work for wee-hours hard drinking I went. If some of the younger writers invited me to party I showed. At night I'd handle my shift in a tee-shirt and jeans. During the day I'd dress in one of my two suits and find a vacant desk from which to work my stories. It got to the point where these famously driven Washington journos were starting to notice my prodigious work ethic. "Are you sleeping under a desk?" someone asked.

Not to mention the catastrophic early onset of male pattern baldness at age 21. Looking back, it might have been one of those gifts in disguise. Without hair, I looked older and less healthy, more in line with the other sleep-deprived go-getters who were my older role models in the newsroom. All of us wore our eye-bags like badges of our unflagging fidelity to the mother *Post*.

At the moment, in Woodward's office, I was wearing my three piece Glen plaid law school interview suit and no shoes. I'd spent the hot, Indian summer day trampling through landfills in Virginia and Maryland, and a sewage treatment plant in DC, hunting for evidence of U.S. government-owned furniture and office equipment that had been illegally removed by a garbage hauling firm from a storage area at the U.S. Department of Agriculture—part of an investigation I'd undertaken during my off hours. My crusty wingtips were stashed in an airtight film bag in the copy aide station. I know I must have reeked.

Fortunately, in this particular line of work, smelling like sludge is sometimes a plus. Beneath the fold of this morning's paper was my first front-page story. The previous day, I'd sat for nearly eight hours in a windowsill at U.S.D.A. headquarters, at 14th Street and Independence Avenue SW, staking out the dumpsters three stories down in the internal courtyard. Late in the afternoon, my confi-dence flagging, my ass killing me, I witnessed at last the act of theft a whistle-blowing secretary had called the city desk late one night to report. (That I kept the tip for myself instead of handing it over to the night city editor is another long bit; besides journalism, the *Post* was all about office politics, played for keeps by people who covered the D.C. professionals. My first mentor at the paper, Tom Sherwood, had instructed, "People here don't stab you in the back, they stab you in the chest." More valuable training for life.)

When Woodward had summoned me to his fishbowl, I was sitting at somebody's borrowed desk, typing—on an IBM Selectric self-correcting typewriter and six-ply paper—the second day follow-up to my story: The General Services Administration had undertaken an investigation into the theft of the furniture. I was 22 and probably high on methane fumes. I'd hardly slept for the last eleven months. Woodward knew me fairly well; I'd stalked and dogged and cajoled him at every opportunity. I'd even attended a party or two at his house, albeit as a sub class of invitee, a member of the support staff. (And once, at football, I got him with a pretty good cross-body block.) For months I'd written features and small town news stories and police shorts. Every time I scored a byline I'd stolen into this very fishbowl at night and left the clipping on his keyboard with a note. (How many times do you figure I rewrote *those* notes?) Finally, with this investigation, I had the kind of story it took to get noticed at the *Post*. To get noticed by Bob Woodward.

He sat on the edge of his desk and looked down at me, his thin lips upturned into a wizened smirk. His chewing gum crackled and snapped. He pointed to my article on the front page. "You've done what I said you had to do: You've proven yourself indispensable to the *Washington Post*."

I felt faint and out of breath, a little nauseous. I was never very good talking to teachers. "Does this mean I get a raise?"

The bestselling author looked at me peevishly, like maybe he'd just made a huge mistake. "You can have what I get: One dollar a year."

Though it would be some time before I was given an actual desk, business card, nameplate, and phone number—I was too young to care or understand at the time, but Woodward had bestowed upon me this battlefield promotion without the necessary clearance from the business side; there was no actual "reporter slot" for me to fill— I thus began in earnest a period I now see as my six years of journalism graduate studies at one of the very finest newspapers in the world. I remain a proud alum.

Years later, I was doing a story for *Esquire* about the entertainer Roseanne Barr. Once labled television's "domestic goddess," she'd grown increasingly erratic. During the course of an interview at her snow-dusted cabin at Lake Arrowhead, CA, she revealed to me that she suffered from multiple personality disorder. Over the next six months or so we did a longer piece. ("The Multitudes of Roseanne," *Revenge of the Donut Boys*.)

One day I had to call her, I can't remember why. Maybe to make arrangements for our next meeting. As usual I was put on hold by one of her minions for twenty minutes. As usual when she finally picked up, there was no salutation.

"All hate is just fear," she sneered, *apropos* of nothing. "All fear is insecurity."

Over the course of my career, I've met a number of people you might think of as mad geniuses. With Roseanne it always felt like I was a step slow. She'd taken to calling me "You Idiot." Somehow, it felt like a term of endearment. I asked her to repeat herself.

"What are you, deaf now, *too*?"

All hate is just fear. All fear is insecurity.

Warming my hands by the cultural fires of so many diverse characters and groups and settings over nearly four decades in journalism, I've observed how strongly our world depends upon our hate and fear, our cultural stereotypes and clannish platitudes, our political correctness, our mythology and pat misunderstandings, our notions of what is supposed to be true, what is considered to be true, what other people say you should think and do, what is gospel.

No matter where I have gone, by keeping my mind open—I call it *suspending disbelief*—I have unfailingly returned home from every assignment with a new sort of understanding, a new insight, something I'd never have even imagined unless I'd walked without judgment the proverbial mile in someone elses's shoes. You can't know what your neighbor is saying if you're yelling back at him... or avoiding him... or trying to kill him. You have to listen, even if it hurts. At least then maybe you'll *really* know who and what you're dealing with.

Pulling together the titles for this collection— a list on my computer screen, playing idly with different fonts as people do—my eyes came to rest on the headline of my favorite piece in this batch, "The Someone You're Not." The assignment and the headline were courtesy of my wonderful *Esquire* editor of fifteen years, Peter Griffin. When I got the call, I was going through the unexpected breakup of my two-decade marriage. Due to the nasty circumstances, I'd been advised not to vacate my house. Confined here, talking on the phone to Ray Towler, a man just released from prison—in advance of my own release and subsequent journey to visit him in Cleveland—I couldn't help feeling as if Ray and I were on the same path, sharing the first steps of different journeys toward new and, hopefully, better lives.

As sometimes happens in the writing game, I stared at the symbols on my screen for a while and a thought sputtered to life. *The Someone You're Not:* All of the articles in this collection share the same theme—the notion that everyday people, and newsmakers alike, are rarely who we make them out to be. Not Todd Marinovich. Not Paris Hilton. Not you or me. In real life, everything and everyone is deeper and richer and more complicated.

Labeled, lampooned, lumped into category, judged out-of-context, ridiculed, embarrassed, or merely over-simplified, every subject in this gathering of pieces is someone who feels grossly misunderstood, publicly or privately, in one way or another. I think of it as *under*-understood. People just don't take the time. They're too busy being focused on themselves, on the the trials of everyday life. It's just easier to subscribe to the common wisdom. We all do it, consciously or not. The world is too big to have things otherwise.

Thankfully, my editors and the publications they represent—starting with Woodward and the *Post*, and on through today with David Granger and Griffin at *Esquire*—have afforded me the time to look deeply. By learning to suspend my disbelief, I've tried to move past conventional understanding, past stereotypes—past hate and fear and insecurity. I've tried to learn how not to judge—at least for long enough to hear a person out. Invariably, when I do, I've always found something to love, or at least to understand—a way to relate to the essential human core that unites us all.

Mike Sager, La Jolla, CA, August 15, 2012

The Man Who Never Was

Todd Marinovich was once known as RoboQuarterback, engineered from birth by his father to be the greatest of all time. But his career never happened; twenty years later, he's a recovering junkie. A cautionary tale of fathers, sons and sports, this is the thirty-thousand word "novella" version of the 2010 ASME award winner for best profile, the inspiration for ESPN's award-winning documentary "The Marinovich Project."

"So what ended your career?"

The Fallbrook Midget Chiefs were fanned out across the practice field at Potter Intermediate School on a sunny autumn day in Southern California, two dozen eighth graders in red-and-white helmets and bulbous pads, some with downy moustaches and hairy legs, others a head shorter and still singing soprano, none of them yet old enough, in their last year of Pop Warner eligibility, to discount the plausibility of a Division-I college scholarship and a career in the National Football League. Whistles trilled and coaches barked, mothers camped in folding chairs in the welcoming shade of the school building, younger siblings romped; a trio of adolescent females, dressed distractingly, flitted and prowled along the sidelines. Fathers hovered here and there on the periphery, wincing with every blow and dropped ball as if experiencing it themselves, gathering material for the inevitable post-mortem on the ride home.

Into this tableau ambled an unusually tall man with faded-orange hair cropped close around a crowning bald spot, giving him the aspect of a tonsured monk. There was a certain glow on the faces of the four who accompanied him—a man in riding togs, a forty-ish mother with fake boobs, a short guy with a tape recorder, an older man with bull shoulders and a pronounced limp. The tall man himself wore dark sunglasses. His face was all angles, his fair skin was sunburned and heavily freckled, his lips deeply lined; the back of his neck was weathered like an old farmer's. He was six-foot-five, 212 pounds, the same as when he'd reported for duty twenty-one years ago as a redshirt freshman quarterback at the University of Southern California, the Touchdown Club's 1987 national high school player of the year. The press had dubbed him RoboQuarterback; he was the total package. His Orange County record for all-time passing yardage, 9,182, stood for more than two decades; had he played the second halves of many blowouts, it would still be untouched.

Now he was thirty-nine. He wore a T-shirt and surfer shorts, rubber flip-flops. He moved across the parking lot to the field in the manner of an athlete, loose limbed and physically confident—a lanky, coltish, nonchalant stride that revealed nothing of the long and tortured trail he'd left behind.

A coach hustled out to meet the party, the offensive coordinator for the Midget Chiefs. He was wearing a black and silver baseball cap with an Oakland Raiders logo on the front. Around his neck was a Raiders pendant. His name was William Hopkins but everybody called him Raider Bill. "Todd Marinovich!" he enthused. "Would you mind signing these?"

Raider Bill produced a Sharpee and a couple of 8-by-11 plastic sheets, the kind collectors use, with individual pockets and loose-leaf binder holes. In all of the pockets were bubble gum cards featuring Todd in his playing days, number thirteen at USC, his grandpa's old high school number; number twelve as a Los Angeles Raider, before the team moved to the Bay Area. As Todd signed dutifully, everybody gathered and copped a squat. Like a speaking stick, somebody tossed Todd a football.

"Hi, my name is Todd. I'm an old player. I played *waaaay* before you guys were even born." Without his sunglasses, resting now atop his head, his blue eyes looked pale and unsure. Raised much of his life on the picturesque Balboa Peninsula, connected to the mainland by a bridge and a three-car ferry, he spoke in the loopy dialect of a surfer dude. He once told a reporter in jest that he enjoyed surfing naked at a spot near a nuclear power plant in San Onofre, California. "The water's warmer down there," he'd explained, goofing with the dude. The quote circulated around the world. Thereafter, among his other transgressions—nine arrests, two felonies, a year in jail—Todd would be known derisively for naked surfing. "One thing that I am today and that's completely honest," he told the Midget Chiefs. "I won't BS you, I won't lie to you, I'll tell you exactly my experience. Because that's all I have, my experience. I wouldn't change anything for the world."

As he spoke, Todd fondled and flipped and spun the ball. It seemed small in his hands and very well behaved, like it belonged there. When he was born, his father put a big plush football in his crib. Marv Marinovich was the co-captain of John McKay's undefeated USC team of 1962. He played offensive tackle and defensive end, every minute of every game. The team won the National Championship; Marv was ejected from the Rose Bowl for fighting. After a short NFL career, during the height of the Cold War, Marv began studying Eastern Bloc training techniques. The Raider's colorful owner, Al Davis, made him one of the NFL's first strength-and-conditioning coaches. Before Todd could walk, Marv had him on a balance beam. He would stretch the boy's little hamstrings in his crib. Years later, an ESPN columnist would name Marv number two on a list of "worst sports fathers." (After Jim Pierce, father of tennis player Mary, famous for verbally abusing opponents during matches.)

Marv sat at the back of the Midget Chief gathering, resting his bum knee, eating an organic apple he'd just picked in a nearby orchard. His own pale blue eyes were focused intently on his son's performance, as they had been from day one.

"I don't know if you guys have heard of Mater Dei high school, it's a prominent sports school," Todd said, speaking of the perennial OC powerhouse. "I played football as a freshman on the varsity, which was kind of a big deal back then—I was the first freshman quarterback in OC to ever start a varsity game. I broke a lot of records. Then I chose to go to USC and I played in some really big games. I beat UCLA. I won a Rose Bowl. It's quite an experience playing in front of one hundred thousand people. It's quite a rush. You've got the ball in your hands and everyone is holding their breath, wondering: *What's he gonna do next.* After my third year of college I turned pro. Here's a name you probably know: I was drafted ahead of Brett Farve in the 1991 draft. I was picked number one by the Raiders. Farve went in the second round. I played for three years.

"The best thing about it was my teammates. Howie Long, Marcus Allen, Ronnie Lott—there's a long list. A lot of guys I'm still in touch with today. There is something about the team game of football that is like none other."

Having said this last bit, Todd scanned the young faces that surrounded him. In a little over a minute— about the time it once took him to run the 440 (his father's suggestion, the longest sprint event in track)— he had summarized the entire first half of his life. He looked down at the football in his hands, not quite sure what to say next. He gripped the ball along the laces with his left hand like he was going to throw it. His long, reddish-pink fingers brought to mind something oceanic, like a squid. He pump-faked once and then again, and then he took the ball and spun it magically on his palm. "Any questions?"

A moment of dumfounded silence gave way—several kids raised their hands, oohing and ahhing the way they do at that age. Todd pointed the ball at a kid, who asked if Todd had fumbled a lot and everyone laughed. Another kid wanted to know how far he could throw. Another asked about his greatest moment. Raider Bill asked Todd how he got along with his coaches, eliciting a huge guffaw from both Todd and Marv, which made everybody else crack up as well. Then Todd pointed the football at a kid with freckles.

"You said you only played three years in the NFL," the kid said, more a statement than a question.

"Correctamundo," Todd replied, at ease now, loosey-goosey, playing to his crowd, well into the spirit of things, not really thinking about what was coming next, which you could say has always been his biggest strength also his biggest weakness, an ability to exist solely in the moment, without fear or thought of consequence.

"So what ended your career?" the kid asked.

"What *ended* my career," Todd repeated. His smile faded as he searched for the right words.

"My Dad came from the old school."

Thirty years earlier: September, 1978.
The blue-and-white Newport Beach Cheyennes were scrimmaging against the best fourth grade Pop Warner team in Orange

County. After a season of flag football, Todd was in his first year of organized tackle.

Todd was the quarterback, a twig-figure with flaming orange hair and a sweet touch on the ball, even then. Nine years old and painfully shy, he was a head taller than everyone in his class at Newport Elementary, where a white sand beach served as the playground. Todd rode his bike to school every morning, six blocks along the boardwalk.

The opposing team was anchored by their middle linebacker, one of those elementary school Goliaths often encountered in youth sport—genetically gifted, physically mature for his age, two things you can't coach, the saying goes. With the clock waning and the score close, the Cheyennes' coach opted to give his second string offense a chance. In this scheme, Todd moved to fullback.

Over in his usual spot near the end zone, away from all the other parents, Marv's eyes bugged. *Why isn't this idiot coach going for the win?*

The Marinovich family had recently returned from living in Hawaii, where Marv, after six years coaching with the Raiders and one more with the St. Louis Cardinals, had done a two-year stint with the now-defunct World Football League's Hawaii Hawaiians. As Marv sorted out his working status, his family of four was living with the maternal grandparents in their four-bedroom house on the Balboa Peninsula. Once a summer beach shack, it had been converted over the years into a utilitarian, two-story clapboard and faux stone house with four bedrooms. The Pacific Ocean was two long blocks from the front deck; Newport Harbor was two short blocks from the back door, its docks crowded with yachts and pontoon party boats. The peninsula was chock-a-block with houses of every style, from tawdry to luxe. There was the ferry port, the museum, the carousel; a bustling commercial and nightlife district; USC and Raiders flags flapping everywhere in the briny breeze. John Wayne once had a huge house just down the channel. Rock Hudson was here all the time. In summer came the throngs: it was a non-stop party.

Todd's mom was the former Trudi Fertig. The holder of several high school swimming records in the butterfly, she was a late-fifties prototype of the classic California Girl. Blonde, beautiful, and gregarious, a Delta Gamma sorority sister at USC, Trudi was equally at home in a swimsuit or in white gloves—a much-sought after coed who quit college after her sophomore year to marry the captain of the football team. As an NFL wife during the opening days of the Hugh Hefner sixties, she'd become dear friends with the likes of Virginia Madden and Geri Belitnikoff, game gals who fancied dry martinis and blue humor. They called their hubbys "the boys" and weathered their pre-feminist behavior in martyred silence. Al Davis was constantly fussing over Trudi and winking her way. Years later, he'd draft her kid into the big show.

Trudi's father was C. Henry Fertig, the retired police chief of nearby Huntington Park. It was he who'd passed down the carrot top, a product of his German and Irish ancestry. The Chief, as he would come to be known to all, graduated high school during the Depression and received a football scholarship to St. Mary's. He wanted to walk on at USC, but his father, a blacksmith, insisted he work with his four brothers in the family business. As a young cop, the Chief put himself through night school at USC and received a degree in public administration. (Later, to support his growing family, he moonlighted in security at MGM Studios; there are pictures of him with Spencer Tracy, Peter Lawford, Bob Hope, and Frank Sinatra, the last on the set of *Anchors Away*.) Over the years he would become "the most visible of all the Trojan alums," according to an article in the *Orange County Register*. Before every USC game you'd find the Chief, wearing his cardinal-colored shirt and bright gold pants, tailgating in his regular spot on Hoover Street in front of the L.A. Coliseum, the fabled stadium where the Trojans play their games. (Upon his death in 1998, at the age of eighty, the alumni association laid a brass plaque on the spot.)

Following his retirement from the police force, the Chief became the golf course marshal at the Newport Beach Country Club, which was owned by a wealthy friend. He also served as the unofficial mayor of the Balboa Bay Club—known as a drinker and a storyteller, he had a million connections; he knew a lot of secrets, both in Hollywood and around Newport, during a more gentle era when private indiscretions by famous people often went unpublicized. On a summer afternoon, in the thick of tourist season, while watering his front planters, the Chief would get to talking with a vacationing stranger on East Balboa Boulevard and end up bringing him inside to show off his collection of USC memorabilia. "He's giving another $2 tour," his wife, Virginia, would announce ruefully. Among the chief's most prized possessions: a collection of pro helmets from former Trojans who made NFL teams and an autographed jersey from USC Heisman winner O.J. Simpson. The Chief was particularly close to Todd and his sister Traci, another redhead two years older. They called him Poppa. He taught Todd to ride his bike while Marv was away at summer football camp; he also gave the boy his first taste of USC tailgate parties and professional boxing. As young as six, the Chief was giving Todd mini-cans of Coors Beer. Later, during the middle school years, as Marv turned his focus increasingly to Todd, the Chief taught Traci to play golf. She became the first high school girl in Orange County to letter on a boy's varsity golf team.

The Chief's son, Trudi's brother, was Craig Fertig. Craig was the third-string quarterback on Marv Marinovich's 1962 Championship team. Two years later, as a senior starter, he was the architect of one of the greatest Trojan victories of all time, a comeback win in 1964 against arch-rival, undefeated Notre Dame. After that memorable season, Fertig was asked to join McKay's staff as an assistant coach. He would be associated with the program for nearly fifty years as a coach, assistant athletic director, and TV commentator until his death, the result of organ failure due to acute alcoholism. Most of his last days would be spent drinking in the Chief's trophy room, next door to the spare bedroom in which he was living on the ground floor of the Balboa house.

The saga of the Marinovich clan was no less epic: Marv grew up on a three thousand-acre ranch in Watsonville, in northern California. On a clear day, from a high spot on the property, you could see all the way south to Monterey. The spread was owned by Marv's grandfather, J.G. Marinovich, a Croatian who had risen to the rank of general in the Russian army. According to family lore, J.G. was a cruel man who'd overseen the battlefield amputation of his own left arm. At some point, he immigrated to California and bought land. A few years later he made a fortune selling it to the railroad.

J.G. had three sons. Marv's dad was the middle. Mervin "Slip" Marinovich was a tender, easygoing man who lived his entire life under the thumb of his powerful father. In his youth, Slip was a star athlete, a two-way lineman at Watsonville High, one of the few freshmen in the school's history to go straight to varsity. Slip's coach at Watsonville also coached Marv (and the sons of many other alums). He would often regale Marv's team with inspirational stories about Slip, stressing his drive and his heart. Ironically, Slip Marinovich died at age forty-two of a ruptured heart valve. He could have been saved by a new surgery involving the transplantation of a pig's heart valve. The long time farm boy declined.

Marv and his younger brother and sister, Gary and Gloria, grew up on the ranch with their extended relations. There were separate houses for each family, three lakes, huge flat fields for pickup games, a remote cabin to which Marv and Gary could ride on horseback and stay a week unsupervised. Marv's dad never required his son to work as his own father had required him; Marv remembers rainy days making huge pyramids in the barn with bales of hay, chicken fights in the lake with the neighbor kids, wrestling with three thousand-pound show bulls in the corral—trying to back them up, wrestle them to the ground.

Like his dad, Marv played the line both ways as a high school freshman. Marv's senior year his team went undefeated. Marv was selected to play in an all-star game held at the Rose Bowl in Pasadena. Following that game, he and five other mates from the victorious northern team were recruited to play for Santa Monica Community College. That fall, SMCC went undefeated and won the 1958 National Junior College Championship. From there Marv transferred to USC.

After an impressive sophomore season, in which he moved up 15 slots on the depth chart to start at tackle, Marv was suspended from the team early in his junior year for fighting with a teammate. Since his youth, when he frequented a gym in Watsonville and learned to box and wrestle from an old pug known as the Greek, Marv had a reputation as a brawler. In high school he was the two-time state heavyweight wrestling champion. By college he was six foot three, 240, though in the program they listed him as 225, so he would have an additional edge against opponents.

Marv loved to fight. He'd fight anybody, any time. People said it was like he had a switch; trip it and he was unstoppable. As it would turn out, this was a great quality in a football player, but not so great in real life. Junior year, when Marv went home to Watsonville to serve out his suspension, he spent the major part of his exile at the ranch carving a large bust of a Trojan from a piece of redwood gathered off the acreage—he'd already taken a number of fine arts courses at school; art was a secret passion that would follow him the rest of his days. Some years later, when his grandfather J.G. harvested all the redwoods on the property to help build a local college, Marv was so incensed that he never again spoke to the old man.

Upon his return to USC, second semester junior year, Marv begged Coach McKay to allow him back on the team for spring practice. McKay refused. Marv implored. Finally, McKay allowed him to play on the scrub team against the first string. Marv wrecked such havoc at practice—witnesses say he was actually foaming at the mouth—that McKay called him into the office and reinstated him to varsity. "We give up," the famous coach told Marv. "We don't want you to go against us anymore—we can't afford the injuries." Though McKay showed open contempt for Marv thereafter, the players voted him their captain; McKay, flummoxed, broke tradition and appointed a co-captain as well. The ensuing undefeated 1962 season is in the record books. Marv was awarded USC's Most Inspirational Player award and went to the All Star game at the Hula Bowl. Despite his personal feelings, McKay called him "one of the nation's finest and most unheralded lineman," according to news accounts from the time.

Marv was drafted by the Los Angeles Rams of the NFL and by the Oakland Raiders of the upstart AFL. To prepare for the mission that was ahead—making the pros and kicking everyone's ass—Marv did as he had always had done. "I ran, lifted, pushed the envelope cardiovascular-wise and aerobic-wise, flexibility-wise. I maximized my effort to the Nth degree," he recalled. One exercise from his regime: thirteen hundred-pound squats, with the bar full of forty-five-pound plates, with one hundred-pound dumbbells chained and hanging on the ends because he couldn't get any more plates to fit. "And then I would rep out," he recalled. "Unfortunately, I hadn't yet figured out that speed and flexibility was more important than weight and bulk. I over-trained so intensely that I never recovered."

After a disappointing first year with the Raiders, Marv walked out of camp during the summer of his second season, disgusted with himself and his diminished abilities, uninspired by the professional atmosphere that made football seem like business instead of the love match it had always been for him. The following year, signed by the Rams, he ended up leaving camp voluntarily. His playing days were over. Washed up at twenty-four.

Determined not to let his own fate befall others, Marv turned his sights to the task of finding a better way to train athletes. Impressed by the performance of the Soviets and East Germans at the 1964 Olympics, he began studying Eastern Bloc techniques. From there, his lifelong work would lead to groundbreaking advances in the field of conditioning and training—much of the core- and swimming pool-based conditioning programs in use today owe nods to Marv's ideas.

Marv's unyielding personality and lack of social and business skills would lead, over the years, to a difficult life, both personally and professionally. His temper is well known. There have been two divorces, verbal and physical altercations with all manner of people of different ages and sexes, civil suits threatened but not pursued. In 1976, Marv and his brother Gary were fired from their coaching jobs at Crespi Carmelite High School in Encino. Gary, drafted as a halfback by the Cleveland Browns, had previously coached OC's Bishop Amat to the state championship; his star players were Pat Haden and John McKay, Jr. Later, during a Crespi game against Amat, the Marinovich brothers felt as if their team had given up; at the end of the game, they refused to send any more plays into the offensive huddle. "Call it yourself," was the message; Babe Laufenberg, who would go on to play in the NFL, was the team's quarterback. The next day, according to news accounts, the Marinovichs punished the team with sprints and hills late into the evening. As it happened, many of the players were scheduled to take the SATs the next day; the parents complained bitterly. To this day the affair is known in local football lore as "The Incident at the Water Tower." The Marinovich brothers resigned "for personal reasons" and "basic policy differences with the administration of the school."

Nevertheless, Marv's genius has been long recognized. Under the graces of the Raider's Davis, and later working on his own, Marv developed a system for evaluating athletes and for getting them into "balance," thus maximizing their athletic potential. He has developed several workout machines. There is a long list of athletes he has helped, including baseball's Steve Finley and basketball's Tyson Chandler. His most recent reclamation project: superstar defender Troy Palamalu of the Pittsburgh Steelers. Palamalu has posted an enthusiastic video for Marv's process on YouTube.

Into the middle of Marv's quest to unlock the secrets of human physical potential came his own two children, Traci and Todd. "Some guys think the most important thing in life is their jobs, the stock market, whatever," Marv would later say. "To me it was my kids. The question I asked myself was, How well could a kid develop if you provided him with the perfect environment?"

Since college, when he went to bed early and followed all of the training rules religiously, Marv had been early adopter of what was known back then as "the health food craze." For the nine months prior to Todd's birth, on the fourth of July 1969, Trudi ate nothing but natural food—no salt, sugar, alcohol or tobacco. In an era when parents followed unquestioningly the teachings of sixties-guru Dr. Spock, the couple read all manner of alternative books, talked to experts, tried to forge their own path. Trudi breast-fed for a year, then switched directly to raw milk. No formula, no baby food—just fresh-cooked vegetables and fruits. Like a pioneer wife, Trudi baked all the family's bread from whole grains. When he was teething, Todd was given frozen kidneys to chew to soothe his gums. There was no walker in the house: Marv wanted Todd to crawl for as long as possible; he believed crawling would improve hand-eye coordination. Todd's blood was tested regularly for vitamin and mineral deficiencies. Trudi sent Todd off to birthday parties with carrot sticks and carob muffins. Everything consumed was organically grown. "I paid extra to get him eggs from chicken that had been out in the sun and grain fed," Marv recalled. Of course, no burgers or boardwalk pizza or fast food was allowed; no candy, no Slurpees, no junk. And even before he could stand, Marv had Todd throwing with both hands, kicking with both feet, playing with medicine balls. At age three he started sit-ups and pull-ups and light hand weights.

"As a kid it was just part of the routine," Todd recalled. "We did something every day. I could have the rest of the day off if I just did something first. We were either running on the beach or in our little garage doing some strength work. There were days obviously I didn't want anything to do with it. And that's when he gave me the look, like 'Well, fine, but you're gonna get your ass kicked when you start to play sports.'" On his fourth birthday, Todd ran four miles along the ocean's edge in thirty-two minutes, an eight-minute pace.

Having grown up around football players his whole life, Todd begged to play Pop Warner: like most boys, from an early age, he wanted to be a pro. In fall of fourth grade, Marv signed him up for the Newport Cheyennes. Though Marv wasn't coach, he never missed a practice—like his own father, Slip, before him, who watched every Wildcat workout from the driver's seat of his pickup truck, Marv was always around, hovering on the periphery.

And so it was, late in the game against a team remembered now as the best fourth grade team at the time in Orange County—anchored by a young Goliath of a middle linebacker—that the coach sent a play into the huddle. The second string quarterback squeaked it out to his teammates, hopefully loud enough for all to hear. It was a running play, a handoff to the halfback. As fullback, Todd's job was lead blocker.

The ball was snapped. Todd led the halfback through the hole.

He'd just cleared the line of scrimmage when Goliath-boy stepped into the gap and delivered a forearm shiver very much like the one that had gotten Marv ejected from the Rose Bowl. Todd was wearing a quarterback's face guard, with minimal protection; the forearm reached its mark undeterred.

Todd crumpled to the ground. The whistle blew. Bright red blood flowed copiously from Todd's nose.

As Todd was being cleaned up, Marv convinced the coach that his Todd needed to go back into the game. Immediately. At quarterback.

"Everybody was babying me, you know, asking 'Are you all right?'" Todd recalled. "I didn't know if I was all right or not. But they threw me into the game and told me the play, and I had to call it in the huddle.

"I went up to the line. It was the last few seconds of the scrim-mage. We were only down by a few points. My nose was still bleeding all over the place. I took the snap and faded back. I threw a perfect spiral into the back corner of the end zone. That has always been my favorite route. I remember seeing the ball. It was like slow motion. It was spiraling and there was blood just flying off of it, splattering out into the air.

"When the catch was made, everybody got real quiet for a second. Then everybody got all excited. We ended up winning. I remember the parents cheering," Todd said.

"I guess that set the tone for things. The attitude. 'Cause my dad came from the old school. You never lay down on the field. If you're hurt you play through it. And if you can't play through it, if you're hurt to the point you can't go on, you better walk or limp or crawl your ass off that field and make way for somebody who can play. You don't ever take a play off. Ever. You give what you have and then you give a little more. That was just the way it was done."

"Was all the hard work worth it?"

September, 1984.

Todd gathered himself as best he could and rose to one knee on the synthetic turf at Orange Coast College. He'd just been blasted by two big studs from the celebrated front line of the Fountain Valley High School Barons, ranked number one in Orange County on this opening day of football season.

The band was playing, the crowd was roaring. Cheerleaders were throwing kicks and cartwheels. Todd fought for breath; he was literally seeing stars—tiny motes of phantom light floating across the inky darkness of the sky. He felt like he was in one of those war movies, where the hero has just survived a bomb blast and everything goes silent and slow-motion. The game had been hyped by the local newspaper; someone had come up with the idea of staging the contest in LeBard Stadium to accommodate the crowd. Two months after his fifteenth birthday—three days before he'd even set foot into a ninth grade classroom for the first time—the six-three, 170-pound freshman was starting at quarterback for the Santa Ana Mater Dei Monarchs, the largest Catholic high school west of Michigan.

In a sports-mad county known for its quarterbacks, Todd's freshman start was an all-time first. In its fifty-eight year history,

Mater Dei had been named the number two high school athletic program in the nation by *Sports Illustrated*; the football team had won nine state championships and two *USA Today* national championships, with five undefeated seasons. Two Monarch quarterbacks, John Huarte (Notre Dame) and Matt Leinart (USC) went on to win Heismans. This season, a new coach, a former West Pointer known for developing quarterbacks, had been hired to revamp the Mater Dei program, which had fallen off in recent years, in part because of a weak passing attack. Todd was to be The Answer.

Sometime around seventh grade, Todd had set a goal for himself: to start at quarterback as a ninth grader on a varsity team. Marv put up a chart in the garage listing the different stations of the diagnostic cross he had devised: forty yard dash, bench press, squat, agility drill, vertical jump, etc. Under each was listed the quantitative standards that Marv, based on his experience working with athletes of all ages and abilities, called "Varsity Level." If Todd could achieve those marks, he told his boy, he would achieve his goal.

Now here he was, in Monarch red-and-white, wearing number seven after John Elway, who he had met as a sixth grader, when the future Hall of Famer was the quarterback at Stanford University and came down to Southern California to work with Marv. Todd and his family had been driving past this stadium his entire life. The lights were glaring; seven thousand people cheered in the stands, TV cameras and reporters roamed the sidelines, the smell of hot dogs wafted on the balmy ocean breeze. It was football night in America, So-Cal style. Even the *Los Angeles Times* was in attendance.

At the moment, midway into the first quarter, everyone was holding their breaths, a collective stunned silence: Would this skinny youngster make it past the hype to survive his first game? Todd himself felt as if he'd just been body-slammed by a winter wave onto one of those cement-sand beaches they have on the North Shore of Oahu. His ears were ringing, his vision was blurred, he wanted to puke. Later he would recognize the symptoms of his first concussion. Numbly he hauled himself to his feet. Marv's conditioning was designed to train the body and the mind to push beyond pain, beyond fear, to new limits of accomplishment. Throughout his career, Todd would be known for his extraordinary focus and will—qualities that would both enable and doom him. Two years from now, the left-hander would lead a come-from-behind victory with a broken thumb on his throwing hand. Five years from now, he'd throw four college touchdowns with a fractured left wrist. Sixteen years from now he'd throw ten touchdowns in one game, tying an Arena Football League record, while suffering from acute heroin withdrawal.

Acting on instinct, the fifteen-year-old Todd peered out of the echoing fiberglass cavern of his Riddell helmet and searched the sideline, looking for the signal caller, his next play.

One of his teammates, an upperclassman, grabbed him by the shoulder pads. "Our team's on this side, dude," he told the freshman phenom, spinning Todd around 180 degrees to face the Monarch bench.

By the time Todd reached sixth grade, he was playing football, basketball and baseball, depending upon the season. Tall and ambidextrous, it seemed at first that hoops would be his calling.

He started in a Boys Club rec league in Newport. Marv coached; the team was named the Red Rockets, for Todd's hair, which took its curl from Marv's nimbus of brown. The next season, Todd joined an area all-star team; Marv insisted he play up two age-groups so as not be typecast as a center. Eventually the family moved to Huntington Beach so Todd could play on a team with other gifted middle schoolers coached by Gary McKnight, who would later go on to establish a basketball dynasty at Santa Ana Mater Dei. In three years, playing in tournaments from San Diego to Las Vegas, the all-white South Coast All Stars went 177–7. Todd was a knock-down shooting guard. McKnight, who would win five state championships in more than twenty-five years of coaching, has said that Todd was one of the best shooters he's ever seen. "Coach told me right from the start, 'You're in range when you step into the gym. I'm gonna take you out if you don't shoot,'" recalled Todd, who carried a cooler of organic food and snacks with him to traveling games to accommodate his strict diet.

Like many star athletes, Todd repeated seventh grade to gain an advantage in age and maturity. With the onset of adolescence, Marv ramped up the training. "It was brutal," Todd said. "There were no days off." They worked on the beach and in the garage; Marv brought in a series of experts. A pitching coach from the Texas Rangers broke down Todd's throwing motion with video and computers and found it 4.53 inches too low; his stroke was re-tooled accordingly. A New York physiologist advised Todd to rotate his hips faster to get more velocity. A vision specialist in Westwood sought to improve his peripheral vision. He'd have Todd wear prism glasses, stand on a balancing beam in a dark room, and bounce a ball while reciting multiplication tables. There were nutritionists, psychologists, massage therapists. After Marv caught on with the LA Rams, overseeing player development, Todd got the chance to work out with Pat Haden and Vince Ferragamo at summer camp. "I'd grown up around all these pros, and now I'm running around at practice, and they're like, asking me to step in for throwing drills. I was totally into it. How could you not be?" Todd said.

"Todd threw a nicer ball than either of those guys," Marv recalled.

At hoops games, Marv was always in the stands. "There were hand signals," Todd said. "Get after it. Be explosive. Stop dogging it." If Todd was slacking on defense, as he sometimes did, Marv would become vocal. He'd always disdained the prima-donnas, the guys who loved to score but wouldn't do the dirty work. "He'd call me Timmy," Todd said. "Like I was being timid, you know, like Tiny Tim." He'd call out from the stands in a high, mocking, girlish voice, "'Come on Timmy!' and I would just, my fuckin' skin would fuckin' crawl." Typically, after practice or a game, Marv would take advantage of the drive home to critique his son's performance.

Since his own playing days, Marv had a reputation for excess saliva. "Foaming at the mouth," is the phrase most often employed by those describing it. Trudi recalled one trip home from a tournament: "It's a long drive from Vegas. And Marv is repetitive. It was never how many points Todd scored, it was 'Did he hustle? Did he give his all?' He would get so excited the spit would fly. He'd just go over it and over it and over it again. I could see Todd turn him off. He knew how to do that. We'd get back home and I'd have to clean the spittle off the inside of the windshield."

One evening on the way home from basketball practice, Marv came down on Todd for dogging it. "It was like, 'You didn't run during practice, so now you're running your ass home," Todd recalled. "I ran on the beach by the water's edge. I could see his headlights. He'd drive along Pacific Coast Highway and pull over and wait to see me come by. Then he'd drive up to the next spot and wait there." Depending who tells the story, Todd ran either five or nine miles. "It was nothing. I'd been running since I was four. I could run all day. I was glad to be out of the car and not have to deal with all the spit and verbal abuse. I was just like, 'Cool, fuck it. I'll run home.'"

At some point during the summer of eighth grade, the South Coast All Stars were at a traveling tournament. In the downtime between games, the guys were out on a field, getting some fresh air, screwing around with a football Todd happened to bring along. At one point, somebody went out for a bomb. Todd waved him farther downfield...farther still. It was one of those moments you've seen a zillion times: Keep going!

At last he heaved a pass.

The ball flew about fifty yards, a perfectly arching spiral that settled into his receiver's hands as gently as a mother bird coming to roost on her nest.

"Coach McKnight's eyes got huge," Todd recalled. "He was like: *'That's your sport.'*"

The summer before ninth grade, Todd started summer football camp as the Monarch's fifth string quarterback. His typical workout week, as reported in an article in the *Orange County Register*, looked like this:

Four days of weight lifting, three days of light body work and running. Daily sessions with Mater Dei's assistant basketball coach. Twice-weekly sessions with a special shooting coach. Two hours daily throwing the football. Twice-weekly sessions with a quarterback coach. Thrice-weekly sprint workouts with a track coach.

There were also Mater Dei summer AAU club basketball games and twice daily football workouts. "I don't think any of the kids were ever jealous of Todd because they knew that when they left that field or court or gym, Todd was still going to be there for many many hours," Trudi recalled.

During this time, the other members of Todd's extended family stood by powerlessly. Nobody really wanted to butt heads with Marv. But that didn't mean that there were no efforts to subvert him.

The Chief took Todd deep sea fishing. He regularly fed the boy donuts, beer, pizza, and other fun junk. Though Trudi is embarrassed to admit it, she herself took Todd to McDonalds from time to time. Trudi worked hard as a waitress during the frequent periods when Marv wasn't employed. Like a great artist or the proverbial mad scientist, Marv had a sort of creative tunnel vision. He cared only about his craft, his life's work. "He didn't do reality too well," Trudi likes to say. For her part, she tried to make both of her children well-rounded. There's a classic family picture of Todd in his baseball uniform playing violin in a grammar school recital. Classical and jazz music was played around the house, there were frequent trips to museums. Violent cartoons were forbidden; encouraged instead were old Hitchcock and Agatha Christie movies. Every once in a while, Trudi would "kidnap" Todd and Traci and flee to San Diego for the weekend. The trio would go to the zoo and SeaWorld, to movies. They would sit in public places and watch people and make up elaborate back stories to explain their lives. Often they would stay at the landmark Hotel Del Coronado, where Trudi and Marv had honeymooned, in a comped suite befitting his status as newly-crowned national champion. (According to Trudi, Marv could really cut a rug in those days.) "Todd and Traci just ran around and went to activities with all the other kids," Trudi said of the Hotel Del. "I would lay in the sun and read. It was a breath of normalcy."

Trudi continued: "I have told Todd repeatedly that his dad never did anything purposefully to hurt him. To me it was misplaced love. Misguided love. And I should've never let him get away with it. But I was under Marv's dominance, too. It's not an excuse. It's just a fact of life that I was young; I was nineteen when we married. And here's this dominant figure. Look at the generation I came from. Women were subservient. My mother was a housewife who stayed home until I went away to college. She catered to my dad. This is what you did. That's what women did."

Though Todd's sister Traci has written of hearing Todd alone in his room at night crying, Todd never appeared to be at odds with his training. Sure, he would bitch and moan sometimes like any teen, he recalled. But mostly, he did what he was supposed to do with dedicated effort. He gave 110 percent, as coaches like to say. He seemed to want it just as much as Marv wanted it for him.

"Sports was my first love," Todd said. "Whatever game it was, if it was a basketball tournament or handball with the girls at recess, I was in it all the way, I was playing it, and loving it, I was trying to beat them. I had that competitive thing. I just wanted to compete. People have a misconception, you know, that sports was forced on me but it wasn't. I wanted to do one thing: play football. That was my absolute goal. Marv never made me do it. It was all about me..."

And so it was, on September 7, 1984, that Todd realized his goal—at age fifteen, before ninth grade had even started, he was making his debut as a starting quarterback under the lights at a college stadium in front of seven thousand fans. Shut down completely in the first quarter, the Mater Dei Monarchs started the second quarter losing 14–0. Then Todd led the team on two consecutive drives for field goals. A Monarch interception for a touchdown brought the halftime score to 14–13.

The game bogged down in the second half, an early-season penalty-fest. Fountain Valley added another field goal and posted a 17–13 win at the final gun. Todd would end the day nine of seventeen for 123 yards and two interceptions, the second of which foiled an end-of-game drive. Said the *Register*: "Without Marinovich... the Monarchs wouldn't have had an offense to speak of... He did show composure under pressure, however, and proved he could both read defenses and get the ball to the open man."

After the game, Todd remembered, "We went back to Mater Dei and they had a ceremony—it was in this grotto where the team goes and does its prayers and all that. And then I walked over to my parents. I don't remember if it was my mom or if it was Marv, but somebody asked, 'So, did you enjoy it? Was all the hard work worth it?'

"Without hesitating the answer was, 'Yes!' It was *absolutely* yes," Todd said. "It was one of the most exhilarating experiences, an energy that I wish everybody could experience, stepping out on that field, the crowd just erupting. In all reality it's almost God-like 'cause you have control of everybody's emotions—you have the ball and everybody in that stadium for the most part is watching the ball. And what I do with that ball determines how they react. As time went by, I really started enjoying playing in opposing stadiums even more than being at home. That was the ultimate. You're against the odds, you're hated. Almost as good as the eruption you get at home is the *silence* you get on the road when you've just shoved it down their throats and the place is still—it's just absolutely stunned and still."

As he stood so proud and shy with his parents, off to one side, drinking everything in, Todd's new teammates drifted over and surrounded him.

"They were all these upperclassmen. And they're congratulating me and stuff. And it's like, growing up, the term my mom used, she would describe me as 'terrifyingly shy.' That's why I always loved being on the team. Being part of it. It was the only way I could make friends because I was so shy. And then it's even worse, you know, always being the young guy coming in, the guy people have heard of—plus I'm supposed to be the quarterback barking orders. And so here come all the new guys from the team, and they're all around me and my parents. That's another memory that's just as good: All the guys coming up to us. And they're like, 'Hey, Todd, let's go! Come out with us after the game. It's party time!'

"I looked at Marv and he didn't hesitate. He just gave me the nod, you know, like 'Go ahead, you earned it.' He understood because he was part of it, he was a pro, he knows that the quarterback has got to be part of the boys—even though he was a little apprehensive. I mean, I was just fifteen. They were all eighteen."

Off Todd went, into the night with his new friends.

"I thought I'd found the miracle drug."

January, 1988.

It was the opening night of the public school basketball season. After two years at Mater Dei, Marv had engineered Todd's transfer to Capistrano Valley High School in nearby Mission Viejo. With fifty-eight seconds remaining in their game against rival El Toro, the score was tied at sixty-one.

Todd flashed into the paint, took a pass from the wing. He made the lay-up and drew the foul. The whistle blew. Three thousand fans in the arena at the University of California, Irvine went nuts. The six-five, 217-pound senior pumped his fist in celebration.

As a quarterback, Todd had led the county in passing his freshman year at Mater Dei. By the end of his sophomore year he'd thrown for nearly forty-four hundred yards and thirty-four touchdowns. But the Monarchs record was mediocre. Marv believed their offensive line was weak, offering no protection. He was afraid Todd would be hurt. "I was getting pounded my sophomore year and I didn't need to be getting pounded," Todd recalled. "The problem was the philosophy of the blocking scheme. Their idea was to send a lot of guys out and hopefully you get rid of the ball before they hit you; rather than let's send fewer receivers out and protect the quarterback and give him more time. I remember coming home from a game against Bishop Amat. I was taking off my shirt, and my mom just was like, 'Ah!' I had welts all over my back and ribs. And I was wearing all the gear—the rib padding, the flak jacket, all that—and I was still getting pummeled. I even bent two metal knee braces. Marv made me wear them. I *hated* those things. But I was glad I had them. I was getting hit so much, the knee braces got bent."

When Todd left, his Mater Dei coach was bitter: "Todd loved the place and was featured in our offense," Chuck Gallo told reporters. "The killer is that we put two years of our program into him and we can't finish what we were going to do."

The coach of Todd's new football team, the Capo Cougars, was Dick Enright, a long-time friend of Marv's. Enright was a former USC player, San Francisco 49ers O-line coach, and head coach at the University of Oregon, where he groomed Dan Fouts. Enright ran a pass-oriented pro-style offense that stressed protecting the quarterback. Under Enright, Todd would break the all-time Orange County passing record. (By sitting Todd out of victories, Enright managed to ensure his second-string quarterback, whose career had been derailed by Todd's arrival, a D-II college football scholarship.) Todd was named a McDonald's All American; he was the Touchdown Club's National Player of the Year. (Todd's high school passing mark would finally be broken by Mater Dei alum Matt Barkley, the first freshman to start as quarterback in a varsity game since Todd. After his graduation in 2008, he followed Todd to USC.)

The real hoopla began after Todd's first football season at Mater Dei, when People magazine published a full-page article about Todd.

It was all there—the father, the diet, the training, the single-minded focus. In short order, Todd was a household name around Orange County.

Three years later, in December, 1987, when the January issue of now-defunct *California* magazine hit the stands with Todd's picture on the cover, the hype rose to unimagined levels. The headline "ROBO QB: The Making of the Perfect Athlete." It was picked up by the wires. A parade of media came to town. They called Todd the bionic quarterback, a test tube athlete, the boy in the bubble. His mad scientist father had trained him since birth! He had never drunk a Coke or eaten at McDonalds! His mommy used to give him organic muffins to take to birthday parties! All over the world, people were talking about Todd's amazing story. In truth, the carrot-topped phenom was leading a double life.

Back during freshman year, after the ceremony in the grotto at Mater Dei, after Marv had given him that understanding nod, Todd and his older teammates "went directly to a kegger and started pounding down beers," Todd recalled.

"I had the German-Irish blood. The Chief had been giving me beer my whole life; I used to go to the fights with him and drink these six-ounce mini-Coors. I felt I could handle my own alcoholically. It was great. Here was this new cool aspect of the high school experience. It all started from there. It became the thing: I really looked forward to giving it all I had at the game on Friday nights and then continuing through the weekend with the partying. It opened up a new social scene for me, being able to shed all these insecurities through alcohol—liquid courage. I wasn't scared of people anymore. All of a sudden all these senior girls were chasing me. My freshman friends were like, "What's going on, dude?"

Todd started dating the sister of his friend, Matt Spence, who'd moved over from QB to running back when Todd came to the Mater Dei Monarchs. (When Todd transferred to Capo, Matt and several other players came with him.) At first, Lanie Spence disliked Todd for taking her brother's position. "I thought he was a geek. Then I fell in love with him," she said. When his parents decided to divorce, during his sophomore year, Todd became even more attached to the Spence family. "I remember the night we told him we were separating," Trudi recalled. "He was in tears. He said, 'I need you both.'" Lanie recalled giving Todd his first surprise party for his sixteenth birthday. She invited a hundred people. Todd walked into the house and everyone shouted. Rattled by the attention—a stadium full of strangers was fine; a room full of friends was something else—Todd went directly to the table of presents and began opening them. Lanie recalled how she and Trudi came over to stop him. "We told him, 'Wait a minute, Todd. You're supposed to come into the party and say hello to everyone and let us sing to you first.' He was very much like a little kid in a lot of ways," Lanie said.

It was at Mater Dei that Todd began smoking marijuana. By the time his junior year rolled around, "I was a full-on loady," Todd recalled. He was living in an apartment with Marv near Capo. "Probably the best part of my childhood was me and Marv's relationship my junior and senior year. After the divorce, he really loosened up. It was a bachelor pad. I had the bedroom, Marv had the sofa in the living room. He was dating, I was dating. His little code was, "I'm entertaining tonight." That meant I got a free night out."

Every day before school, Todd would meet a group at a friend's house and do bong hits. They called it Zero Period. Some of the guys were basketball players, others were into surfing, skateboarding, and music, the holy trinity of the OC slacker lifestyle. They dressed as retro Dead Heads, used the word "dude" like punctuation. They seriously loved concerts. The unbridled release of the mosh pit was as close as you could ever get to playing football—with no pads or practice.

"Pot just really relaxed me," Todd said. "It just enhanced whatever I was doing. It didn't, at that point, take away from anything. I never played high or practiced high. I was always down by practice time. But pot just allowed me to be social. It wasn't as hard on my body as drinking. It allowed me to laugh, to be carefree, to not be worried about whatever there was to worry about. I could show up and be accountable but still smoke. I was sold on it. I thought I had found the miracle drug. I was like, 'This right here is the best thing in the world.' I thought it was a damn crime that pot was illegal. I started drinking less and smoking more. I'd found my thing. I was in love."

As Todd was growing up on the west side of the county, there was another well-known father-son football combination getting a decent amount of press. Bob Johnson was the coach at El Toro High School. He had two sons, Bret and Rob. They lived on the other side of the Saddleback Valley. Like Todd, Bret was a senior. He was also named All American at quarterback. Eventually he would go to UCLA, transfer to Michigan State, end up in the Canadian Football League, a disappointment. His younger brother, taller and more talented, would enjoy an eight-year career as a journeyman quarterback in the NFL. As Todd was growing up, the elder Johnson seemed to take umbrage with all the publicity that Todd and Marv were getting. He always made a point of contrasting his boys with Todd, touting them as natural athletes who were not pressured as children. Over time, much would be made of the rivalry between Todd and Bret; that Brett would attend rival UCLA kept the fires burning. At one point, one of local newspapers decided to photograph the two celebrated QBs together. At first, the story goes, the six-foot Bret refused. Todd was always making fun of how short he was; Bret didn't want to pose next to him. Finally, on the appointed day, Bret arrived late to the photo shoot, already wearing his football cleats. Todd and others at the shoot believe he'd stuffed his cleats with paper or some other material in order to give Bret more height. Why else drive in football cleats?

The Johnson/Marinovich rivalry had risen to a crescendo during the past football season. Todd and his Capo team had blown through the league, posting a perfect 9–0 record, including a 22–21 victory over the Johnsons and El Toro. The battle of the All-American quarterbacks played before eight thousand fans; it was the first high school game ever televised on ESPN, the first broadcast of "Scholastic Sports America." A few weeks after the game, however, allegations surfaced that an acquaintance of Coach Enright's had videotaped an El Toro practice, and that Enright had viewed a few minutes of the poor-quality tape before casting it aside. Capo's victory over El Toro was subsequently reversed; the game was recorded as a forfeit. Enright was suspended and then resigned. He retained his county job as a Phys. Ed teacher at Capo. He never coached again.

In the face of the turmoil, and without Coach Enright, the football Cougars went into the league championship game against another close rival, Mission Viejo, and suffered their first loss of the season, 28–21. With 3:53 left in the second half, the Cougars were in the middle of an inspired comeback drive toward a touchdown when Todd broke the scholastic passing record. For most of his senior year, the Register had run a regular feature on the sports page called "Marinovich Watch," chronicling his march toward the prep passing mark held by Ron Cuccia of LA Wilson since 1977. The local media was on hand to record the moment. A time-out was called. The principal came onto the field and held a little ceremony for Todd, who was furious. "The ceremony killed our momentum," Todd said. "We never recovered." After the final gun, in the locker room, interim coach Eric Patton—a huge man, a former All-American lineman at Notre Dame—wept as he addressed the team.

At one in the morning after the loss, Coach Enright heard a knock on his door. He didn't live far from the school; earlier, he could hear the roar of the crowd—it struck him as odd, he wasn't used to being at home during a game. Now he found Todd on his doorstep, sopping wet from the rain.

"I tried to win it for you coach," Todd said, and then he collapsed, sobbing, into the ample arms of the big man...

Now, just weeks later, it was the opening game of basketball season; Todd had another crack at arch-rival El Toro and the Johnson brothers, who also played basketball.

The Capo Cougars had a dominating front line, with a seven-foot center and a six-ten power forward. Todd played either the two or the three. Four days ago, in a pre-season tournament, Todd and his team had upset number one Mater Dei, the first public school team to do so in six years. Todd had twenty-five points against his old coach, Gary McKnight, aided by the newly instituted three-point shot. Going into tonight's game against El Toro, Capo was ranked number one in the county by the *LA Times*.

Bret Johnson was the point guard for the El Toro Chargers. His brother, Rob, a six-four freshman, was nearly the tallest in the lineup. Despite the height advantage, the game had come down to the wire. Todd had just broken the tie with a lay-up. The Cougars were up two; Todd had one foul shot coming, the "and one." The El Toro coach asked for a time out, hoping to rattle Todd.

In the stands, Trudi didn't worry. Ever since he was young, she recalled, "When the game was in the balance, you wanted Todd on the free throw line." He shot nearly ninety percent—with either hand.

This time he relied on his left. Swish. 64–61.

El Toro inbounded the ball; it was stolen by a Capo player. He fed Todd diving to the basket. A hard foul sent Todd to the line again for two shots. There were thirty-seven seconds left to play.

The crowd was screaming, pounding the floor, shaking signs, the usual high school hoopla. Behind the basket, dozens of El Toro students, many of them recognizable to Todd as football players, were wearing orange wigs to mock him. As Todd went through his foul shot ritual—the dribble, the breath, the visualization, trying to block everything out but the rim— something broke his focus. The fans were chanting. It sounded like his name.

"Marijuana-*vich*!

"Marijuana-*vich*!

"Marijuana-*vich*!"

"I was supposed to be shooting free throws, but I was really glancing into the stands, trying to see if my father was noticing," Todd later recalled.

He put it out of mind and nailed both free throws.

El Toro and the Johnsons were toast.

"I don't hear any booing now."

November, 1990.

A hush fell over the Rose Bowl crowd of 98,088, half of which was wearing UCLA's True Blue, the other half USC's Cardinal Red. No matter what the teams' records or national ranking, this was always the biggest game of the year, a rabid cross-town rivalry dating back to 1929, the inaugural year for both programs, when USC won 76–0.

With sixteen seconds to play in the sixty-first annual Crosstown Showdown, the score was 42–38 in favor of UCLA—a state school, leafy and sculpture-bedecked, set between Wilshire and Sunset Boulevards, near Beverly Hills. From the opening kickoff, the advantage had seesawed back and forth as the teams traded touchdowns. UCLA was led by Tommy Maddox, who had beaten out Todd's OC nemesis

Bret Johnson. (After an unproductive career in the NFL, Maddox sold insurance for his father's company in Houston. Later, he'd make a brief comeback with the Arena Football League.) With 3:05 left in the game, Todd hit freshman Johnny Morton (a future NFL All-pro) in the end zone for the go-ahead score. The next series, after an abortive Trojan goal line stand, the Bruins fullback punched it over to take back the lead.

Following the kickoff, Todd began operating at his own twenty-three. On third down, he completed a twenty-seven yard pass to Gary Wellman, a fast white boy—five-nine, 170; he'd later play for the Houston Oilers—who'd been his favorite target during this red shirt sophomore year. Then he hit Wellman again for twenty-two yards. They were in striking distance for a touchdown. A field goal would not be enough.

The football was spotted near the left hash on the UCLA twenty-three yard line. Trojan coach Larry Smith called for a time out. Todd and his corps of receivers jogged over to the sidelines. There was a certain looseness in their gait, an unselfconscious sense of grace. They'd been training their whole lives for moments like these.

Coach Smith was a flinty, white-haired Ohio native who stressed discipline and fundamentals. He'd gotten his first break under Bo Schembechler, coached at Tulane and Arizona before arriving at USC, one of the few head coaches in the school's history with no previous ties to the expensive private university, set like a jewel in the middle of dicey South Central LA. Two years from this day, after suffering a humiliating defeat at the hands of Fresno State in the Freedom Bowl, Smith would tell reporters: "Names and logos don't mean anything," an insult to a school and a football program that prided itself on its deep tradition (and deep-pocketed alumni). He would be fired shortly thereafter, ending his six-season tenure. He died in 2008 of leukemia and lymphoma.

Of all the coaches he'd ever had, Todd hated Smith the most. Smith made no secret of his own feelings about Todd, either. In Todd he smelled a dangerous non-conformist—his job depended on this freak. He seemed determined to break the kid, going so far as to specifically outlaw flip-flops on road trips. (When the announcement was distributed to all team lockers, everyone deposited their copies into Todd's locker.) Over the last two months, Todd had been repeatedly drug tested. He'd been suspended for an unimportant game against a weak team; he'd been benched as a starter for one set of downs. There'd been a huge row before another game about some adhesive tape Todd put on his shoes. "It seemed like a destructive type of interaction was going on" between Todd and Coach Smith, Marv recalled. "It's hard to tell who was the adult in that situation."

"So what do you want to do?" Smith asked his quarterback.

Todd looked at him incredulously. His ruddy, freckled, sunburned face flushed to an angry reddish-pink. "You're asking *me* what *I* want to do? Why start *now?*"

Todd turned to his guys, standing behind him in a mini-huddle. There was Wellman and Morton and Joel Scott, along with halfback Mazio Royster (three years with Tampa Bay). Todd loved his teammates. They were the ones he battled and partied with. They believed in him. They treated him like he was a normal person, albeit a normal person who could sometimes work miracles. Ever since his fourth game as a redshirt freshman, when he'd engineered a brilliant last minute comeback in a hostile environment against Washington State, his teammates believed in Todd and his magic. The eighteen-play, ninety-one yard march downfield—seven crucial completions, including a touchdown pass and a two-point conversion— is recorded in college football history as "The Drive." President Ronald Reagan, who watched the game from his bed while recovering from surgery, phoned Todd afterwards to congratulate him. Todd was found riding his bike across campus and summoned to Coach Smith's office. The two-term Republican president—famous for playing football icon Knute Rockne in the movies— told Todd that his performance was one of the most exciting he'd ever witnessed. He gave the twenty-year-old his digits and invited him to stop by the Western White House if he was ever in Bel Air.

"This is what we're gonna do," he told Coach Smith, yelling over the crowd. "*You're* gonna stay the fuck over here while we go win this game..."

Although Todd thought about other colleges—Stanford, Arizona, Washington—in the end, no other school really had a chance.

Todd's sister and his first cousin were already attending USC. His uncle Craig Fertig was a coach—there was some minor hoopla when Craig was seen at one of Todd's high school football games; technically, it was a recruiting violation for Todd to be talking to a college coach. The Chief had put it to his grandson like this: "Where do you want to live when you're done with school?" When Todd answered "Southern California," the Chief asked him, "Does it make sense to go somewhere else and make a name for yourself and then leave?"

When Todd went to SC for his official visit, his hosts took him down on the field of the empty Coliseum—where Todd had tailgated with the Chief and watched games his entire life—and had his name announced over the loudspeaker system; they even piped-in the roaring crowd. His student host was an All-American wide receiver. He walked Todd over to somebody's apartment on campus. There was a party going on. "They had a three-and-a-half-foot purple bong," Todd recalled. "And I'm like, 'I'm at home.' I went right over to the bong. I had my own weed on me."

Once summer football and classes began, the shy boy who used to hide behind his mother's hip fell immediately into harmony with his new surroundings. "I liked the camaraderie. They had guys who were part of the system, but they also did things on their own terms, kind of like 'fuck the system we're doing it our way.' The guys knew I was talented. They knew I had that fuck-you-to-the-system-mentality, too. They brought me into their inner loady circle. Not everybody on the team got high, but there were a few guys who dabbled with it and then there were the hardcore guys. They were All-Americans. They all played well. And they happened to love smoking pot. They sat me down in the beginning and they said, 'If you're confronted with anything, we got one word for you: Deny, deny, deny.' I knew I was in the right spot. I loved it."

His first year at SC, Todd was redshirted. He got to suit up for home games but didn't play; there was no pressure. The starting quarterback was Rodney Peete, a fifth-year senior who would spend sixteen years as a journeyman in the NFL. (Troy Aikman, meanwhile, was across town at UCLA.)

After all those years of hard work, Todd was having the time of his life. He was fifty miles away from home, totally unsupervised. He was taking freshman courses; the classes were large and easy, he went when he felt like it. He painted a mural on his dorm room wall; soon he was painting murals for others. His cousin, Mark Fertig, son of Craig, was on the baseball team; Todd partied with them. Other guys he knew from home were in fraternities; Todd partied with them. There were tons of girls to party with too, beautiful and wealthy and well-dressed SC girls, all of them eager to meet the tall, cute, redhead freshman phenom. Directly across the street from the athletic dorm was the 502 Club, a pub that served as the unofficial frat house for the football team. Todd was only eighteen but the owner let him in. "We'd go there after games. It would just be raging. We'd pick out the people we wanted to have stay and then we'd lock it down and kick everybody out."

Coming into football season in Fall 1989, Todd's first official playing season with the team, the projected Trojan starting quarterback was Pat O'Hara. O'Hara, also from OC, had served his time behind Peete. Now it was his shot. But ten days before the opening game, during a routine scrimmage, O'Hara suffered what would be a career-ending knee injury. Todd got his first start against number twenty-two-ranked Illinois.

Smith played it conservative, staying on the ground with future NFL star Ricky Irvins, the latest in a string of great runners to attend Tailback U. Todd's first college pass was an interception; he ended up going 14 of 27 for 120 yards. The number five Trojans offensive line was admittedly terrible, allowing four sacks on the wiry freshman. In the end, Illinois ground out a 14–13 victory.

It didn't take long, however, before RoboQuarterback began living up to his promise. By season's end, Todd had completed sixty-two percent of his passes for twenty-six hundred yards and sixteen touchdowns, leading Trojans to an 9–2–1 record, a Pac-10 title and a Rose Bowl victory over Michigan, during which Todd engineered another late, seventy-five-yard scoring drive that ended the legendary coach Bo Schembechler's career with a loss. Todd was named All-Pac 10 and the national freshman player of the year.

When the next season rolled around, Coach Smith raised eyebrows when he told the media he was not yet settled on his starting quarterback. News of Todd's partying had spread across campus;

Smith was partial to clean-cut, frat boy Shane Foley, the reserve QB, also out of OC.

Todd ended up starting. Their first contest was against Syracuse in the Meadowlands in New York. Despite returning only seven starters from the previous season—leading the exodus was defensive stalwart and future All Pro Junior Seau, who turned pro after his junior year—the Trojans prevailed, 34–16. Todd torched the Orangemen for 337 yards. In the swirl of the Big Apple media attention, there was much talk of Todd's Heisman chances, speculation about turning pro. Upon his return west, the USC sports information office, at Todd's request, asked reporters to please stop raising those topics. Trojans faithfully began wearing buttons declaring "In Todd We Trust."

After several up and down weeks on the field, problems off the field started to surface. By now, Todd had happily declared his fine arts major. The problem was, all the classes were held in the afternoons, at the same time as practice. Todd was given a key to the studio and allowed to work independently. However, he was not formally excused from classes; each miss was recorded. He was often seen working through the night on art projects, both for school and on his own, like the giant wall mural he did at Julie's Trojan Bar and Grill. Another problem was Todd's living situation. Because he had procrastinated handing in his student housing application, he didn't get any housing (a free part of his scholarship package). He'd ended up sleeping for weeks on friends' sofas, moving about like a nomad, attending classes less and less frequently.

Finally, citing the missed classes, Coach Smith suspended Todd. Conveniently, the team was scheduled to play Arizona State, a weak team. Coach Smith told Marv privately that he suspected Todd was using drugs. Over the course of the season Todd was urine tested at least ten times by the team and the NCAA. Over the course of the next fifteen years, Todd would become expert at circumventing urine tests, substituting clean urine for his own.

By the time the Cal game rolled around, on November 3, 1990, there was a full blown quarterback controversy at USC; everyone had an opinion, it was well covered in the press. Foley started the home game and threw for a touchdown on the first series. Todd went in for the second series. As he jogged onto the field, his own fans began to boo. Todd couldn't believe what he was hearing. In the huddle, his guys were incensed, especially the All American lineman Pat Harlow, a future New England Patriot. "Do you understand what's going on?" Harlow bellowed. "They're booing our boy!" Harlow was so angry, Todd recalled, that he was frothing at the mouth.

Todd kept his cool. On his first play from scrimmage, he hit Wellman across the middle for an 85 yard touchdown. Instead of running down the field and celebrating in the end zone with the guys like he usually did, Todd showed no emotion at all. He just walked off the field quietly with his head down. Harlow made a bee-line for the stands. He threw his helmet into the band section and gave the fans a huge double finger. Up in his usual seats, Marv became engaged in a shouting match with a Trojan alum who had booed Todd. A complaint was later filed. Marv's seats were moved to another section...

After his little conference with Coach Smith— sixteen seconds to play in the sixty-first annual Crosstown Showdown, the score 42–38 in favor of rival UCLA—Todd and his corps of receivers jogged back to the huddle. The ball was on the 23. Todd called his play.

Wellman, his favorite receiver, was in the slot. The pass was designed to go to him. Morton, a six foot freshman, another fast little white boy, was split left, the decoy. Morton had been pestering Todd all afternoon to throw his way, telling the QB he could beat his man, "just like every receiver does every game," Todd recalled. Three minutes ago, Morton had finally gotten his chance, a twenty-one yard streak that had broken his ten game touchdown drought. Now he wanted the ball again. Unfortunately, the play called for an eighteen-yard comeback route, a pattern that would leave him short of the goal line, momentum taking him in the wrong direction. Breaking out of the huddle, he appealed to Todd; seeing the coverage, Todd agreed—the route was quickly changed. Instead he'd run a post-corner. "I winked at Todd, letting him know I could make the play," Morton recalled.

The ball was spotted at the left hash mark, close enough that Todd could look into the eyes of the UCLA cornerback who was covering Morton. His name was Dion Lambert. He'd go on to play four years in the NFL. As Todd approached the line of scrimmage, fully intending to go to Wellman, he pointed teasingly at Lambert, as if to say, *I'm coming your way.*

Lambert shook his head, *No way. Ain't nothin happenin' over here.*

The ball was snapped, shotgun style. "While it's in the air," Todd recalled, "I'm seeing Wellman get jammed at the line. Whenever a receiver doesn't get a clean release you got to go away from him, cause it just screws up the timing. So I looked back to the other side and I saw Morton on his corner route. He was making his post move. Lambert had slipped and fallen down. When there's two deep coverage, you're assuming your receiver is going to beat his man. The question is, What's the safety going to do? Is he gonna bite on the post that the receiver's selling? When Johnnie Morton went to the post, I saw the safety just drive on it, thinking I was throwing there. That's when I knew I had it."

Todd lofted the ball deep into the left corner of the end zone, near the very section where the Chief and his wife Virginia happened to be sitting, a textbook pass, his trademark. "It's been my favorite pass since I was playing Pop Warner," Todd said. "You really can't stop it."

After the game, Todd told the press: "I don't hear any booing now."

"They say in the history of the Raiders it was the best rookie party ever."

As his season of disharmony at USC drew to a close, Todd was increasingly at odds with Coach Smith, who would later say that Todd "took twenty years off my life."

At the Hancock Bowl in El Paso, the two were caught by cameras in an emotional sidelines confrontation. Smith's version was that Todd refused to go back into the losing effort against Michigan State in relief of Foley. Todd's version was that he told Smith, "I won't play for you but I'll go back in and play for my guys." The tape was replayed again and again on ESPN and elsewhere. Thereafter Todd missed a required team meeting and failed to register for the next semester of classes. His GPA had fallen to .70 on a four-point scale. Finally, Smith suspended him "indefinitely" from the team.

On the evening of Saturday January 19, 1991, Todd called his ex-girlfriend Lanie Spence, now a volleyball player for the University of New Mexico. Lanie was home visiting her parents in Mission Viejo; Todd suggested a movie. Lanie had for years made no secret of her dislike for Todd's partying. It was the main factor that had broken them up in high school. Tonight they couldn't agree where to meet; Todd ended up hitting the bars on Balboa Island with his cousin, Marc Fertig, and two other Trojan football players. The boys were headed home at 4 a.m., no more than ten yards from the front door of the Fertig family beach house, when two black-and-whites from the Newport Police Department came screeching through the alley with their lights on.

"I had a little nug on me," a marijuana bud, Todd recalled. "And in my small Levi's pocket I had a bindle of coke this guy had given me. It was half a gram. He was a fan. I hadn't seen him in a while; that sort of thing happened all the time. We were just walking home, relatively quiet, not making any trouble at all. The cop went right for my pocket, like he already knew the drugs were there; somebody must have tipped somebody off."

After several court dates, Todd was charged with two misdemeanors and allowed into a diversionary program for first-time offenders, which included counseling and AA meetings. School was finished. He declared himself eligible for the NFL draft and signed with a big time agency, IMG, which represented Joe Montana, Jack Nicklaus and Wayne Gretzky.

Since his arrest, Todd's stock had fallen; he was projected as a third round pick. For the first time since freshman summer, Todd went into training with Marv. (All through college Marv had attended practices, sitting quietly by himself in the bleachers but making no remarks to Todd unless his son came to him for advice.) To help them out at receiver, they hired an NFL veteran who lived in the area. Their plan: to skip the NFL combine and hold their own exhibition before the draft. "Marv was like: 'If you just keep working out and dedicate yourself in these next two months, somebody will take a chance on you, guaranteed. They know you can play. Somebody will give you a shot,'" Todd recalled.

On March 20, 1991, Todd walked out onto the field at East Los Angeles College with a new look. His long, curly, matinee-idol locks had been shorn in favor of a bright orange buzz cut, invoking the clean-cut Johnny Unitas, an image makeover suggested by Tom Condon, his agent at IMG. There were representatives of eighteen teams present. Trudi set up a table with lemonade and pastries. Todd was in the best shape of his life. "We went through the passing route tree and hit them all," Todd recalled. "We didn't miss a pass. We put on an aerial show."

The *LA Times* reported reverently the next day that Todd "heaved the ball flat-footed through the uprights from the fifty yard line." Why someone would need to do that was not explained. The only NFL owner in attendance was Al Davis. He arrived late, according to the *Times*. Bypassing the knot of scouts and coaches standing around on the field, Davis climbed up into the stands and sat between his old friends Marv and Trudi. "I kind of knew right then that the Raiders were gonna pick me," Todd said. "I was totally psyched. I wanted to play for them."

The first time Todd met Howie Long—the future Hall of Fame defensive end, film actor, and media personality—Todd had just been selected number one by the LA Raiders, the twenty-fourth pick in the NFL draft. It was July, 1991. Most of the top picks that year were defenders and lineman—number one overall was defensive tackle Russell Maryland. The only quarterback taken ahead of Todd was Dan Maguire, the six-foot-nine brother of baseballer Mark. (Huge but not mobile, he had trouble staying out of the way of the pass rush.) Future all-pro quarterback Brett Favre went in the second round, at number thirty-three, to the Atlanta Falcons.

Long was known as the heart and soul of the Raiders. Drafted number one by the team, he would play with them for his entire, thirteen-year career. At the point he met Todd, he was the only player left on the roster who'd moved with the team from Oakland to LA. On draft day, after partying all night in a hotel room with friends, Todd was brought, bleary-eyed, to the Raider facilities for a press conference. It was all very familiar; like USC, the Raiders played their games at the Coliseum. Along with all-pros Marcus Allen and Ronnie Lott, both of whom were Trojan alumni, Long would become Todd's closest mentor and confidant on the team.

Upon meeting, the first thing Long told Todd was how psyched he was to have Todd in black and silver. The Raiders had not won a Super Bowl since 1984. The previous season, they had suffered a 48-point drubbing in the AFC championship game. "I went to the Super Bowl early in my career and I thought I'd go back," Todd recalls Howie telling him. "I'm getting down to the end now and I want to get another chance at it." Howie urged Todd to be ready for the season. "We need you now," he said.

And then Howie switched topics. "He said, since I was from USC I must have a good chronic connection," Todd recalled, referring to strong, locally grown marijuana. "Then he told me, 'You better bring a couple of righteous ounces to training camp. Eight weeks of two-a-days gets pretty long."

After a short holdout, Todd signed with the Raiders for $2.25 million, including a $1 million signing bonus.

There is a funny story about Todd waltzing into summer training camp in Oxnard in flip flops, surfer shorts, and a backpack, making a bee-line for the front office to sign his contract and collect his bonus check. As he was walking back to his vehicle—the first car he'd ever owned, a Toyota Land Cruiser that IMG had fronted him—he peeked inside the envelope, bracing himself for the thrill of seeing a one plus eight zeros on a check made out to him.

But something was wrong. The colorful cashier's check numbers tallied only $676,000.00! *They're stiffing me!* Todd fumed. He turned around and marched back into the office to complain.

"They all ended up laughing at me," Todd recalled. "They were like, 'Have you ever heard of Uncle Sam?' I'd never had a paycheck before. I'd never even had a *job*."

The guys at camp called him Rook or Red. Sometimes they called him The Kid. The quarterback job was Jay Schroeder's to keep, despite his unraveling in the AFC title game against the Buffalo Bills the previous year, when he threw five interceptions. Backing him up was Steve Beuerlein, another OC boy from the Trinity League. The team was stacked with future Hall of Famers. Though it looked as if two-sport wonder Bo Jackson was washed up with his bad hip, owner Al Davis had stolen Lott and Craig Morton away from the Forty Niners—between them they owned seven Super Bowl rings. Sportswriters were predicting a strong season for the '91 edition of the bad boy Raiders—the team itself is another California institution known for its outlaw fans and second-chance heroes; a perfect fit for Todd, not necessarily in a good way. He'd be brought along slowly, announced coach Art Shell, another Al Davis guy, the first black head coach in the modern history of the NFL.

Todd loved training camp; there was no pressure. It felt like freshman year all over again. The facility was fifteen minutes from the ocean. Following the morning practice, while the other guys crapped out, he'd put his board on top of the Rover and go surfing. Following the afternoon practice, Todd said, he and a few others would go back to one of the players' suites. "We'd fuckin' twist one up, hang out and laugh."

At the time, all players took an NFL-mandated urine test during the first days of training camp. There were no further tests, unless you made the playoffs. Due to Todd's arrest, the NFL required him to take urine tests weekly. There was a bonus clause in his contract if he stayed clean for the entire year. Todd kept Gatorade bottles of clean urine, donated by non-pot smoking friends, in his refrigerator at his Manhattan Beach house, one block from the ocean, which he'd purchased for $900,000. Throughout the season he had a routine. Every Monday, he'd pour the pee into a small sunscreen bottle he kept for the purpose. When he got to practice, he'd put the bottle in a cup of coffee and leave it in his locker to warm up while he went to the team meeting. Afterwards, he'd stash the bottle inside his compression shorts, beneath his package, and go do his pee test. Usually he'd ask the supervisor to turn on the water in the sink to aid his shy bladder. "I got it down to a science," Todd said.

As tradition dictated, at the conclusion of camp, the first draft pick was required to throw a party for the team. With Trudi's help, Todd spent fifteen grand on a whopper. He rented a ranch. For the big eaters he brought in a company that did barbecue on a huge grill on a flatbed truck. He turned the barn into a stadium with hay bale proscenium seating. Marcus Allen helped him get the girls. In the spirit of team multiculturalism, Todd hired ten white strippers and ten black strippers. Given their star-studded audience, the girls became somewhat competitive; a strip battle of sorts ensued, each team of girls trying to outdo the other with their moves. The grand finale: three porn stars with double headed dildos.

"It was out of hand!" Todd recalled. "Little groups started breaking off. We went all night. They say in the history of the Raiders it was the best rookie party, ever. I definitely left my mark."

Following a trip to Tokyo for an exhibition game against Miami (and a memorable experience with a Japanese comfort girl and her exceedingly well-trained vulva) Todd made his first professional appearance in an exhibition game on August 12, against Dallas. As it happened, the game was televised on Monday Night Football.

Todd entered with fifteen minutes remaining in the contest and moved the Raiders downfield, completing three of four passes for sixteen yards—the last of which was a perfectly executed play-action rollout for a touchdown. Following the game, Beuerlein was traded to the Cowboys. Forty-year-old Vince Evans became the Raiders backup QB, with Todd at number three, so as not to feel pressured.

As the season progressed, Todd felt anything but pressure on the field. Off the field, however, he seemed to be pressuring himself to live up to his reputation as an epic partier. Arriving at the hotel for an away game, Todd would go with the rest of the players in a limo or a van to strip clubs or other venues. Upon his return to the hotel with the team, he'd sneak out again on his own. (Sometimes he'd do the old "I'm going for ice" trick with the ice bucket and take the stairs to avoid team security.) As if partying was sport, Todd seemed determined to make himself rookie of the year. There were women, clubs, the early-nineties rave scene, concerts, alcohol and ecstasy, a bit of cocaine. Vets on the team would save him a seat at the pre-game meal just to hear the stories of his exploits the night before. "Every city started running into one another," Todd recalled.

Sometimes, to amuse himself, Todd took pharmaceutical speed before the games. "I wasn't playing so I was doing it just for fun. The warm-ups were like my game. I enjoyed going into foreign stadiums and they'd have great stereo systems and they'd be blasting the Stones or whatever in warm-ups, and I'd take some of those Black Beauties and be throwing the ball seventy-five yards, running around playing receiver, fucking around—and then that was it for the day, I was done. I never played. I didn't even have to hold the clipboard. I couldn't have played in that condition anyway, I was really just too amped for my position. A lot of the guys played on speed, though. Some of the guys liked to mix speed with Vicodin. They could run though a fuckin' wall and not feel a thing."

During the fifteenth week of the season, Todd made his first trip to New Orleans. A long night of Hurricanes in the Quarter ensued; Todd ended up in bed with two stewardesses. He barely made it back for the pre-game meal.

"I walked into the Superdome, which was the biggest indoor stadium we played in—ninety thousand screaming Cajuns—and I was in hell. I mean my head—I was *dying*. I was barely able to make it though warm-ups. I was sweating profusely, trying not to vomit. The noise was fucking brutal."

The Saints that year had one of the best defenses in football. Midway through the game, Schroeder went back to pass and got hit simultaneously from both sides, injuring both ankles. "Coach Shell looks at me for a split second, like *Are you ready to go?* My heart dropped to my toes." Todd recalled. "I shook him off, like a pitcher does on the mound to the catcher. I was like, Are you fuckin kiddin me?"

The next week, December 22, was the last regular game of the season, a must-win against the Kansas City Chiefs; a wildcard slot in the playoffs was at stake. With Schroeder still hurt, Todd made his official debut... and completed 23 of 40 passes for 243 yards.

Though the Raiders lost 27–21, Todd's play was deemed "nearly flawless," by sportswriters. Two of his touchdown passes went to Tim Brown, a Notre Dame alum and Heisman winner who would become known over the years as "Mr. Raider." Brown told the *Times*: "Todd came out and played like he was in the league for ten, eleven years."

Marv was reported to have arrived at the stadium before the gates opened, waiting in line with the other fans to see his boy start. "Needless to say, I've had my Christmas present," he was quoted as saying afterwards.

Crowed *Times* sports columnist Mike Downey: "Sunday was Marinovich's bar mitzvah. The boy became a man."

The next morning, the Monday before the wildcard game—which was also against the Chiefs—Todd went to his refrigerator and discovered that he'd run out of clean piss.

Luckily, one of his former teammates was hanging out at his house. There were always people over; Todd might have turned pro but most of his friends were still at USC. On Halloween, after police responded to a complaint about loud music, he'd been cited for misdemeanor noise disturbance. His failure to appear at the initial hearing would eventually complicate his life further. This morning, Todd's former teammate gladly volunteered his urine; he assured Todd he hadn't smoked pot or taken any drugs. Unbeknownst to Todd, however, he'd been drinking non-stop since his own game on Saturday.

Todd collected the sample, poured it into the suntan lotion bottle, went to practice, did his pee test slight-of-hand.

A day later, the Raiders got a hasty call: Todd's urine sample had registered a blood alcohol level of 3.2, nearly four times the legal limit.

"They're like, 'This guy is a fucking full-blown alcoholic,'" Todd recalled. "They made me check into Centinela Hospital in Inglewood for alcohol detox—and I hadn't even been drinking. All I had was weed in my system. I had to stay in the hospital for two days. The team left without me; they ended up flying me to Kansas City by myself. It was such a fuckin nightmare. This was my life, dude."

The Chiefs played a defense with a "lurker" assigned to shadow Todd's every move. He was picked off four times and fumbled once; the Raiders lost 10–6. Their season was over.

And so was Todd's party.

The team held an intervention: Trudi, Marv, and Coach Shell were there, as were Todd's mentors, Marcus Allen and Howie Long. Todd went to the Betty Ford Center for 45 days. Before he left, he died his hair and his eyebrows black, so as not to be so conspicuous. He'd always hated sticking out the way he did. Years later, after a disastrous stint in the Canadian football league, he'd be trying to cop heroin in a drug ghetto in Portland when a cop would approach and address him by name. "What the hell are *you* doing in this neighborhood, Todd?"

The next season, 1992, Todd started out as backup. He was required by the NFL to pee-test three times a week. The alcohol deal had earned him one strike; the NFL's newly-installed substance abuse policy allows three. During training camp, Todd reportedly suffered a "dead arm," though he showed flashes of brilliance in several exhibition appearances. "Todd is football," enthused receiver Tim Brown at one point. Since Pop Warner, Todd's receivers had always loved him. There was something about him, so confident and vulnerable at once. You wanted him to lead, but at the same time, you felt the need to protect him.

Schroeder got the nod as starter for the season opener. He was benched two games later in favor of Todd, who completed thirty-three of a club record fifty-nine passes for 395 yards and three interceptions in the home opener, a losing effort against the Cleveland Browns, 28–16. The next week, against Lawrence Taylor and the New York Giants, Todd cut his passing hand on a defender's helmet, then had the wind knocked out of him. From the time he was small, from those first Pop Warner games up through the triumphs of high school, Marv always said the same thing to calm his son's jitters: "There's no reason to be nervous—it's not like you're playing the New York Giants." Now, here he was; and the Giants were kicking Todd's butt, two injuries in the opening minutes.

Todd pulled himself together, went back on the field. He hit Brown for a sixty-eight-yard touchdown pass and got his first NFL win, 13–10. After the game, Marv told Todd, "I don't care if you never play another down. You exceeded all expectations of what I thought you could do."

As the season progressed, Todd recalled, "I was trying to obey the league and not smoke pot, so my solution was, I'm just going to take acid 'cause it doesn't show up on drug tests.

"There was like a five to six week period, during my second season, when that's all I did after games—I'd drop a hit of LSD. It didn't stay in your system, so it didn't show up on the urine tests. Plus, I'd have two days to recoup, because Monday we'd just come in for film, and Tuesday we'd have off. So that worked for almost two months. I loved acid. It was one of my most favorite drugs. It went with the music shows I was going to on the weekends, on Sunset Boulevard and all over. The problem was, the effects linger for so long in your brain. I remember coming to practice and sitting down for the team meeting and seeing Art Shell up there do an arm movement and *wooooooooah*, you know, I'd see his arm making a trail. All of a sudden you'd get a zap and things are moving around."

Todd went on to win one more game as a starter, against the Buffalo Bills. By early November, he was benched; coaches complained he hadn't yet conquered the complicated pro system. By late November he was demoted to third string as Shell and the coaching staff became more and more disillusioned with his play and off-field antics.

"Being tested three times a week, I was like *fuck*, you know?" Todd recalled. "They were tying my hands. At this point, my solution to life was pot. It was my coping mechanism, it was my way to deal with life. It just allowed me to be comfortable in this loud, chaotic world. And especially in the world that I was living at that time. I was indescribably on Front Street. It was pretty much just like a gauntlet. Being from this area, playing here in college and now with the Raiders, I couldn't go anywhere. And if I did I was loaded. It just made sense for me. I had been doing it since I was fifteen or sixteen. Back then I was like, 'Thank God I found this.' I couldn't fathom living life sober. So it was pretty much pick or choose. I had to have some kind of drugs."

Again Todd came up dirty in an NFL urine test. This time, they skipped the intervention. He went straight to rehab for forty-five days. Strike two.

That spring, the Raiders signed free agent Jeff Hostetler and dealt Schroeder to Cincinnati. In the third round they drafted quarterback Billy Jo Hobart from Washington. Over the summer, Todd traveled the world, going from the South Pacific to the Caribbean to Ireland, a country where a tall redhead could easily disappear.

Upon his return to summer training camp there were four quarterbacks in Oxnard. Even so, Todd was slated to be on the cover of the NFL's 1994 calendar. "There could be a book written about all the things I've supposedly done that I haven't done. It's reached mythic status," he told the *Times*. "I'm not an angel, far from it. But some of the best players are out there were doing what I was doing, which was only having fun. People like that used to be called characters. Nowadays, it's more like convicts. Attitudes have changed. I've got God-given talent to throw a football. Yes, I've gone out and had a few drinks with the boys, and I've made a few mistakes. But it's been hard. It's been a major tarnishing experience."

Toward the end of August, 1993, Coach Shell was hospitalized for complications of diabetes. A few days after that, Todd failed another urine test. Ten days later, on August 30, Todd was let go. MARINOVICH PROJECT ENDS, said the *Times* headline: TEAM SAYS IT WAS OFF-FIELD BEHAVIOR THAT WAS DETERMINING FACTOR.

After eight games, eight touchdown passes, and nine interceptions, RoboQuarterback's NFL days were over.

Before the move was announced to the press, Al Davis spoke with Todd. He told the youngster he'd had him under surveillance, his phones tapped. "He had a list of all my friends and their nicknames. They were watching from this parking structure across from my house. Al said he knew it was only a matter of time before I got popped again on the league substance abuse policy. He said, 'I've never had to have this conversation with somebody as young as you about off-the-field conduct," Todd recalled.

Davis tried unsuccessfully to reach Trudi and Marv. He found Todd's grandfather, the Chief, in the press box at the Coliseum. "I've known Todd since he was a kid," Davis told the Chief. "But I'm going to cut him. He's been missing meetings. He's not doing what he's supposed to do."

The Raiders' director of football operations told the press, "The Todd Marinovich chapter in our history is now over... We have a history of succeeding with cases like Todd's but this time we didn't. The National Football League is a fast and unforgiving business. We felt it was time to go in a new direction."

"They were like, 'You're suspended for a fucking year for violating the substance abuse policy,'" Todd recalled. "It was my final year on my contract where I'm making the most money, like 750 grand. And they were like, 'We're not going to pay you if you can't play. We're letting you go.'

"To me it was like, fuck it, you know? Knowing they'd been watching me... That's what really pissed me off. That's why I just kind of threw up my hands and said, 'I'm done.'

"I'd been playing a long time—my whole life. I'd accomplished my goals. I started as a freshman on varsity. I'd played in the Rose Bowl. I played before a hundred thousand fans. I played against the New York Giants and beat them. I never said I wanted to play forever.

It was always just assumed that I was going to make a career and play fifteen years—but that assumption wasn't made by me. I just wanted to play at the highest level and have respect from the best guys that played the game, and I had that. Even in college it felt like the shit you had to put up with in order to play on Saturdays wasn't worth it. And you know, that's how it was in the pros. Those few amazing hours on Sunday were being outweighed by all the bullshit, and I just went, 'You know what? This fuckin ain't worth it.

"Plus, I thought I had a ton of money," Todd said. "In all reality I didn't have a ton of money, but what the fuck did I know? I packed up the Land Cruiser and drove to Mexico to surf."

"Heroin became my full-time job."

After leaving the Raiders, Todd sold his three-story, European style house in Manhattan beach for nearly two hundred thousand less than he'd paid for it and took off to travel the world.

After the signing bonus, he'd collected $350,000 for his rookie year and $500,000 for his second, less taxes and agent fees. The fact that he'd been dismissed by the Raiders for drug use was kept under wraps by the league and the team. In the world at large, nobody quite understood what had happened to RoboQuarterback. The easy answer was that Marv had burned him out too early with all the preparation, that Todd's drive had petered out, that he was just sick of trying so hard all the time, sick of the game of football, sick of old guys who couldn't even play anymore telling him what to do. Some people insisted that his strict upbringing created an equally strong desire to participate fully in all things hedonistic.

Whatever it was, upon leaving football, Todd acted as if he'd just been shot out of a cannon. He didn't even entertain an offer from the Steelers to sign and wait out the suspension.

He flew to Cancun, Mexico, to participate—along with Jim Kelly, Doug Flutie, and Evander Holyfield—in an Addidas Super Stars competition. After that, he traveled where whim dictated. Jamaica, South America, Hawaii, Colorado. He was in the thrall of new experiences and new ideas and new challenges. At each destination, he felt as if he'd found a new perfect place where he could become the self he was truly destined to be. On the north shore of Oahu, at the Bonsai Pipeline, he was nearly killed when he was caught in an undertow created by twelve-foot waves. "Panic was about to set in. My legs started cramping. I finally hit the reef and had some leverage to push my way to shore. It was the most scared I've ever been. I think back on it, how you can be here one minute, gone the next. It's good for you," he would later tell the *Times*.

The near-death experience got him thinking. He flew home and started training again with Marv; his agent worked the phones. By May of 1994, it was announced that he'd made a deal with the Winnipeg Blue Bombers of the CFL, runners-up in the last two Grey Cups. Initially, the Blue Bombers had offered the job to Florida State QB Charlie Ward, who went undrafted by the NFL. Ward instead elected to try the NBA. All was going well with his workouts until Todd tweaked his left knee in a pickup basketball game. A few weeks later, on the first play of the first day of Blue Bombers training camp, Todd's cleat got caught in the grass during a drop-back passing drill and his left leg crumpled. "It was freakish," recalled quarterback coach Mike Kelly. "It was like Stephen King wrote it. At first I said, 'You're kidding, right?' and then I looked at his eyes and I knew he wasn't."

"It was the most excruciating fucking pain I'd ever felt in my life," Todd recalled.

The Bombers offered to keep paying Todd if he stayed in Winnipeg and had the surgery, but Todd elected to go home. He'd torn both the ACL and the meniscus; he didn't want to take any chances. Doctors advised him to wait a month before having surgery. About two weeks before the scheduled date, it was July fourth, Todd's birthday. When he was young, Trudi used to delight him by saying that the Independence Day fireworks displays were in his honor. Todd was riding his beach cruiser on the crowded boardwalk at Newport Beach, taking care to guard his knee, when a little girl ran out in front of him. Trying to avoid the girl and protect the knee, Todd fell on his left wrist and broke it.

After reconstructive surgery on his knee, Todd went home to the little house he'd bought for himself in Dana Point, one half block from the sand. (While on painkillers, he scratched his face badly with the cast on his hand.) He bought himself a black Labrador puppy—to replace a boxer, named Blitz, the family had given away abruptly when he was four years old. (In elementary school Todd wrote a heartbreaking account of having to give up his very best friend.) Because his new dog had huge black paws, Todd named him Mims, after the six-foot-five, 300-pound San Diego Chargers lineman Chris Mims. Several years later, the ex-footballer would be found dead in his downtown Los Angeles apartment. Todd went everywhere with Mims. Over the next twelve years, the dog would be his most constant companion.

Todd's best human friend at this time was probably Marv. As always, Marv was training top athletes and making new advances in his field, but his income was never certain. If someone asked him to work with an athlete he'd do it because it needed doing. Without a place to live, Marv moved into Todd's. For a ten-month period, four hours a day, Todd and Marv worked together in absolute silence in Todd's garage, sculpting and sanding an eight-foot tall piece of mahogany that Todd had bought. "We called it 'going into the time warp,'" Todd recalled.

They created a large, abstract work, some parts smooth, some gnarled and gouged, a fitting representation of their lives. Todd also spent time drawing and painting, doing portraits of his idols, Hall of Fame quarterbacks Kenny Stabler, George Blanda, Dan Fouts, and Joe Montana.

One day during his rehab, Todd's old friend Marco Forster stopped by and gave him a guitar, something to keep himself busy during his rehab. Marco had been one of the Zero Period guys at Capo High; he was still into music.

Todd taught himself how to play. He began jamming with Forster and his friends; within three months, they started playing shows. They called the band Scurvy. Trading on Todd's fame—his nihilistic, all-star-gone-bad persona was perfect for rock 'n' roll—the band went on to headline such famous LA clubs as Bob's Frolic Room II and the Whisky A Go Go.

On stage, Todd stood uncomfortably off to one side and played rhythm guitar and sometimes sang. Forster played bass. The other members were Stoner Peterson, drums; Machine Riles, lead guitar; and Chimes Felix, lead singer. According to a review, the band featured "Van Halen-esque harmony," combined with "Steve Earle-like heavy country," along with "the occasional bass line that sounded like Ministry on Ritalin. The combination lives up to none of the influences, not even the cheese rock of Slaughter, off of which they seem to have ripped a play list," said the *Register*. The band's songs included several Todd originals: "Leavin & Teasin," Todd recalled, was "a Billy-Ray-Cyrus-meets-Judas-Priest mess." "Out of Gas," included the line "we're out of tune with funny hair, a state of mind I can't compare." Todd rented a warehouse for practices and financed a five-song demo. The group began taking meetings, trying to find a record deal. "He sent me a tape and, well, I guess there is an age gap there," Marv told the *Times*. "But if he enjoys doing his music, then I've got to respect that."

Meanwhile, like his friend Forster, Todd started doing heroin. He loved the calm and the easy of heroin; it made him feel comfortable in his own freckled skin. It also helped Todd combat his extreme stage fright. He liked it so much, he began smoking it every day.

"I didn't know about this thing called withdrawal," Todd recalled. "After a couple of weeks of using, one day I didn't have any. And I started to get sick. I was like, 'What the fuck is going on?' I thought I had the flu.'"

Todd found a connection in Santa Ana who would deliver. Before long, he was smoking an eight ball a day, three and a half grams—a golf-ball size chunk in a baggie, about $300. Eventually, to cut down on his expenses, the guys showed him how to inject.

Early in 1997, Scurvy was practicing every day in the warehouse. They were in negotiations with Sony for a record deal. It looked like a lock. Then Marco got popped on a heroin beef. The band was done. "Heroin became my full-time job," Todd said.

It was Swallows Day in San Juan Capistrano, March 24, 1977, a celebration of the time every year when the birds return to the historic mission after wintering seven thousand miles away in Argentina. There were parties, foods, a big parade. Todd, twenty-seven, lived in a small house in nearby Dana Point. To celebrate the three-day weekend, he had a few friends over; somebody got the idea to go to the grammar school playground next door to play some hoops on the eight-foot baskets.

As the game got going, the motley crew of loadies transformed themselves to ballers; guys were jamming and alley-ooping and playing hero. Todd of course could not miss, inside or out; as ever he seemed to have a laser scope guiding his aim. Then one of the guys, John Valdez, hurt his back going for a rebound. He went down like a ton of bricks.

Valdez was twenty-nine; he weighed about 275. The pain was so bad he couldn't walk. With much difficulty, the guys hauled him back to Todd's place. He didn't have any money or any insurance; the emergency room was not an option.

Valdez lay on Todd's bed moaning. In agony, he appealed to his host: "You got anything to help the pain?"

Todd left the room and returned with his works and his stash of Mexican black tar heroin. "I fixed myself first," Todd recalled. Because he was ambidextrous, he could shoot up with either hand; it was helpful to be able switch arms to find a good vein; years later he'd be using a mirror to shoot himself in the neck.

"I remember it being strong stuff but of course I didn't give him the same amount I gave me, I just gave him a fraction of the amount. I hit him and I remember missing a little bit when I started hitting the plunger. He went, like, 'Ow!' And I was like, 'Sorry, dude.'"

By this time all the partiers but one had left. Todd went outside to the porch to have a cigarette. When he came back in to check on Valdez, Todd recalled, "He's frothing from the mouth. He's fuckin blue."

Todd ran outside and retrieved the garden hose—it was easier than lugging the large man to the shower, as they always do in movies. As Todd was spraying him down, he remembered a conversation he'd had with Valdez that very day about the way Valdez had once brought somebody back from an OD—he'd slapped the living shit out of him until he regained consciousness.

Todd dropped the hose onto his bedroom floor, the water still running, and proceeded to smack Valdez across the face.

"I'm rearing back, I'm fucking hitting this guy with everything I've got. And I swear, I could see the struggle going on within him, I could see his spirit struggling to leave his body. I don't tell this story much; people think I was hallucinating. But on heroin you don't hallucinate—you do not fucking hallucinate on fucking heroin. And with all the adrenalin that was pumping through my system at the time I was alert and aware and totally on it. I could see his spirit leaving the top of his head; it was almost like he would just become this flesh bag with no life inside, and then the spirit would come back. The only way I could describe it is like when you see heat waves on the beach—when you're low to the ground and the heat waves eddy up and warp your vision a little bit. It was like that, and it was colorful. I actually saw it, the life-force or whatever, as it would leave the top of his head, and then I would smack the shit out of him and I would see it actually coming back into him. It seemed like a long time but it was probably only a few minutes. And then I realized, you know—it got to a turning point. I knew I was going to fucking lose him."

Todd yelled to the last remaining partier: "Call 911."

John Valdez started foaming at the mouth. The 911 dispatcher coached Todd through CPR.

Soon, the paramedics arrived, followed by the fire department and seven sheriffs deputies.

The first ENT on the scene asked Todd what Valdez had been ingesting. Todd said Valdez had been drinking, and maybe he'd done a little bit of heroin, too. The medics gave Valdez a shot of Narcanon, which usually brings around an OD victim, but nothing happened. Valdez was breathing, but only barely. The medics put him on a gurney and wheeled him out.

As this was happening, one of the deputies came into the room. He was holding a trash bag full of marijuana clippings.

The day before Todd had helped another buddy harvest his crop of homegrown marijuana. As a thank you, the buddy had gifted him a trash bag full of clippings—not the actual buds but the leaves and shake; the by-products, smokeable but not as potent. Todd had stashed the bag haphazardly in his garage rafters, along with his surfboards.

Given a bag that size, filled with that amount of product, the deputies assumed immediately that Todd was a commercial grower. "Where are the plants?" they demanded.

Todd's bed and his apartment were flooded. He was not stupid, he could see where this whole thing was going. He appealed to the deputies, who were acting as if they recognized the former Robo-quarterback: "I'm not a grower," he explained. "See, this buddy of mine—"

Just then, another deputy entered the room. He was carrying two spindly, half-dead marijuana plants that Todd had set up in his laundry room with the kind of grow light you can buy in any drugstore to help your houseplants through the winter.

Todd was charged with felony marijuana cultivation, and also with two misdemeanors relating to a syringe and prescription drugs not in Todd's name that were found in his apartment. (The next day, out on bail, Todd visited Valdez in the hospital. Valdez told of being in a place that was "really warm and comforting and going toward a white light," Todd recalled. "He wasn't fighting it. And then he said he was rudely brought back into reality by the medics shocking him with paddles.")

On September 3, a bench warrant was issued for Todd after he failed to show up for the third time to his pre-trial hearing. Two days later, Todd plead guilty and was sentenced to six months. He served two in the local jail, and then another month at the James A. Musick Facility, a one hundred-acre minimum security prison known as the Farm.

"The day before every game I'd make my needle exchange."

Todd served three months at the Farm, living in a filthy, six-man cell. He washed his clothes in the shower with a bar of soap. The toilet was one of those steel numbers without a seat; he had to do his business in front of everyone. In a county facility with few resources, he spent his time picking vegetables and repairing irrigation sprinklers. During his off hours, Todd did pushups and sit-ups on a towel on the concrete floor of his cell. As much as possible, he reversed his schedule and slept during the day to avoid conflicts. The deputies were worse than the inmates. Some showed compassion, many were former high school footballers who'd dreamed of turning pro; a couple had even played against Todd in high school. "They were like, 'Oh, you had it all and now look at you.'" Todd recalled. "They took a lot of pleasure in me being there."

Over the years, Todd had always been a model rehab patient; locked down and given rules to follow, he would always excel. Jail was no different; he ended up getting additional time off for good behavior, then spent three additional months in a sober living facility. When he was released from the Farm, Trudi and his dog Mims picked him up. The first thing Todd did was go straight to the beach and run along the water, the way he'd done with Marv since he was four. "I just wanted to keep running," he recalled. "It was a rush. I was high."

By the time Todd paid for his fines and treatment, all of his money was gone; he appealed to the NFL for reinstatement and began working out with Marv. For fun and conditioning he returned to pickup basketball. During a game one afternoon, Todd up pumped faked a guy and he bit—he jumped up high in the air to block the shot...and came down right on top of Todd. Herniated disk.

In April, 1999, just shy of his thirtieth birthday Todd was cleared by the NFL to play. He worked out for five teams; the Chargers and the Bears showed real interest. Due to his bad back, however, Todd failed the physical. No deals could be made. He ended up signing with the British Columbia Lions of the Canadian Football League, a team once led by Doug Flutie. Todd would be the backup to Marcus Allen's little brother, Damon, a CFL legend.

Somewhat drug free for the first time in years, Todd found Vancouver to be a beautiful city. He brought along Mims; he rented a little place right on the beach in a town called White Rock, forty minutes from the city. His roomie was a Canadian; there was a rule in the CFL, there had to be a minimum number of Canadians on each team. About two weeks into his stay, Todd's roommate took him "to check his babies." It turned out he was growing BC bud, a potent strain of marijuana that was popular on the west coast.

There was a full-on operation: two thousand square feet, grow lights, reflective Mylar, huge buds strung from the ceiling with fishing wire to dry. "I had never seen that much bud in my entire life," Todd recalled. "I was like, 'Oh yeah, I'm living with the right guy!'" On the way home, the guy took Todd to a downtown head shop to buy a bong. As Todd stepped out of the car, his foot crunched a bunch of little vials scattered in the gutter. His junky radar sputtered back to life.

In downtown Vancouver, Todd soon discovered his own personal land of Oz, where drug laws were liberal and junkies bought and used heroin openly—the cops only got involved if somebody keeled over in the middle of the street. The heroin was from the Golden Crescent area of southeast Asia. It was called China White. It was infinitely more potent than the Mexican black tar Todd had used before—and relatively cheap, smuggled into Vancouver's huge international port.

Before long, Todd had settled into a routine. "The day before every game, we would do a walk-through in the Dome—that would be my day to make my needle exchange. All my years of being a dope fiend, the hardest part was always getting needles—they were harder to score than anything. It got to where I was picking up a pack of fifty needles every week. I was getting good coke and really pure heroin and combining them. That's all I wanted to do. I woke up, fixed, went to practice. I would take a couple of syringes with me already prepared. I was in a fucking trance, playing by instinct. Thank God I was just backing up; Damon was a great athlete, one of the best players they ever had in that league. I was just the clipboard guy, playing the opposing quarterback in practice."

There was no urine testing in the CFL; a number of his teammates used crack and pot regularly. Todd's heroin use put him in a class by himself. He'd be partying with the guys and everybody would be all sprung from coke, and he'd go into the bathroom and fix, return all calm. Once, during halftime, Todd got one of his pre-made rigs out of his locker and went into the bathroom to shoot up. Because he didn't have any powered coke to add to the mix, he'd bought some crack. Sitting on the toilet, half listening to the chalk talk, he shot up the heroin. As the team was starting to leave the locker room for the second half, Todd struggled with the screen in his glass crack pipe—he wasn't getting a good hit. Then the pipe broke and he lacerated his left thumb—his throwing hand. By the time he got out onto the field, the game had already started. With his thumb wrapped in toilet paper and still bleeding he took up the clipboard, his only duty. "I didn't even know what play they were calling," Todd recalled. "Nobody looked at the shit I wrote down anyway."

The worst part were the away games. "I ran out of drugs a few times on the road. Those flights back were pure agony. That's where the training of the mental toughness came in handy. I couldn't whine and act sick. I just had to get through and get home so I could go hook."

At the end of the season, the team had a party. Todd was standing there, "gowed out of my mind," meaning that he was "somewhere between a nod and full-on slumber." In all reality, Todd recalled, "I had become a celibate heroin monk. I would go downtown, cop, come back to my pad, not leave till the drugs were gone. I wasn't eating at all. I spent a lot of time in this Astro mini van I had. I'd just climb into the back and fix. Me and Mims. There was no furniture in my place, just a bed and a TV. My life revolved around dope and my dog. He'd want to go down to the beach, so I'd take him down there for hours. He saved my ass because it was always in the back of my mind that I needed to take care of him; he would get me outside doing more healthy things that I really loved."

Standing there gowed at the end of the year party, Todd became aware that the general manager of the Lions was motioning for him to come over and chat. *Oh shit*, Todd thought. *The jig is up.*

The GM was a good guy who'd recruited him to come to BC. He smiled and put a hand on Todd's shoulder—Todd was too tall to wrap an arm around, though at 173 pounds he looked like a wreck, his orange hair long and greasy, hanging in his face.

"I know we signed you for one year with an option for another year," the GM said, looking grave. And then he issued a toothy smile: "We'd like to pick up that option."

Todd looked at him, mustering all the focus he could. "You got to be fuckin crazy," he said. "I can't stay here."

About a week later, Todd's good buddy and teammate Moe Elewonibi drove over to Todd's beach house. Six-four and 300 pounds with dreadlocks, Elewonibi was born in Lagos, Nigeria, attended high school in BC. At Brigham Young University he won the Outland Trophy as the nation's top collegiate interior lineman. Problems with drugs and alcohol shortened his career in the NFL; he fell in fast with Todd from the moment they'd met at Lions camp. Moe couldn't bear to see Todd wasting away like he was.

Elewonibi packed Todd and Mims and a whole bunch of China White into his truck, determined to drive Todd home to OC and get him some help. They left on the afternoon of December 31, 1999, New

Year's Eve, the dawn of the new millennium. As you could well imagine, their three-day drive south is an epic story in itself. Todd went into rehab again.

In March, 2000, Los Angeles was awarded an expansion team in the Arena Football League. The owner, Casey Wasserman, was the grandson of media mogul Lew. At twenty-five, he was the youngest owner of a U.S. professional sports franchise. Because of a labor dispute, the team had only six days of practice before the first game. Training camp opened with only twenty-eight guys. Todd signed a contract for $60,000. "It's still football," he told the *Times*. There were four quarterbacks in camp. Scott Semptimphelter, a backup the last two seasons in Nashville, would likely be the starter. "That takes some pressure off me," Todd said. He was just happy to be working.

The season started in late March. In mid-April, in San Diego, another young quarterback with a tremendous upside, Ryan Leaf, had self-destructed. The Chargers asked permission from Wasserman and Brock to meet with Todd as a possible replacement. The Chargers coaches were impressed; Todd's hopes were raised when he was pulled off the Avenger team plane in Chicago to talk to his agent about terms. In the end, the Chargers elected to go in another direction, selecting JuJuan Seider from Florida A&M in the sixth round, and signing free-agent quarterback Mike Burton from Division III Trinity University. Though Todd's arm was not questioned, the Chargers said privately that Todd's history off the field was a concern.

Todd settled into his new role as third oldest player on a rag-tag Arena League squad—his teammates included a former school teacher, a real estate investment broker, a graduate of engineering school, an OC truant officer, and a former volunteer at the Vancouver Aquarium.

In late April, after a small Jacuzzi party at his apartment complex in Marina Del Rey, Todd was arrested by police on suspicion of sexual assault after a nineteen-year-old woman claimed he forced her to have sex. The charge did not stick. A used condom collected by investigators from Todd's bathroom trash, usually an indicator of mutual consent, helped sway the decision, as did the testimony of her friends. "Based upon the ambiguity of the complainant's behavior, Marinovich had a plausible defense that he reasonably believed the victim was consenting to sexual intercourse," the assistant district attorney told the press.

In June, Todd was awarded the Avenger starter's job. Under his stewardship, the team notched its only three wins of the season, including a record-setting performance in a 72–66 victory against the Houston Thundercats. On and off the wagon since the beginning of the season, by the time of the Houston game, Todd was again a full-blown heroin addict. Usually, he carried a stash with him; this weekend, he'd miscalculated. By game time he was suffering from full withdrawal—shaking, sweating, vomiting, muscle cramps, diarrhea. During warm-ups he shit his white football pants; the equipment manager gave him a new pair but warned they were his only extras. "Remember, this is the Arena League, not the NFL," he told Todd. (The difference was clear to Todd also; from day one, he chose to wear clownish, red high-top Chuck Taylors with his red-white-and-blue Avengers uniform.) At game time, RoboQB strapped it together and went out onto the field. He threw ten touchdowns, winning the game in overtime and tying the league record, which was still intact when the league died for financial reasons in 2008.

The Avengers finished the season 3–11. Todd had appeared in eight games, passed for 2,552 yards and forty-five touchdowns. Thirty two years old, he was named to the All-Rookie team; the Avengers made him their franchise player and offered $100,000 for a second season.

On December 13, 2000, Todd went to the team's office to sign the papers. He left with his signing bonus—$35,000 cash in a manila envelope. Longtime junkie that he was, Todd headed straight to downtown LA.

He copped a couple balloons of black tar heroin, pulled his Toyota truck to the curb next to a little park, the only white face in a Mexican neighborhood. "I had just plunged the plunger of the needle and I'm feeling it—getting my rush, you know, and I see five-oh (the cops) coming my way. They slow as they pass, and I'm pretending to do something in the glove box. I start the car and take off real slow, but they pull a U and get behind me and he flips it, you know, turns on the lights and the siren. And I'm like, *Fuck man, I'm fucked.* The cop gets on the bullhorn. He's like, 'Todd, pull the vehicle over!'"

Todd was charged with felony possession of heroin. In March, 2001, he pleaded no contest and made a deal to enter a court-approved drug treatment program. For the first time outside of an AA meeting, he spoke publicly about his six-year struggle with heroin addiction. The LA *Times* headlined their story: SCRAMBLING FOR HIS LIFE; TODD MARINOVICH REVEALS A SECRET: HE HAS BEEN HOOKED ON HEROIN FOR SEVERAL YEARS.

In the article, Todd made sure to say that contrary to popular opinion, Marv was not to blame for his troubles. It was Todd's shyness, his desire to fit in, that led to pot, he said. With heroin it was something deeper. "I can only compare it to what the womb must feel like. The outer world disappears and you are completely at ease."

The 2001 edition of the Avengers team was even worse than the inaugural squad.

Though Todd was living with a volunteer minder named Garo Ghazarian—a former lawyer whose own drug addiction had led to his disbarment—Todd was doing drugs on and off, missing his court mandated pee tests, failing to make counseling sessions and AA meetings. He seemed determined to get thrown into jail again. Unlike rehab, where structure seemed to give him purpose, being at large in the world seemed to be too much for Todd to handle. He liked to live in the moment; it was too much trouble to live otherwise. So messy, so many obligations. It was as if he didn't understand the notion of cause and effect. Or maybe he just didn't care. Every time he slipped, there was someone to pick him up and set him back on the path. His talent at once saved and damned him. He knew everything that could be known about quarterbacking a football team, but very little about living real life...

Going into the Gaylord Entertainment Center for a game against the Nashville Kats, on May 18, 2001, the Avengers were 0–4. Their coach, Stan Brock—once an interior lineman with the 1995 Super Bowl champion San Diego Chargers—had just been fired. The new coach was Robert Lyles, whose previous head coaching position had been at Treadwell High in Memphis, Tenn.

The Kats were 3–2. Ranked only fourteenth in scoring in the league, at 40.8 points a game, they ranked first defensively, giving up only 31.6 points a game. With 1:57 left in the first half, the Avengers were trailing, 28–20. They had the ball on their own two yard line. Todd was flushed out of the pocket by a heavy rush; on the small field, literally the size of a hockey rink, there was nowhere for him to scramble. A diving defender caught him by one foot; as Todd was going down, he chucked the ball downfield, at the feet of his running back. The ball bounced on the turf and hit his man on his thigh-pads.

The ref threw a flag: intentional grounding. Todd went bat-shit—he chucked his quarterback's hand towel at the ref, who in turn ejected him from the game. As Todd was being escorted from the field, the PA announcer informed the crowd: "This is the second week in a row that Marinovich has been ejected." The previous week, enraged by another bad call, Todd had thrown a clipboard onto the field. He went straight to the locker room, showered and dressed.

"Off I go into Nashville," Todd recalled. "I go to a bar and it's all about Jack Daniels, just getting blitzed. When I start getting hammered, I start thinking about doing what I really want to do—drugs. The day before I had gone to the Country Music Hall of Fame. I bought a CD of one of my favorites, Steve Earle. And I remember listening to one of the songs about going down to some street in Nashville to meet the devil. Of course if you're a junky, you know what he's talking about.

"I get into a cab and I say take me to Such and Such street, and the cabby looked at me, like, Are you sure?, so I knew I had the right place. And lemme tell you: I had been into some ghettos before. But dude, this was a Saturday freaking night and it was sketchy. I'd been in sketchy, but this was even sketchy for me and I was solo. The cabby's like, 'Do you want me to wait?' And I'm like, 'Nah. I'm good.' I get out and walk over to this liquor store where they're all fucking just boozing and fucking hanging out. And it's the projects, bad. They're a little apprehensive at first but they can tell that I ain't a cop, I'm just fucking a crazy white boy looking to score.

"I let my first forty dollars go. I wanted heroin but this was a crack spot. The dude took my money and walked. I realized that shit wasn't coming back. After that, I just kind of leveled with the dudes. I'm like 'Look, I'm going to kick you down, there's no reason to fucking run off with my money. Let's just go somewhere and party.' So we went to some fleabag ghetto motel and got some crack and some weed and some forties of malt liquor and we started partying. Meanwhile, my phone starts blowing up. It's Garo. He's like, 'The game's over. What happened to you? Where the fuck are you?'

"Garo finally comes and finds me and gets me in the wee wee wee hours, I don't even remember what time. We get back to the team hotel, and we go to sleep. When we wake up, we discover that the team left us. They just left us at the hotel. No wake up call, nothing. When the team leaves their fucking quarterback in Nashville, you know you can see the writing on the wall. It cost Garo like $1,500 to get us home."

By 2004, Todd was out of money and moved back to Balboa. He had no fixed domicile. He haunted the beaches and alleyways of his youth, a stoned apparition. In the summers he lived at times under a palm-frond gazebo, washing at the public bathhouse. Other times he couch-surfed. He knew a million people; fewer and fewer knew him back anymore. He didn't really like to go to the family house on Balboa if he didn't have to. He hated the way Trudi looked at him, with such hurt in her eyes. She just wanted her boy back. "It was really hard to see him like that," she recalled.

Sometimes Todd did stay at the house. Trudi, Grandma (the Chief's wife), and Uncle Craig Fertig were living there together. Todd and Craig would sit and drink in the Chief's trophy room, which Todd called The Shrine. At some point, Craig would accuse Todd of stealing some money and Trudi would change the locks. Thereafter, Trudi saw her son infrequently; sometimes they'd meet at one of the ornamental benches on the island and she'd bring him food on a paper plate.

Because he had no car and no license, Todd had trouble scoring heroin, which was more rare and more expensive due to the war on drugs. As time passed he discovered a ton of meth around Newport Beach. "People were practically giving it away," Todd recalled. "It's totally different drug, depending on how you ingest it—you can eat it, snort it, smoke it, or slam it. All four are fucking completely different highs, or not completely different, they're all obviously stimulants, but each one has different features. Smoking is the most mellow. People smoke it in those little round bowls. I did it every which way until I came across somebody who was slamming it. After all my speedball usage (coke and heroin combined) I knew that using a needle is in itself an addiction alone. That's all I wanted to do. Because after the initial big time adrenaline rush that you get, after three or four days of being up, meth takes you to that same nod-state that heroin gives you. So you get to that dream trance warm euphoria, though you have to ride it out for fucking seventy-two hours to get there.

"When I was sprung, I spent all my time skating. Skating was probably the most fun that I've ever had on drugs. That and sex. Meth makes you just fucking perv. Fuck. It's sick. It turns normal people with some morals into just fucking sick perverts. That's all I wanted to do, you know, is look at porn or create my own. God. What you see on the news, that type of shit? I think speed's behind most of these violent fucking perverted crimes.

"When I grew up Marv was totally against skateboards. It was too dangerous. I might break something. But I loved it. It was recreation, it was also transportation. It was a way to burn off all that fucking energy that I had from the meth. And it was fun! It was like surfing on fucking concrete. I loved it. I would skate for fucking eight hours a day. Miles and miles. I was fucking gone. Usually my best time was late at night. I knew all the cops' shifts; the shift would change between 3 and 3:30 a.m. There'd be no cops on the island, and I'd have the whole fucking boulevard, all smooth, no rocks or seams, and I'd be just carving up and down the street in board shorts and maybe tennis shoes, my Chuck Taylors."

Todd's knowledge of police shift times proved not to be so flawless. A six-five redhead living on the same tiny island where he grew up so prominently, Todd was never very far from public scrutiny; every cop and nearly every resident in town knew he was an addict on probation.

In September of 2004, Todd was arrested by Newport police for skateboarding in a prohibited zone. Police found meth and syringes on him.

It happened again in May, 2005: Accosted by police in a public bathroom, Todd fled on his beach cruiser and was apprehended fifteen blocks away. Police found drug paraphernalia in his toiletry kit but no drugs; one of the cops was an old Capo Cougar teammate. Todd was charged with violating probation. In June, 2005, thanks to the efforts of twenty-three of his old USC teammates, who put up $4,600 required for Todd to enter an inpatient treatment program, Todd avoided going back to jail. Three months later, he walked out of the sober living facility where he was living and disappeared for three weeks. Eventually he gave himself up. He was sentenced to his second stint at the Farm, where he picked vegetables and repaired irrigation equipment.

On August 30, 2007, a pair of Newport police riding in an unmarked minivan saw Todd, by now thirty-eight years old, skateboarding on the boardwalk. It was about 1:15 in the morning. Todd was carrying a guitar case, wearing a backpack. As Todd well knew—having lived here for a lifetime—skateboarding is not allowed on the boardwalk.

The officers gave chase.

"All of the sudden two fucking blue uniforms pop out of this freaking tourist van," Todd recalled. "I had just been over to my hook spot; I was holding. I take off. One cop is running at me, and the other one's crossing the boulevard, trying to head me off. I cut back on the skateboard and then popped off, dropped my guitar case, and fucking ran down this alley. And then one of them yelled: 'Todd! Freeze.' That's when I heard the *pop pop pop*. I thought they were fucking shooting. But it turned out to be a taser. My leg started spasming but it wasn't too bad, I kept running. I guess the taser had hit my backpack; only some of the electricity got through. I went and hid on somebody's second floor balcony. I saw the fucking light come on and a guy came out, looked at me, and shut the door real fast. I was like *Oh fuck! I got to find a new hiding spot!* By then there were helicopters, the whole nine yards. Then I heard the dogs barking. That's when I gave up. I didn't want to get bit. I've seen too many people come into fucking Orange County Jail tore up from dogs. So I just laid down on the fucking ground and they found me. That was it. I gave up."

It was Todd's ninth arrest. He was charged with felony possession of a controlled substance, and misdemeanor counts of unauthorized position of a hypodermic needle and resisting a police officer.

"Believe me, dude, I've been there."

September, 2008.

Evening in the suburbs. The dishes were drying, a TV was droning in a back room, the washer cycling through another load of dirty clothes. A fifteen-year-old boy sat at the dining room table, doing his honors geometry homework with a mechanical pencil.

Todd sauntered into the room, his rubber sandals flapping against the hardwood floor. He stood a moment watching the boy scratch out an answer, and then he placed his big, freckled mitt on the kid's shoulder. Todd's knuckles were raw and torn from his job cleaning barnacles off boat bottoms in Newport Harbor. He worked early in the mornings before the sun got too high; he wore a wet suit and goggles, used a long air hose, drove a dinghy on his rounds from motor yacht to sailboat. He'd be down there all alone for a half hour at a time, his bubbles slowly circling the hull—lost in repetitious physical effort, cocooned by the silent salty water, he made no bones about comparing it to the calming effects of heroin; for all his love of the big game and the big stage, he has always been most comfortable when he was alone. (In college, after the Syracuse game in the Meadowlands, when he threw for 337 yards and three touchdowns, Todd was asked by the press to name his favorite moment in New York. "Lying on my bed in my hotel room for two hours and listening to Led Zeppelin," Todd said into the bouquet of microphones.)

Todd was now thirty-nine. As of tonight, he'd been sober thirteen months.

Following his last arrest, he was diverted to a special drug court run by a county judge who takes special pride in his low recidivism rate. Hanging over Todd's head—a suspended sentence of two years in jail. His schedule was nearly as crowded as it was during the summer before ninth grade: Pee testing three times a week. Mandatory attendance at sessions with his special drug court group, at one-on-one therapy, at group therapy, at meetings with his parole officer, at AA meetings. The goal: If he completed the program successfully, in another eighteen months, he could have his felonies dismissed or reduced, opening up his opportunity for coaching at a public school.

Todd made about $40 a boat, six boats a week. Lately, his other main source of income was coaching young quarterbacks. There were four students right now, kids of varying ages who dreamed of playing someday in the NFL. All of them had promise; Todd's services cost $40 an hour, more than you invest in a kid for fun. Jordan Greenwood was one of his most talented.

"Dude. You gotta minute?"

Jordan looked up attentively, the way a ninth grade boy will do, part reverent child wanting to please, part young man with ideas of his own. They were in the great room of a renovated ranch house near the city of Orange, a few miles southeast of Anaheim, in the central part of the county. From their particular vantage point, at 9 on a Wednesday night, Jordan and Todd could look out the sliding glass doors toward the pool, the Jacuzzi, the two Labrador retrievers romping in the yard... and beyond that to the bright lights of Handy Park little league stadium, where Jordan played as a kid... and beyond that to Route 55, the Costa Mesa Freeway, an eight-lane river of mighty asphalt linking Los Angeles and the coast with the Inland Empire, part of the fifty-four thousand linear miles of roadway that rule the rhythms of daily life in the county.

Framed there in the tempered glass was the perfect rendering of the real OC, which is, at its best and worst, a place that exists primarily to grow and house families, home of the California lifestyle. Orange County has the most athletic field space per capita of any county in the nation. The Board of Education is the largest employer in the county. It could be said that OC is to genetics as Napa Valley is to cooking—a place that specializes in great ingredients. Common wisdom has it that the most beautiful people in the world come to Hollywood to get famous—most don't make it. Instead they move to OC, get jobs, and make beautiful children. And great quarterbacks.

Jordan is five foot eleven and a half, 150 pounds. His cheeks are free of any whiskers; he's got a bit of growing left in him. His dad, Scott, is an insurance guy with a soul patch beneath his lip and a custom painted, spit-shined, 550-horsepower Baja desert racer in the garage, beside a yellow Hummer. He is not tall for a man, but his wife is tall for a woman. People say that a lot of boys get their height from their mom's side (though that might just be people who have short fathers). Mom's name is Andrena. It was she who stuffed the double stuffed potatoes served tonight for Todd, his girlfriend Alix, and your reporter. Scott grilled strip steaks for the men, salmon for the ladies. Jordan had one of each for the protein. Andrena likes to joke that her name sounds like a black church lady in the south. In fact she is Italian. Her parents used to own this house as a rental property. She attended the high school nearby. Scott's from Fullerton, about four miles northwest, up the 5 freeway.

Jordan is their younger son. He's a freshman at Orange Lutheran, one of the schools that competes in the Trinity League against Todd's old team Santa Ana Mater Dei. It costs dearly to go there, but not as much as a secular private school. Jordan started playing tackle football at age eight in the Junior All American program, which is more competitive than Pop Warner. His first year, against an all black team from Compton, Jordan broke a long run for a TD. "Look at that white boy go!" enthused the local announcer over the PA. Coaches from other teams would come up to Scott after the game and whistle appreciation: "We really need to keep an eye on him." From there he went on to the All Conference team. He also played soccer. One game he had three goals in the first ten minutes.

About a year ago Jordan was referred to Marv. Todd was brought in on day two. He hadn't been sober very long but he was up for the distraction. Todd watched Jordan throw and thought to himself, *This kid's got something. I could really help him.* The first order of business: completely remake Jordan's throw—which gave Scott a heart attack.

Scott was Jordan's first coach, his manager, his financier, his constant booster. Scott played quarterback in high school. He'd taught Jordan his stroke—what he believed to be a perfect throwing motion. Like a good basketball shooter, you never want to mess with the shot: Everybody knows that. But Todd showed the Greenwoods the mechanics that he and Marv had worked out years ago with the same man who'd adjusted Nolan Ryan's throwing motion. Given Todd's history, he was probably the best-trained quarterback who ever played the game. Maybe not the most *successful*, but certainly super-prepared, having been tweaked by experts of every stripe. Scott went ahead and agreed, and for the next six months, Todd and

Jordan rebuilt his throw. Every night, Jordan had to stand in front of the mirror and repeat the new motion—which had a lot to do with keeping the elbow out and properly squared and whipping the hand forward—one thousand times a night. Each rep had to be perfect. It was up to Jordan. Nobody could do it for him.

Meanwhile, as a family, the Greenwoods looked at all the schools in the area and talked to many of the coaches. In the end they decided on Orange Lutheran, another perennial powerhouse in the county. One recent Lancer's graduate, Aaron Corp, competed in 2009 against Mater Dei's Matt Barkley for the starting job vacated by USC's Mark Sanchez, by now a successful pro.

As everyone had hoped, Jordan started the football season strong. At summer practice there were four quarterbacks on the freshman team. Jordan worked harder than any of them; after every practice, he was the one left picking up the balls.

Over the first three exhibition games, the coach rotated all four. Fleet of foot, Jordan was perfect for the Veer offense; he scored fifteen touchdowns, including a seventy-yard run against Long Beach Poly, an inner city team the county folks like to call "very athletic." Then came the fourth exhibition. The entire extended Greenwood family came out to watch. Jordan did not play. Not even one down. You can guess how everyone felt, especially Jordan, who tried not to show any emotion. Scott got super pissed. He threatened to go see the coach at Villa Park, the public school in the neighborhood. The coach over there was new, himself part of a family football dynasty. Andrena, however, counseled patience. "Let's see what Todd thinks," she'd said, picking up the phone to invite him to dinner.

Now Todd folded himself into the chair next to Jordan. He wore his big sunglasses atop his head. The orange hair was not so bright anymore, like a colorful curtain faded over the years by the sun.

Over the course of the evening, during the grilling and soft drinks, during dinner, the adults had done all the talking. Jordan stood by Scott's side, listening, dutifully fetching whatever asked—the meat, the tin foil, the serving plate. During dinner Jordan ate with the gusto of a teenage athlete; he may not have even been paying attention as the adults talked about his future. Should they stay at Orange Lutheran? Should they go to Villa Park? How do you deal with such inexplicable coaching decisions? When it's your kid, it's not just sports: It really makes you feel like you want to kill somebody. The Greenwoods were at the edge. After dinner there was a final conference with the parents out front. Then Todd came inside to be alone for a few moments with his charge.

"What's the worst part of your experience over there at Orange?" Todd asked, keeping it vague to start.

Jordan looked down at his math book. "I don't know," he said. He commenced drumming the eraser of his pencil against the text book.

"Not playing?" Todd ventured.

Jordan looked up, made eye contact. "Yeah, mostly."

"What else?" Todd asked.

Shrug. "I dunno."

Todd lowered himself into the chair next to Jordan. "Believe me, dude, wherever you are, I've been there."

One way or another, Todd knew exactly how Jordan felt. How many times had he agonized about a coach's seemingly-arbitrary decision making? It just seemed instinctive to want to reach out to this kid and help. "In all my years," he would later say, "when I look at the people who coached me, I had maybe one or two who really had played themselves, who really knew what the game was about from the player's point of view. So many coaches out there, they're like, fucking up the kids. It's terrible. The parents and the coaches. Football is archaic in their mentality. The idea that the loud yelling coach is acceptable—I don't know where that comes from. Maybe it goes all the way back to a Vince Lombardi-type era when it was in-your-face kind of discipline. When it was happening to me, the thing is, it doesn't help. *It does not help.* It's just a superiority thing, like they know everything, the coaches. They're trying to make you bend to their will. But when there's a correction to be made, and they're berating a kid verbally about it, there's no teaching going on. None at all. They don't see football for what it is. At it's highest, it's an art form. A way to express yourself.

"Its hard because it makes the kid not wanna play. I've heard more stories of people who tell me they just stopped playing because of a certain coach or a team's philosophy that just drove them off the cliff. I don't think you have to do things like that. I think you can be different as a coach. You can have knowledge about the actual game itself, and you can also have a side of you where you can convey it to somebody young and not be a dick. I think that's what I'd like to try to do. I think I could really help."

"So what else?" Todd asks Jordan. "What else is bothering you."

"Well, the thing is," Jordan said haltingly, "the coach, at the beginning of the year, he was like, 'If you put in full effort and show the attitude, you're gonna play.'"

"Right," Todd said, leaning in.

"But this other quarterback—I put in like twice as much effort as him. I'm not being cocky or anything, but I have a way better attitude than him. He kind of gets in trouble in like classes and stuff."

"Um-hum."

"And then the coach still like starts him over me. That's like the thing I don't understand. The coach stresses effort and attitude, but he doesn't really like apply it."

"I can see that being frustrating," Todd said.

Jordan looked at him. You could tell he was trying not to cry. He likes Todd because he's really calm. Besides all the mechanical stuff, Todd has taught him a lot about the game. Like if you throw a bad ball, execute incorrectly, read the coverage wrong, whatever, you just have to get over it and go to the next play. The other day Todd even gave him a book of inspiring quotes—that was real cool too. To him, Todd felt as much like a friend as he did a coach. .

"Listen dude," Todd said, as warm a *dude* as was ever uttered. "Things can look pretty overwhelming right now because you're so young, but believe me, you can have a great career—possibly at Orange Lutheran. You never know. I wouldn't cash my chips and be bitter just yet. Some days, stuff just looks all wrong. We're all gonna be here for you. Your parents aren't gonna guide you in a way where you end up with a bad coaching experience. I'm not gonna let that happen either. You are gonna be fine. You just have to believe in yourself."

"I know," Jordon said, brightening a bit.

"It's gonna be fine," Todd enthused, giving him a brotherly shove. "Now do your homework before you flunk out!"

"Someday people will realize what a genius you are, Buzzy."

October, 2008.

Moving day in San Juan Capistrano. Todd and Marv Marinovich were biding their time in the shade of a thirty-foot U-Haul truck. They were at one of those self-storage places where you rent a locker about the size of a small garage, with a high ceiling and a roll-down metal door; the lock is sold separately.

It's a long story, and there are several sides, and some people are not talking, but Marv's stuff is in storage because he was asked to leave the private high school out of which he'd been working for nearly two years. There was a beef with his young partner, a display of temper. The young guy was embedded in the school's fabric. Marv was asked to leave rather abruptly. Todd ran over there in his girl-friend's truck and hauled out as much of Marv's equipment as he and a friend could carry—heavy machines, exercise equipment, training balls, hand weights, a lifetime aggregation of training stuff.

You might not know this about storage facilities: some places charge you the low introductory rate for the first month. Then the next month is five times higher. Neither Todd nor Marv had that kind of cash. Luckily another friend of Todd's—there are friends of Todd practically everywhere in OC—volunteered his father's garage. Another friend donated the money for the truck rental. Marv is here to help load; then he must leave for an appointment to train a kid. You can read all about Marv's successful techniques on the new web-site his former partner has posted, SportsScienceLab.com.

Since Todd got straight, he'd stepped in to help Marv as much as he can. Marv was never very good with dates and bills and check-book balances. Todd helped him buy a new computer and set it up. He took him to the doctor several times. Usually a robust man, Marv had been feeling tired lately; he may have an irregular heartbeat. "All those years I was so out of it. It felt great to be able help Marv," Todd said simply. "He has always been there for me."

At ten in the morning it was already hot. Somehow, when the storage locker was hastily rented, custody of the key was not properly monitored. After an ill-fated attempt to drill out the lock—it looks so easy in the movies—they had to call a locksmith. They don't have the money for that, either.

Todd squatted in the shade of the rental truck like a gang member on a prison yard, smoking an ever-present Marlboro Red. He smokes like an addict; you've seen the behavior at break time outside at AA meetings. He sucks the smoke down hungrily; he'll talk with a butt dangling from his lips, carry heavy boxes with a butt dangling, swish three pointers with a butt dangling, the smoke trailing off, causing him to squint one of his pale blue eyes.

Marv was standing against the building, in a sliver of shade. Though he is nearing his eighth decade, he looks twenty years younger. He has a full head of curly gray hair. Until this recent spate of not feeling well, he's always worked out on a rowing machine and ridden his racing bike for miles along the coast. He lived at the time in a tiny apartment in the shadow of the centuries-old mission, part of a system used by Spanish monks to settle and pacify California. A much younger woman occasionally found her way to his place for sleepovers. When you get to know him well, you see that Marv has three possible speeds. Stone silent, giggly, and spitting mad. Because of his feelings about processed food, his body being a temple and so forth, he will not have so much as a glass of water in a restaurant—which made our first meeting, in a restaurant, somewhat strange for the waiter. Another time, when Todd and I went to lunch at a rural golf course, Marv elected to pass his time in the heat of the car. He sat there like a stone until we returned.

"I don't know if I told you this," Todd said, filling the time with talk. "They finally put the kid in over at Orange Lutheran."

"You went to see him the other night at his house?"

"Jordan. They let him play. And he threw for one touchdown and ran for two. They won 48–14. Spanked 'em!"

"It took 'em that long to figure it out?" Marv asked. The two men snorted in derisive harmony. They share many of the same nonverbal expressions—and also the same dismissive feelings about the quality of most coaches.

"I'm gonna start giving him the personal training right at his house," Todd said, taking a last deep drag, then carefully ashing the coal, field-stripping the butt, placing the filter in the pocket of his surfer shorts. "They've got a pool and a gym in the back of their house. He's perfect for the water work."

"You're gonna get rid of all the—"

"Weights?" Todd interrupted.

Marv cringed theatrically, then sort of laughed at himself. Weights are his big bugaboo—remember how he ruined himself before he went into the pros? He sees it all the time in the kids he trains. They go away to college, bulk up... and lose four inches off their vertical jump. To all appearances, Marv is a sweet and personable man who loves Todd very much. He really has no one else besides Todd and Traci, who lives several hours away, and Mikhail, his son with his second wife, a former dancer who also bore him a daughter. Mikhail is a six-six sophomore defensive end at Syracuse. He has the right stuff, Marv says, though he came to football late. He was arrested in 2007 for getting drunk and breaking into the college gym with a friend to lift weights after hours. Thereafter Todd advised the kid: "Don't be stupid. You're a Marinovich. You have a target on your back."

"He can't mess himself up too much with light dumbbells," Todd said about Jordan.

Marv grimaced and shook his head, unrelenting on the point. "Tell that to Tyson Chandler. When I got him, he couldn't even get his arms behind his head. It was screwing up his whole shot. He had to torque his body and sort of fling the ball."

"Light shrugs and stuff?" Todd asked. "That's good, no?"

Grimly: "You're putting the body out of equilibrium."

"The thing is, the joker needs to put on weight," Todd said. "He's only 150. Too light for varsity."

Marv giggled like a school girl. "You haven't become one of those guys who always say—" and here he waggled his sausage-like finger, doing an imitation, complete with southern drawl, of one of those kinds of coaches they both hate: "'If he had another ten pounds on him he'd be great!'"

Todd laughed. "That's funny, Buzzy. You're getting to be a real comedian in your old age."

When Todd was born, he was listed as Marvin Scott Marinovich on his birth certificate—Trudi changed it a few years later to Todd Marvin. Early on, Marv nicknamed the boy Orange. It was like, "Hey Orange, time to go practice your free throws," Todd recalled. Over time, for reasons unremembered, Marv started calling Todd Buzzy, a reference to Buzzie Bavasi, the legendary Dodger general manager known for engineering the team's move from Brooklyn to LA. (Though Todd didn't play high school baseball, he was drafted as a pitcher by the Angels.) For some reason, when Marv began calling Todd Buzzy, Todd began calling Marv Buzzy as well.

Nowadays, when Marv calls Todd's cell phone—Todd's ringtone is the first few bars of the Monday Night Football theme—Todd will pick up and say, "Hey Buzzy, what's up?" Around others, he still calls him Marv, as he has since he was small. "I can't ever remember Todd calling him Dad," Trudi recalled.

Todd rose and changed positions, taking a place next to Marv in the shade against the building.

After a short silence, Todd began telling Marv about an art history course he is taking at Orange Coast College. It's as a requirement of drug court, he mentioned to his father, but he can count the credits toward his college degree, if he ever wants to finish. Like Todd, Marv was a fine arts major at USC; they share a keen interest in art. About a month ago, Marv was working on a painting but he couldn't get the sky right. He had Todd come over to help; it took about five hours until they were both satisfied.

The other night in class, Todd told Marv, they were learning about Dadaism, the anti-art art movement born in Switzerland during World War I. One of the icons of the movement was this dude named Marcel Duchamp. He did a cool painting called Nude Descending a Staircase.

"When he was coming up, Marcel's older brother and his friends were the ones recognized as the famous painters. They thought Marcel sucked," Todd explained. "But in the end, everybody recognized that Marcel was the true master."

"After he was dead, I'm sure," Marv said.

"When I heard that," Todd said, ignoring his father's comment, "the first thing I thought of was you, Buzzy. Someday people will realize what a *genius* you are."

Marv raised his thick eyebrows archly. "Have you been drinking something?"

And then the two of them, Buzzy and Buzzy, had a big laugh.

"It's like you're too old to play now so you don't have to do drugs anymore."

Driving north on I-5, past the rugged mountains of Camp Pendleton, Todd and I were returning from offloading Marv's stuff. The large U-Haul truck juddered wildly on the uneven asphalt. I was driving. Todd was in the passenger seat. Even at fifty miles per hour in the slow lane, the ride was torturous. It had been a full day; the mood in the cab could rightfully be called slap-happy. Todd noticed that if he sang a note and held it, the pounding of the road would make his voice quaver rhythmically. It was a silly, joyful thing that turned the discomfort of the ride upside down; I remember my son doing the same on this stretch of road when he was about five.

You could say Todd missed his childhood. Sports took away his first twenty years. Then drugs took the second twenty. Imprisoned inside the junky equation, the constant cycle of need and scam and self-loathing, he missed his adulthood, the decades of experience and personal growth that shape most men as they near forty, as Todd will be next July fourth. When he was young, Trudi used to tell Todd that the Independence Day fireworks were all for him. Today she estimates that since he's been straight, these past thirteen months, Todd has matured from an emotional age of about sixteen to maybe twenty-four, the same age as his fiancé.

Alix is an OC girl with pretty blue eyes. She is pregnant. They are expecting a boy. They plan to name the child Baron Buzzy Marinovich. They have cleaned out the Chief's trophy room on the first floor of the beach house and made a little nest for themselves, complete with a new mini kitchen where the bar used to be. They watch a lot of DVDs, live frugally. Todd seems anxious to catch up on the small normal things he missed. In the hallway between their two rooms sits the redwood Trojan bust that Marv carved many years ago when he was suspended from USC's football team from fighting.

Todd says he's finished with drugs—the frantic hustle, the lies, the insidious need, the way the world perceives you as a loser. Each time he went to jail he walked the gauntlet of deputies, many of them high school football players. "You had everything and you threw it away," they told him. It was hard to hear. It's even harder to consider thoughtfully. The pain of regret is searing.

"I'm gonna get through this program," he said, his voice quavering comically as we bounce up the road in the U-Haul. "The day is coming when I'm not gonna have to piss in a fuckin bottle."

From the driver's seat, sensing his good mood, I asked: "How much effect do you think that Marv and sports and all contributed to you turning to drugs?" I'd been saving this line of questioning since our first interview, six months earlier; I'd had my first meeting with Marv nearly a year before that. "If you look at your life, it's interesting. It appears that to get out of playing, you sort of partied away your eligibility. It's like you're too old to play now so you don't have to do drugs anymore. Has the burden been lifted? Nobody's counting on you to win the game for them anymore. You can come out of your cave."

Todd looked out the windshield, down the road. The truck bounced. Thirty full seconds passed.

"No answer?"

He looked at me pleadingly, as if to say *Do I really have to do this?* Sometimes he brings to mind Richie Cunningham of *Happy Days*. Sometimes he brings to mind Marmaduke, the loveable great dane who doesn't understand just how outsized he really is. "I don't know how to answer that," Todd said at last. "I really have very few answers."

"That's kind of what it seems like."

Twenty seconds.

"No thoughts?"

"I think more than anything it's genetic. I got that gene from the Fertigs. My uncle, the Chief. They were raging alcoholics. And then, the environment plays a part in it for sure."

Now it was my turn to be silent. My son was fourteen at the time; a competitive athlete but not the star. Finally I said to Todd: "I guess, as a father, it's hard to know how much pressure to put on your kid. You want to challenge him to step up, to realize his potential. But it's like, how much can you step up? How much pressure can you take before you just want to run away and escape?"

This time Todd's response was immediate: "*Ye-ahhh*,"—a loopy, OC surfer dude expression that translates roughly to *No shit, Sherlock.*

He lit another Marlboro Red, sucked down the first sweet hit. He rode in silence the rest of the way home.

February 2009

Three months later, feeling pressure from all directions—the deaths within one week of his uncle, Craig Fertig, and his grandmother, the Chief's wife, Virginia Fertig; an upcoming gallery show; Marv's health problems and loss of his driver's license; his new life with his expectant fiancé— Todd drove on a Sunday afternoon to his old hook spot in Santa Ana and bought some black tar heroin.

He pulled over, smoked his first hit. Then he threw the dope out the window and called his parole officer, who advised him to drive directly to the county complex and give himself up—sixteen months of sobriety lost up a tin-foil tube.

The sign of hope is that he gave himself up so swiftly. The last time he binged, he was in the wind for three weeks. This time, he'd envisioned the consequences and stopped himself—albeit one hit too late. As every addict knows, progress comes in tiny steps; it is difficult to explain the difference to non users.

As he drove across town to surrender himself—he will get another week at the Farm, six months in a sober living facility, and will lose a step in his court program, adding time and expense to completion—Todd saw in his mind a picture of Alix, the swell of her belly, and he realized something: He wants to be a father to his son. He's never before had such a powerful reason to stay sober, a reason outside of himself. For once in his life, it's not all about him.

Epilogue

In December of 2011, with Todd's cooperation, ESPN Films aired "The Marinovich Project." The film told the unvarnished story of Todd's unique ascent to stardom, the dark descent that followed, and the complicated bond he shared with his father, Marv.

By now, with the addition of a newborn daughter, Coski, Todd and Alix were the parents of two children; Todd's gallery show of his paintings was at last a reality. By all accounts he'd been sober for nearly two years. His world was clearly focused on his children, upon whom he doted.

In the words of the documentary's producers: "Even as we started filming, we looked at this story through the lens of the myth we had been sold for decades: part Frankenstein, part Icarus...

"What we found was a real life love story between a father and a son."

(2009)

Ugly

Warren Durso is the kind of guy you have to know to love, a five-foot-seven-inch, 175-pound, Italian sausage sub from upstate New York. He has a big cement-block head; his neck is reminiscent of a bullfrog's; life has not always been kind. But somehow, when he looks in the mirror, he sees a man who is six-foot-four with ripped abs. The soul of us all uncovered, the naked underneath.

Warren Durso, sitting behind his MacBook Pro in a fifth-floor room at a Holiday Inn near the Los Angeles Airport, a double he's sharing on a week-by-week basis with his producing partner. Three projects have been green-lighted; the money spigot is expected to turn on soon. Almost everything he owns is stowed on his side of the closet.

He takes a call on his cranky iPhone, due for an upgrade, and employs his British accent, one of a number of eccentric mimicries collected over the years on his vocal palette: "Hello, *lovely.*"

A woman's voice crackles through the speaker: "Hello, *ugly.*"

Durso sputters, momentarily lost for words, a somewhat uncharacteristic condition. By age two he was holding full conversations on the telephone. By four he was reading the newspaper out loud. By ninth grade, he was so full of defiant theories and know-it-all ideas that his English teacher sometimes gave up and surrendered him the floor. His senior year, he ditched 180 days of school. When the principal threatened failure, Durso reminded his nemesis that such action would mean another year of dealing with... *him.* Later he would marvel at the weird numeric coincidence with his jail sentence, resulting from a willful misunderstanding with a rental-car company during a Jack Kerouac-inspired adventure—180 days. Maybe hitchhiking across country with his friend and two drum sets wasn't such a good idea after all? On the third night in the lockup he was abducted from his cell. Thankfully, his assailant "was too excited to perform." (Durso still remembers his name.) By the fourth night, he was safely ensconced in protective custody, where he stayed for the duration of his sentence, earning a reputation among the other trustees for telling jokes. His father and his uncles were great jokers— often at his expense. In high school it saved him from the bullies. Eventually he became known around the San Diego County Jail as the Joke Man, as in "Joke Man, motherfuckin' tell me a joke." Nobody else messed with him for the duration of his stay.

"You're such an *asshole*," he manages.

"This is what you tell me, yes?"

She is twenty-seven years old. She is hot hot hot. A former Miss Something— Bulgaria? Peru? Albania? Somewhere suitably cutthroat and baroque; clawed her way to Hollywood to seize her dreams. She's writing a screenplay—action adventure, call it *Dance of Vengeance*. Naturally she intends to star.

Durso is fifty-three. He's punching up her pages. A lot. As you can imagine, her English is a little rough. In the past he's run screenwriting workshops, so he appears to know what he's doing, even if he doesn't have a ton of writing credits, or even any at all on his IMDb page, though he is SAG-eligible, and has been in movie scenes with Danny DeVito and Kim Basinger, and spent almost two decades making a scrape-by living as one of those comedians you've never heard of who can make you wet your pants—a veteran utility guy, in other words, a comic's comic, the kind of dude who knows all the famous dudes but never became one, who commands the standard fifteen dollars a set at the Comedy Store in West Hollywood when he still feels like doing stand-up. (They total your sets over four weeks and send you a check.)

Over these last four months, working closely with this young and gorgeous foreign beauty, it appears Durso has grown a tad enamored. Maybe more than a tad. Her script is almost done—he stayed up into the wee hours last night working on the final sex scene. (Somehow, his partner managed to sleep through the clickety-clack.) All that's left now is the final murder, the revenge piece. Durso wants to finish but he doesn't want to finish, if you know what he means.

"I'm a lot cuter with the lights out," he says, seeking to recover from her fond salutation. If a man can brag and apologize at the same time, this is what he sounds like. Through the parted curtains in his room he can see the portico of the motel, and also the McDonald's drive-through that shares the same alley entrance. In the middle distance, cars and trucks ride the cloverleaf like toys on an enormous toy track, merging on and off the 405 freeway. A crayon-yellow sun and blue sky complete the vista.

"*Vhat?*" she asks.

"I'm a lot of fun naked," he enunciates, "but the lights have to be out."

"*Vhat?*"

"Will you please turn up your hearing aid to eight?" He holds the phone up and speaks loudly: "I said I'm *definitely* a lot of fun naked, but the lights *definitely* have to be out. That's my rule."

Static emanates from the speaker.

He laughs to fill the void, a nervous guffaw issued through his shapely Roman lips, forgetfully parted to reveal his several missing teeth.

Durso is grabbing coffee in a shop near his office on Wilshire Boulevard—a small drip with room. Through the storefront windows, down the street to the west, you can see one of those iconic signs that mark the city limits of Beverly Hills. He takes his cup to the fixings bar, gets down to business with the half-and-half and Splenda. To his right, a woman with long dark hair adds honey to her tea.

An accident-prone kid with nerdy black-frame glasses, Durso has been known variously through the years to his friends and tormentors as the Dirt Man, the Dirt Hole, the Turtle (in elementary school for his overlarge green down jacket), the Cheshire Cat (for when he was stoned), and the Penguin (for his turned-out feet and his double-hip-replacement waddle). "When I was younger, my head was always so stretched you could never see the real features," he'll say. "It was like, 'Here comes Durso, don't give him another cheeseburger, he'll explode.'"

When he was fourteen, some cool-crowd guys persuaded him to go rock climbing in the snow. Durso slipped and fell a great distance, had to be rescued by the East Fishkill, New York, volunteer fire department—compound leg fracture, pins and screws, 209 stitches.

He ended up losing forty pounds in the hospital and getting a lot of attention from the girls at school—for a brief Edenic period, he was dating four girls from different grades and his buddies were calling him the Sheik, after the brand of condoms. Then the girls found out and dumped him. "That was probably the high point of my love life," he says.

When he was twenty-one, after an Everclear Punch party, Durso passed out in a living-room chair and his buddies trucked him (in the chair) fifteen miles and left him in a stranger's front yard, where he awoke the next morning, beneath a blazing sun.

When he was twenty-four, his fiancée left and took everything but his drums—it turned out she was having an affair with the girl-friend of the bass player in his band. Years later, Durso ran into the ex. She was tending bar in a dive. She looked at him and sneered, "Oh my God, it's ancient fucking history." Deep down, he thinks maybe that's why he doesn't like to accumulate anything: because he doesn't want anyone to ever take it all away again. Especially a woman.

Somewhere along the line, Durso decided he'd "rather be the dog who wants you to pet his head than the dog who bites your fucking leg." He has this notion that the cosmos eventually delivers everything you need, so if you don't talk to the person next to you, you might be missing your destiny. "It's like, God's letting me know, *There's somebody here you need to hook up with.* But I don't know who it is. He doesn't tell me, like, *It's the guy with the brown hair and the yellow shirt.* It's just, there's somebody there I'm supposed to meet."

In Jerry's Famous Deli in Studio City he approaches a seventy-ish woman wearing a clingy knit minidress, with black and white horizontal stripes and matching kneesocks—turns out she's a semi-famous actress; he gives her his card. On the Third Street Promenade in Santa Monica, he beelines inexplicably for a scowling black girl with a red mohawk of twelve-inch spikes—turns out she is super-sweet; he gives her his card. In the sushi restaurant near work, he chats up a waitress with short short-shorts from Osaka—okay, this one can't understand a word he is saying; he gives her his card. He has more than a thousand e-mail contacts, three hundred phone con-tacts, five hundred LinkedIn colleagues, thirteen hundred friends on Facebook—so many, in fact, that he's thinking of starting a new page.

Lately, he's begun to wonder: How can all of these people really be your friends? Maybe the term should be Facebook *acquaintance*?

Here in the coffee shop, Durso can't help noticing this woman next to him. She's little and cute, with a good figure and nice energy. Yet something about her says lonely hearts. He can't help wondering: Could destiny be knocking? Is this a person he's supposed to meet? It's been more than a year since his ex-girlfriend left town, the last time he had a permanent roof or a steady source of intimate affection. (Her daughter hated him, made his life hell. He has this joke about standing over a girlfriend's sleeping kid in the middle of the night and brainstorming different ways to end its life.)

From his palette of voices he chooses the radio announcer— warm and resonant, available for voice-overs: "What's up, bright eyes?"

She looks at him. Her eyes are indeed bright. At the moment they seem to be saying something like: *Are you fucking kidding me?*

Warren Durso is the kind of guy you have to know to love—a five-foot-seven-inch, 175-pound Italian-sausage sub from upstate New York. Residing as he does in Hollywood, a town infamous for screwy values and astoundingly beautiful people—and people who spend astoundingly in their quest to make themselves beautiful, sometimes with frightening results—Durso is both oddity and every-man, the soul of us all uncovered, the naked underneath.

Looking in the mirror, Durso sees a "big cement-block head" covered by a thick helmet of graying hair, the kind that "grows up instead of down." (Oddly, he shows no sign of male pattern baldness, even at the temples.) His eyebrows are bushy twin caterpillars; his ears are large, low-set, and distinctly elfin. His neck is reminiscent of a bullfrog at full croak—a puffy, stubbled, flesh-colored drape that extends from his cheekbones all the way down to the collar of his T-shirt, as if to shield his precious jawline from general view. His uncle Wally used to tell him he had the kind of nose best suited for picking fruit—meaning he could hang from a tree branch by his "big guinea *beezer*" and pick apples with both free hands. Another Uncle Wallyism: "It looks like you fell out of the ugly tree and hit every branch on the way down."

Some mornings I wake up and look in the bathroom mirror and I'm like, "Forget it. I give up."

I've had girls come up to me in a bar and say, "Hey, you wanna go home with me?" And I'm thinking to myself, 'Damn, I wonder who she'd go to bed with if I said no?'

The first girl I was ever engaged to left me for a chick. It was a long time ago, but I haven't recovered. To this day, I still look in the mirror and say to myself, "I have tits, too. Couldn't we have worked something out?

Stuffed proudly into his size-34/29 jeans—since the mortification of viewing a short film he made in 2008, in which he played himself having sex with a female version of himself (the tag line: Go Fuck Yourself), he has lost 110 pounds—Durso's body is a landscape of pratfall, calamity, and unfortunate genetic recombination. "Sometimes I wonder if I was *born* on the wrong side of the bed," he jokes.

Durso's father, Dominic, was handsome and athletically gifted, the son of an immigrant Italian farmer who died prematurely at forty-six, leaving Dominic to raise his four younger siblings—at the expense of turning down a shot with the Chicago White Sox farm team. Later Dominic Durso became a traveling quality-control inspector for IBM. He was gone a lot. His job was finding fault with things. He always suspected his own third son, younger than his second by seven years, had come damaged from the factory. "He used to say they should have put me on a boat out to sea, which is what they did with all the rejects in the old country, I guess."

(His sainted mother, the former Lucy DiLandro, would always tell him he was handsome, with an award-winning personality. Then she'd make him something to eat. His favorite snack: "Her homemade tomato sauce, the ragu, with either bits of sausage crumbled in it or meatball or vegetable. Crack eggs over top and let'em cook. Add roasted peppers and onions and hollow out a big piece of Italian bread and dump all that in the middle.")

In elementary school, riding his big brother's bike, Durso was hit by a car. In high school, he broke his leg riding a motorcycle, and then again skiing—the leg was reset slightly askew, causing the foot to angle outward. Besides the scar from the compound fracture, he has scars on either hip (replacements at age thirty-four); three scars around his abdomen from hernia operations involving injured testicles ("When you're a little brother, you know, you're always an experiment"); four on his cheek from when he was a toddler and the family terrier dragged him by his pudgy face around the yard; and two more between his eyes, one from a plywood Frisbee that went awry on a windy day, and one from a beer bottle—he tried stop a guy from smacking around his girlfriend in a bar and the girlfriend turned on him.

Either of those last two incidents could have easily blinded Durso, which would have been a shame for many reasons, the most ironic the fact that once people get to know him—once *women* in particular get to know him—they always comment about his sparkling gray/blue/green eyes, set like jewels behind his glasses, within the fleshy recesses of his face, the tricky sort that change color with their surroundings.

"You work around here?" Durso persists.

"Right across the street," the woman with bright eyes says lifelessly.

"That's our building." He points down Wilshire, away from the Beverly Hills sign, toward a postwar brick utilitarian with a billboard occupying the airspace above. It is the oldest structure in their immediate view, which bestows a certain charm.

"I always think that's such a beautiful building," she says, softening.

"Of course, we don't own it. We just rent an office." He smiles pridefully, careful to keep his lips in the down position to cover his gaps—mercury fillings gone bad; he has plans to get a complete makeover at the dentist, he just hasn't had any time. "What do you do across the street?"

"I work for a motivational speaker."

"That must me very... *motivating*."

The timing is perfect—a modest *bon mot*. She laughs openly and with appreciation, and with some amount of relief, no doubt, that this troll who is trying to talk to her is actually kind of funny. She tilts her head slightly, as if seeing him in a new light.

Without hesitation he hands her his card.

Durso is biding his time in the office with his partner, Gino Cabanas; they're at adjoining desks, answering e-mails on their laptops. It's a casting day at the Vine Studio, LLC. They're seeking a hostess for a pilot; this is the second day of interviews, they've hit a lull in the schedule. The place is decorated in eclectic fashion, a sort of found-furniture/packing-boxes/movie-poster motif that somehow befits their mutual state of bachelorhood, with plenty of fruit and breakfast food in the mini-fridge. Sometimes, on an important call, Cabanas—a middle-aged, leading-man type of Cuban extraction who started his career as a theater actor in Miami— will walk circles around the mossy fountain in the interior courtyard, earbuds in place, gesticulating wildly. Sometimes Durso will trail him, listening in.

Their show is called *Jukebox Heroes*. In one sentence, it combines *American Idol* and *The Voice*, only with tribute bands instead of solo singers. Among the classic acts represented will be the Beatles, Heart, Journey, and Earth, Wind & Fire—a dozen in all. Several bona fide rock stars have signed on as mentors; their identities are still supersecret. People love their classic rock. They watch all kinds of crazy stuff on television these days. Why not this?

Durso met Cabanas in 2005, when the latter was directing a film called *Cut Off*, an ensemble piece featuring Faye Dunaway, Malcolm McDowell, and the rapper Kurupt. A comedian friend had been cast in the movie. He helped finagle Durso a one-line part in the hope that Durso could become union-eligible, an important step toward making a viable living as an actor. After false-starting as an air-conditioning mechanic/rock drummer, Durso spent the majority of his adult life as a stand-up comic and strip-club DJ—on the side, he helped his agent manage other acts and set up tour dates. For seventeen years, he lived almost exclusively in hotel rooms, playing USO tours (Dubai, Kyrgyzstan) and far-flung American clubs (the Comedy Zone in Enterprise, Alabama; Comedy West in Bozeman, Montana), burning through twenty-four different vehicles (anything cheap or available, from a Honda del Sol to a decked-out Ford conversion van he crashed on a small bridge). Someday, Durso says, he'd like to buy a house of his own. He'll set up his bedroom *exactly* like a hotel room, the place he feels most at home, the TV remote conveniently Velcroed to the night table.

Durso arrived on location for *Cut Off* in his twelve-year-old Nissan Sentra. He had thirty-eight dollars in his pocket. Given his first shot in a big-time movie, he nailed it—beginning with his chancy decision to cake his face with doughnut sugar before his first take, which cracked up everyone on set. His one-line engagement ended up mutating into six scenes, three of which made the movie. (This is perhaps Durso's proudest personal statistic: *one line, six scenes, three made the movie*—a mantra oft-repeated, proof positive of his worth, even when others can't see.)

After a lot of annoying persistence that got him nowhere—he called Cabanas nearly every week, looking for something, anything to do—Durso finally arrived one day unannounced at the office of Cabanas's production company, located at the time on Ocean Avenue in Santa Monica. "Bro, I'm *supposed* to be here," he told Cabanas. "God has been nudging me and nudging me. *Please?*"

Cabanas, a spiritual man, gave Durso a desk and put him to work in his small but energetic concern. Since then, he has helped produce and finance a dozen short films and two TV pilots, one of them a fine-art competition show called *Work of Genius*. Durso does whatever is needed— writing, casting, acting, arranging, location scouting, phone calling, even shaking the trees for investors. Clearly, after six years together, the men are symbiotic—two fiftyish straight guys sharing their business and a double room at a Holiday Inn, Durso the loyal Sancho to Cabanas's Don Quixote.

At the moment it's well past noon on the second day of interviews. They're looking for a hot girl with both music skills and hosting experience. It is a nonunion project paying less than scale. Yesterday they saw a parade of hopefuls gleaned from Durso's exhaustive search—union members repped by well-known agencies, hopefuls who'd read about the auditions on Craigslist, cuties he'd met on the street, some of them Facebook friends. A sampling: Six five in heels, skinny-skinny, short-shorts, nose piercing, and an asymmetrical haircut—Grace Jones does *Mad Max*. Classic blond beauty, can sing/dance/act, grew up making appearances on the popular Latino variety show *Sabado Gigante*— well past her prime, weirdly augmented upper lip. Iowa native, died black hair and tattoo sleeves, arrived in town six weeks ago— living in a van with her mother and five dogs, parked beneath an overpass in a dicey section of South Central with other vagabond homesteaders.

On the heels of yesterday's cornucopia, this morning has been kind of weird. The first girl bailed. The second hasn't shown up. The mood in the office is sort of like that at a party before anybody arrives.

"They don't call, they don't e-mail, they can't get here on time," Durso says, annoyed. "And then they wonder: *Why am I not working in Hollywood.*"

"This is ridiculous," Cabanas says. His thinning curls are heavily moussed, arranged atop his balding pate. One strand in front falls rakishly over his eye.

"For tomorrow I'll book 'em every ten minutes."

"Line 'em up on the tarmac and make 'em wait," Cabanas says, picking up a stack of eight-by-ten head shots on his desk. He shows one to Durso. "Did you see how she airbrushes the fuck out of her face? In person, there are lots of lines." He indicates the places with his finger, "There... and there... and there."

"When I saw her walk in I was like, *You are nothing like the photograph you sent me,*" Durso explains.

"This girl's a contortionist? Really? Have you seen the photos?"

"Dude, she's doing a book. It's her naked in a chair, doing all these"—Durso grapples for the right word— "positions? It's called An Affair with My Chair."

"This one was kind of overweight," Cabanas says, sifting the photos. "This one was, how to say it nicely—*not the brightest bulb?* I don't think she could do the interviews. This one was talking about going to a concert in '91, when she was twenty, so she is obviously over forty. Did you see the look on her face when she accidentally let the date slip?"

"I know, right? *Busted!*"

"And this one! She was crammed into her outfit like—"

"A stuffed eggplant?" Durso offers. She'd worn all purple. Even though he's joking around—part of his job description is comic relief— there's a pained look on his face, like he's uncomfortable. First of all, he's the one who had to go out and find all these women. He's invested a lot of time and conversation and lots of Web stalking in every one of them, so he feels a certain ownership. Second, he was up most of last night at the emergency room. At the hotel two days ago he walked into a corner of a plastic garbage can and cut himself.

After dressing his shin with Neosporin, he'd continued his daily swimming regimen in the hotel pool. Next thing he knew the cut was angry and infected, and the surrounding area was red and hot and swollen. At the ER they gave him IV antibiotics. The doctor said it had something to do with the fact that his blood sugar was a little high.

"Some of these girls need to get a mirror," Cabanas says, frustrated, letting the stack of photos fall to his desk.

"I guess people see themselves how they want to," Durso offers.

After three nerve-wracking days of scheduling and screening Hollywood hopefuls, Durso sits down to dinner in a Thai place on Sunset Boulevard. Since his dramatic weight loss, and his subsequent viewing of the documentary *Food, Inc.*, he has eschewed all meat and chicken. He still eats seafood; he calls himself a *pescatarian*.

I ask him how many hostess candidates he's interviewed so far.

Tucking into his sea bass, he shrugs. "Forty? Fifty?"

It's kind of funny that you get to judge who's prettiest.

"I know. Isn't that hilarious?"

Do you think it's weird that you're the one casting? He who laughs last?

A sour expression. A long pause. "I don't want to do it. I'd rather not do it."

You don't like passing judgment?

"I'm making decisions on hundreds of girls. They're sending their pictures, all their stuff, hoping that they're gonna get their big break. And it's like, the little chubby girl who sends me her stuff? I have to look at it objectively. I have to say, you know, 'Sorry, it's not gonna work.' I don't want to call them in because I know they're not gonna get the job. I don't want them to waste their gas and their time. I don't want them to get their hopes up. I know how it was for me."

What do you mean?

"I started losing the weight when I started realizing why I was eating myself to death," he says. "The main thing for me was judgment. Worrying all the time what other people thought, their perceptions of me. Getting other people's approval. Always. That and feeling that I wasn't worthy of a relationship because my girl ran off and I never had any closure. They say it's better to have loved and lost than to never love at all. But you also need closure. You need answers to things. Why wasn't I good enough? Didn't I at least deserve a reason for leaving? Say *something*, you know: See you. Fuck you. *Something*.

"For me the big fat ugly guy is still inside. He will always be inside. I didn't realize how deep it went, you know, those feelings of inadequacy, of hopelessness... what the fuck, man? I'm a funny motherfucker. I've done shows all over the world. But still this fat boy is always rearing his ugly head. I slayed him but he's not completely, um... how do I put it? He never comes to the surface 'cause I keep him down. There's no fuckin' way he's ever going to do anything to make me the way I used to be. But it's always a fight."

Durso and his writing partner, the former Miss Something—Columbia? Lebanon? Transylvania?— are hanging out in the restaurant of the Holiday Inn, having a bite to eat, polishing her script. She is taller than he and gorgeous, with long hair and alabaster skin and a smoky foreign accent. One of those affectionate types, she is always touching and hugging and kissing him on both cheeks, always calling him darling and dear and sweetheart. A lot of times when she signs an e-mail, she'll write, "I love you a lot."

There is a lull in the conversation. She rests her hand on his forearm, locks his gaze—since she is taller she must look downward to do so. "Oh my God!" she says enchantedly, as if noticing for the first time, "you have such beautiful eyes."

Durso smiles, remembering to keep his lips anchored over his missing teeth. *Fuck! All right! She's complimenting me!* he tells himself.

When Durso was young, he was very close to his mom and his younger sister. One thing they taught him was not to be an asshole guy. He knows body language. He knows you're not supposed to touch another person, especially a woman, until they touch you— otherwise it's creepy. To this day he never approaches a woman like, *Oh my god, look how hot she is, I wanna fuck her.* Instead, he deals with them first as a bona fide person. Then, you know, he waits for the signs to move forward.

Ever since he met Miss Transylvania at the American Film Market—a gathering where people buy and sell independent movies— they've become more and more friendly. Everything has been so easy; they get along so well, their partnership and friendship just developed organically; everything just clicked. And talk about showing signs. Touching his arm. Rubbing his back while he types. Sometimes she'll all of a sudden run her hands though his thick helmet of hair and scratch his scalp. Oh. My. *Gooooood*. Scalp scratching? Nobody does *that* but a lover. Or someone who wants to be.

And now she's complimenting his eyes?

"Thank you," he says, deeply tickled. "And you—you're simply beautiful all over."

She laughs musically, pats his forearm affectionately.

Lately Durso's been thinking it might be time to settle down. Maybe find a place to unpack. Maybe find someone with whom to share his life. He's looking for quality, for somebody who's going to understand him, someone who totally groks him, like, "She gets me, I get her, we both just *get it*." He's done with all the superficial bullshit, dude. "I'm at a point now in my career where everything's taking off. It's just time. I want someone to share it with."

Durso looks across the table and deploys his richest, sexiest, most resonant voice. To be cute, he addressess her by her honorific.

"So, Miss Transylvania. Can we take this to the next level?"

Her brow beetles. "What do you mean, 'next level?' Like what, go upstairs?"

Surprised: "Do you *want* to go upstairs?"

Clearly she is lost in translation. "I don't understand. Explain to me: What is *next level*?"

"You know, moving to the next level from this friendship we've started?" He uses his hands in the air between them to demonstrate the notion of levels. "'Cause we've hung out pretty much a lot for the last four months. Next level means, like, taking it from friendship to the boyfriend-girlfriend thing."

She looks at him as if he's just hit her in the forehead with a shovel.

As if it had never entered her mind in a million years that she might become romantically involved—much less physically intimate—with Warren Durso, no matter how friendly and funny and helpful he has been...or will *ever* be.

She takes her hand from his forearm, uses it to gesture. "Look at me. Look at you," she says, her thick accent dripping with the serum of her badly phrased truth. "You're an old man. You're old enough to be my *grandfather!*"

"Maybe your father," Durso deadpans, "but I don't think grandfather.

Miss T can't help but laugh. "Okay, maybe not grandfather."

"So you're telling me it'll never happen?"

Durso is meeting a couple of people at the Improv on Melrose. There are pictures of legendary comics hanging everywhere. This week's headliner is Nick Swardson (*Reno 911!*; *Nick Swardson's Pretend Time*). He's an old friend of Durso's. Swardson is sitting at the bar; he's just given Durso a few divided minutes of his attention— like a send-up of somebody in Hollywood talking to somebody they used to know but is now too big to be bothered with.

Mostly men on the crowded floor, standing elbow to elbow. Durso turns around and encounters another acquaintance. He's tall and thin, like Ichabod Crane, wearing a black T-shirt advertising Zildjian cymbals. A leather fanny pack, slung low on his waist like a holster, may later reveal party materials.

Ten days or so since his mortifying scene with Miss Transylvania, Durso is on to other topics. He and Cabanas have found a hostess and a suitable location; in about two weeks they'll be shooting the *Jukebox Heroes* pilot. After that, an infomercial in Miami, and then several other projects are in the wings. When Durso was fifteen, one morning after he'd stayed out all night partying, his older brother was dressing him down. It was the seventies. The family's youngest son seemed hopelessly adrift. "I told my brother that by the time I was fifty, everything was going to be fine. I was off by a couple of years. But now everything is right where I dreamed it would be."

Not to mention this amazing *new* woman he's just met on Facebook.

"She kept popping up as someone I should friend," Durso says.

"It was the universe contacting you," says fanny-pack guy.

"I believe it was," Durso says soberly. "She speaks five languages. She's French, Arab—"

"Where does she live?"

"Beverly Hills."

"Lemme get her number real quick," jokes fanny-pack guy.

Durso takes out his iPhone, makes a few finger taps, shows a picture around.

"*Boing!*" says fanny-pack guy. "Look at that fuckin' picture!"

"Yeah, she's bangin'," Durso says. "And she's got this beautiful accent. Just what I asked the universe for, because I went through this one girl who—"

"Can you call the universe and see if she has a sister?"

The men exchange fist bumps, two regular guys in a crowded bar. I take the opportunity to check out the other patrons. One thing is immediately apparent. Nobody here looks like Brad Pitt.

The dude to my left has got to be 150 pounds overweight; he's sweating profusely and doesn't smell very good. The guy to my right has a prominent forehead and a space between his front teeth big enough to drive a truck through. The guy to his right has acne pustules so inflamed it's kind of nauseating. The guy behind him is four foot eleven, no joke, you can see him moving toward the bar, through the thick underbrush of jeans and Dockers. One guy sitting near Swardson at the bar has a scraggly beard and dreads tied in a topknot—what is he thinking? The guy next to him has a nose suitable for picking apples. And then there's your reporter, a shrimpy guy with a stiff neck, huge nose, not-so-great skin and puffy bags under his eyes—my own mother has never liked one single picture of me. She loves me dearly. But she thinks I need plastic surgery.

"When I'm talking to myself, when I want to confess to the man in the mirror, or I want to affirm the man in the mirror, I'm just looking into my eyes," Durso had told me earlier. "I'm not looking at anything else. 'Cause you know what I see in my eyes? I see a six-foot-four, bald black man with ripped abs. That's exactly what I see. I've trained my mind to not look at what the reflection really is."

The fanny-pack guy takes a hit of his beer. "So when are you gonna see her?"

"I don't know," Durso says. He's drinking club soda with lime. "She might have to leave town, but she's gonna let me know today."

"Sounds kind of iffy."

"She seems pretty cool. When she friended me back, I wrote, 'Thanks for accepting my friend request. I believe everyone meets for a reason and you came up on my page every day for a month. I figured we were supposed to meet.' I also told her about *Jukebox Heroes*, how we were casting it and all."

"What was her answer?"

"She gave me her number.

"So, she wants to be on TV," fanny-pack guy says. "And he wants to fuck her. *Hmmm*. This is so unusual. I can't believe I'm in Hollywood and I'm hearing this kind of thing."

"We've talked on the phone a lot," Durso says. "We've chatted on line. She's just real, man. She's honest. And here's the beauty part: She doesn't want to be on TV."

(2012)

A Girl in Love

Love her or hate her, but do you really know her? In real life, for instance, her squeaky voice is low and sultry. Spend three intimate days and nights with Paris Hilton and her menagerie, including Tinkerbell, Princess Pigelette, her boyfriend, her PR person and the rest. The most publicized Hilton since Uncle Nicky, she may yet become the most successful since her great-grandfather, the hotelier Conrad.

C ontinuing our tour, Paris Hilton throws open the bottom section of a fanciful Dutch door, painted a glossy white, the kind of entryway often found in farmhouses or enchanted cottages in the forest. She leads me into her spacious kitchen.

"Princess Pigelette!" she trills.

A miniature pig trots over, snuffling excitedly though its pink pepperoni snout, its tiny cloven hooves clicking across the stone floor of her minimansion, which is hunkered anonymously in a gated development off Mulholland Drive, at the crest of the Santa Monica mountains in Los Angeles. Outside, through generous windows framed by cottony curtains suggestive of clouds, you can see the pool, the blue sky, the green canyon beyond. The rock hero Slash lives across the street; the mercurial actor Charlie Sheen is a few doors down. Since the so-called Bling Ring broke into Paris's house in 2008 and stole all of the precious things bequeathed by her grandmother, there have been cameras installed in every room. As the eldest Hilton of her generation, the family jewels are her birthright. The teen robbers were caught—one was given her own reality show on TV—but the jewels have not yet turned up. It is not a source of amusement that one of the alleged culprits is starring in her own reality series.

Paris drops lithely to the floor, as if boneless in her comfy cotton Paris Hilton-brand sweat suit, part of a sportswear line selling strongly in Europe, Russia, and the Middle East, some of it in Paris Hilton-brand stores. With her short, black-lacquered fingernails she scratches the wiry fur of her miniature royal dandy, the world's smallest variety of potbellied pig; meanwhile she is mobbed by her entire menagerie of animals—prancing and barking, turning circles, rubbing against her leg, licking her lovely, doll-like face, which is set at the moment in the familiar toothy smile that she usually reserves for personal snapshots, dozens of which are set about her house, each one in its own fun frame. Paris and Mariah. Paris and Jessica. Paris and Carmen. Paris and Fergie. Paris and Nicole and Nicky. Paris and her mom and dad. Paris and her two little brothers, the youngest of whom is a teenager and still lives at home. Paris and her BFFs.

Out in the world, posing professionally, Paris never shows her teeth. A toothy smile means joy and home and BFFs. A toothy smile means crinkly features and weird expressions. "They'll always print the goofiest shot," she explains.

To avoid icky pictures, Paris religiously employs "my little pout," something she's perfected over the last nineteen years, when she first went to work as a model at family friend Donald Trump's agency without her parents' knowledge. Her favorite pose: shoulders back, hand on hip, torso twisted slightly, face turned to the right to better display the exquisitely sculpted jaw she inherited from her father, the grandson of Conrad Nicholson Hilton, founder of the hotel chain and primogenitor of one of America's most prominent families. Sometimes, when she finally returns home or to her hotel suite after a particularly long day of moving about from place to place, stalked by paparazzi, she can still see and feel and hear the pop and whine of the cameras, the blinding fusillade of flashes, the bump and jostle, the chaotic din: *Paris, over here! Look this way! Come on, Paris, give us a smile! Paris, when are you and Doug going to tie the knot?*

"I'll be like twitching because there are so many flashes going off at once. It gets really, I don't know, *overwhelming*," she says.

Even at rest on the floor in her kitchen, she cannot be still. Like the slide show that plays on her desktop Mac, she is constantly in motion. Her head turns a few degrees, tilts just so. She shifts her posture, arches her back; her arms change position. It is as if she is on modeling auto pilot, always posing, unable to stop.

The craziness has subsided a bit since the lunatic years when she and Britney and Lindsay were the most photographed women in the world, since that fever broke after their various meltdowns, including Paris's own twenty-eight-day stay in the county jail for reckless driving. A lot of things have changed since then, but the attention she draws can still be crushing.

Someday, Paris wants four children. For now, these will have to do: There is Princess Annabelle, a rescued Siamese cat. Prada and Dolce are miniature Doberman pinschers, a mother and daughter. Harajuku Bitch (after Gwen Stefani's backup dancers) is a longhair Chihuahua. Marilyn Monroe is a Pomeranian, as is Prince Baby Bear, the only male in the dog pack, a gift from Paris's boyfriend of one year, Doug Reinhardt, who you might remember as the earnest former pro baseball player with the dreamy blue eyes dumped so unceremoniously (and publicly!) by Lauren Conrad on *The Hills*.

Usually the dogs stay outside in the two-story doghouse, built as a miniature of Paris's own house, complete with a balcony and AstroTurf. And of course, a fence. When she was young, Paris and her sister, Nicky, who is three years younger but was raised as her virtual twin, with matching outfits and everything, had a similar playhouse on the back acreage of their large estate in Bel Air, where they lived before taking up residence as teenagers in the family's grandest old hotel, New York's Waldorf Astoria. At one point young Paris, unbeknownst to her parents, ordered a number of different small animals and stocked the playhouse. "I've always wanted to be a zoologist," she says, swatting the fuzzy rump of Prince Baby Bear, who at the moment is attempting to hump Marilyn Monroe, who has no interest, having been responsibly spayed. Often, during photo shoots, if she wants to feel inspired, Paris will think of the human Marilyn Monroe. She'll think of Marilyn's life, and how she loved the camera, and how the camera loved her. And she'll think about how Marilyn loved a baseball player, just like she does. Marilyn has always been a really huge inspiration for Paris, ever since she was little. For many in the places around the world where her products are sold— from Andorra to Azerbaijan, Malta to Morocco—Paris is the *new* Marilyn, an iconic figure representing the wealth and beauty of the American dream.

Marilyn the dog is blond and fluffy—the one who most looks like her owner, in Paris's opinion. She was purchased in Korea. The rest of the dogs are from Japan. "When you buy dogs in America, they're from puppy mills and they always get sick," she explains with the commanding tone of a person who knows—somewhat surprising given her reputation and public persona. In private, Paris only rarely employs her well-known baby-sexpot voice. ("I talk like that when I'm nervous or on TV," she will later say.) In person she has a range of vocal modes that serve as a barometer of sorts, measuring her moods and intentions, moving like a slide whistle from Betty Boop, to Valley girl, to monied boarding-school lockjaw, to bossy eldest cousin playing teacher in a mock classroom full of younger relatives on a landed estate. Absent from the household but not forgotten is Tinkerbell, Paris's famous Chihuahua, credited by some with touching off the international fad of mini-accessory dogs. Tink lives now with Paris's parents, Kathy and Rick Hilton, who have been married more than thirty years and live about fifteen minutes down the mountain. Though Tink is still very involved in Paris Hilton Enterprises—the face of Paris's internationally distributed line of doggie fashions and products— "Tinkerbell can't be here," Paris explains. "She's so jealous of all these dogs. But she comes over all the time and stays with me."

In the corner nearby is a rabbit hutch, the type Paris may have first encountered in Altus, Arkansas (population: 838), where she and her life-long BFF, Nicole Richie, the daughter of family friend Lionel Richie, resided for the taping of their first of five seasons of *The Simple Life*, the show that introduced Paris to the greater American public. Looking out from behind the mesh are two lion-headed rabbits, Thumper and Bambi. With them in the enclosure is Paris's latest purchase, Brigitte Bardot, a teacup-sized minibunny she picked up recently in France during a hellacious ten days that found her flying from L.A. to New York to Paris to L.A. to Rio to L.A. to Las Vegas. For someone so famous for being famous, she seems to actually work quite a lot. "I'm like a machine," she says. "People ask, 'Are you a superhero? Because it's crazy how much you work.' I've been doing it since I'm fifteen. I love to have fun and travel and make money doing it. Who wouldn't?"

On one of her stops, Paris made a commercial for the Brazilian beer Devassa. It featured Paris in a tight black dress taking a beer out of a refrigerator and running the cold can sensuously along her body. Without showing a bit of skin, the commercial managed to offend that notoriously libidinous country's national advertising watchdog, which charged that the commercial violated advertising codes by using sex to sell an alcoholic beverage. And by treating Paris as a sex object.

Loves it, she Tweets to her 1.7 million followers.

Sitting on the floor in her sneakers and her sweats, surrounded by her adoring kingdom of animals, her skin luminescent with the effects of last night's spray-on body bronzing, Paris brings to mind a modern incarnation of Snow White—this one rangy and blonde and *hot*...and clearly in possession of the deed to her own castle on the hill. According to *Forbes*, Paris made more than $8 million on licensing deals, personal appearances, television shows, and other business endeavors between June 2008 and June 2009. Private sources with knowlege of her businesses say her net income is really closer to $10 million per year. Her nine fragrances, they say, sell more than $100 million per year wholesale; this year she will release her tenth fragrance, Tease, with a Marilyn Monroe-inspired marketing campaign. Worldwide, Paris has nineteen product lines, including clothes, bedding, shoes, hair extensions and accessories, dolls, handbags and watches. She is working on a second album with producer Rodney "Darkchild" Jenkins, who has also produced Michael Jackson, Beyoncé, and Lady Gaga. Her television show, *My New BFF*, has franchises in the UK and Dubai. Another U.S. show is in the works as well—a secret but something to do with the family.

From his cage in the corner, an African gray parrot issues a lusty wolf whistle.

"His name is Hank," Paris laughs. "Just plain Hank. Doug named him. He's young; he doesn't talk yet. Who knows what he'll say. Probably a lot of sports because Doug always watches sports and he's up in the bedroom with us on the stand."

Outside the window, a large Hispanic man in a wet suit and diving mask is wading around chest-high in the pool. As Paris and I speak, a couple dozen people are making themselves busy around her house—a PR woman, a personal manager, two assistants, several maids, the gardeners, the party planners, the dance-floor crew, etc. The pool deck is decorated with mod furniture, life-size faux Roman statues, alabaster likenesses of the Little Mermaid and *Peter Pan's* Tinker Bell. The wet-suit guy is putting together pieces of metal scaffolding, a stoic expression on his face. By Friday night, there will be a dance floor and a bar on top of the pool, all of it inside a tent with a Studio 54 theme. (Paris and her mom both had their twenty-first birthday parties at Studio 54 in New York.) One week from now, the dance floor long gone, the weather unseasonably cold, it will be Paris herself wading stoically into her pool for a photo shoot, wearing only a black bikini by Le Bra.

This is Paris's birthday month; she has just turned twenty-nine. Already there have been parties upon parties. The dining table is piled high with flowers and presents from friends. Last week there was a small dinner at her parents' house, followed by a party at club Tao in Las Vegas, attended by more than five thousand paying customers, most of them strangers. Paris was among the first to command a fee for attending a club. She now gets as much as $300,000 to show up and address the crowd, according to reports. The crowning birthday event will be at her own house—the party Friday night for 250 friends.

Now she rises from the floor, goes into the pantry, removes a huge handful of something, and starts feeding it to Princess Pigelette. She giggles as the pig roots in the palms of her hands; the other animals sample the scraps that trickle down, some more enthusiastically than others.

"My house is kind of like a reflection of my life and my accomplishments and what I've done," Paris says in her serious voice. "And I've done it all on my own. When my parents and my grandfather came over for the first time, I was so proud. It just feels good to, like, walk around and be like, I earned all this, you know? I see some of my friends I grew up with from rich families. Their parents spoiled them and they never made them work and just give them an allowance. And now they're like thirty and still living off the parents, having to ask for everything, being on a budget. It's nice to feel accomplished and independent. I don't have to depend on anyone but myself."

Her eyes blaze with the sentiment, big and purply blue, Liz Taylor blue, enhanced beautifully by her Paris Hilton-brand false eyelashes, launching this summer along with her line of sunglasses. Later, I will read in an old clipping that she wears blue contact lenses. Of the hundreds of questions I ask over the course of a month, it was one of the few that went unaddressed by her able new flack, Dawn Miller, an attractive lass from Leeds, England who guards her client fiercely.

Paris wipes the palms of her hands brusquely, one upon the other, cleaning the pig-feed crumbs away and then smiles her toothy smile, the one reserved for friends and family. "Do you wanna go see the second floor?"

The back stairway is decorated with dozens of her framed magazine covers. We enter Club Paris, her own little nightspot.

"I wanted a club in my house because it's easier to have your friends come over—it's more fun than going out."

Prudent, too, for a young woman fast approaching the next chapter of her life; a young woman who, during the early the summer of 2007, spent those twenty-eight days incarcerated in Los Angeles's notorious Twin Towers detention center after being found guilty of violating her reckless-driving probation—a drama that began, she says, with a margarita on an empty stomach after a foodless day of work, and ended one block from the In-N-Out burger franchise to which she was headed. After being stopped by police, Paris blew .08 on the Breathalyzer, which is the legal limit in California. Hence the charge "reckless," not DUI.

Club Paris is dark and sexy and fun, and also practical, she says, since you can dance on top of the black-granite built-ins that line the room, allowing for more dancers per square foot. There is a DJ booth and a fully stocked bar, a tequila-shot machine, several huge TVs, and a shiny brass stripper pole with a raised, black-granite platform. The entire room has been soundproofed to accommodate the neighbors. The parties move inside from the backyard tents after eleven; twoscore security guards, most of them very large black men, keep things copacetic. "If people light a cigarette the guys will be like, 'Put it out.' They watch everyone and make sure they're not trashing the house or going into my bedroom. Since it's a gated community, everyone has to show ID. Sometimes they catch people putting framed pictures in their purse. I'd be embarrassed to jack someone's picture at their party. Like, how desperate are *you*?"

During her upcoming Friday-night birthday soiree, Paris—wearing first a glittery green halter dress and matching bejeweled headband, and later a glittery blue halter dress and matching bejeweled headband—will stow her purse under the platform and dance with unselfconscious abandon for nearly two hours, elevated above the humid and happily loopy throng of Hollywood friends, many of whom will have to park at a shopping center and ride a shuttle bus to and from the party. A select number will receive drive-on valet parking passes by e-mail, including her parents, who will stay until nearly 2:00 a.m., and her younger sister, Nicholai Olivia "Nicky" Hilton, the conservative one, better known as a fashion designer. Wearing a simple striped jersey dress, dancing reservedly on one of the built-ins, the equally beautiful (but less public) Nicky will maintain eye contact with Paris nearly the entire time. Like the primal BFFs they are, it almost appears they are communicating telepathically.

As the dancing continues, Paris will be joined in turn on the platform by several of the BFFs who competed on the first two seasons of the American version of her show. The most famous BFF is named Onch. A diminutive Asian with a shoulder-length bob, he is known unabashedly in Parisworld as her "fairy godbrother." At the party he wears a handmade tiara of Skittles and M&M wrappers. Paris also spends considerable time dancing on the platform with Doug, a mobile-phone entrepreneur and TV producer, a bro's bro out of the high-jock culture of Orange County. All day before the party, Doug will be shooting some very secret pilot or something with TV hottie Hayden Panettiere. The blonde star of *Heroes* will show up at the party with huge fake eyelashes and her hair dyed brown, rendering herself almost unrecognizable. "Hi," she says, "I'm Hayden." Indeed she was, in a frilly hippy dress with a punging neckline.

Faithful to the period theme, Doug sports a huge Afro wig and a shiny polyester shirt unbuttoned to his *pupic*. (On Halloween he and Paris *both* went as Dorothy.) From across the room you can see the sparkle of the hefty diamond earrings Doug gave Paris for her birthday. ("He's finally starting to get the jewelry thing," Paris says.) Another surprise gift from Doug: At 1:00 a.m., the rapper Mickey

Avalon gives a special live performance. He stands on top of the built-in next to the DJ booth and lets it rip, looking a little like a sweaty, hip hop incarnation of Sean Penn's Jeff Spicoli in *Fast Times at Ridgemont High*. His hit song, "My Dick," sets the crowd into a frenzy of call-and-response.

Absent the revelers, Club Paris conjures a fancy, Prohibition-era speakeasy (or a ritzy bordello), with lots of gold-guilt and black-leather banquettes and flickering faux-candle wall sconces—a time of robber barons, heiresses... and Paris's own great-grandfather, Conrad Nicholson Hilton, the son of a Norwegian immigrant general-store owner from San Antonio, New Mexico who became a billionaire hotelier and philanthropist.

"Basically my great-grandfather was a bellboy," Paris explains, thumbnailing the family history. "He was living in Texas and had this dream to own his hotel, so he somehow got a loan from this guy who believed in him and then he started the first Hilton. Over time, it grew into this whole empire, including the Waldorf-Astoria. After that my, grandfather took it over. And then my dad was born—he has five brothers and two sisters.

"My family has always had this thing," she continues, "they're like, they never wanted to spoil their kids. They always wanted their kids to do something on their own. So my dad was actually a bellboy at the Waldorf. He worked his way up. Now he owns like the biggest real estate company in L.A. And he did it all on his own. I think that's where I got it, too, because my parents always made me want to do something with my life and make something of it."

In some sense, Paris's public life is part of her inheritance. Connie Hilton loved the spotlight. He was fond of opening his hotels by dancing a type of polka called the varsoviana. He mingled with celebrities, had an eye for showgirls. His son, Conrad Nicholson "Nicky" Hilton Jr., was himself the focus of intense press interest after he married an eighteen-year-old Liz Taylor, the biggest female star of her era. Only 205 days later, she had the marriage annulled.

Connie's second wife was Zsa Zsa Gabor, the Hungarian beauty queen who became... famous for being beautiful and famous. (And also for getting married nine times.) Zsa Zsa's sister, Eva Gabor, was a TV actress. She stared in *Green Acres*, a popular sit com about a spoiled rich girl forced to move to the country. When the producers signed up Paris for *The Simple Life*, before putting her on a private jet to an unknown destination, she says they gave her these acting notes: "Paris, be the dumbest you can be. Just be a dumb, ditzy blonde—like *Legally Blonde* meets *Green Acres* meets *Clueless*." BFF Nichol Richie was told to be the mean one. (BTW, they are friends again.) "That whole fight was engineered by the producers," Paris says unconvincingly.

Interestingly, Hilton hotels are credited with being world's first international chain—the first to promulgate a distinct world-wide brand and standard for hotel accommodations. In the nightstand of every Hilton in the world there is a copy of Connie's autobiography, *Be My Guest*.

Today Paris has her own Hilton brand. Her autobiography, *Confessions of an Heiress: a Tongue-in-Chic Peek Behind the Pose*, was a *New York Times* best seller. There have been two other books, and a third authored by Tinkerbell the Chihuahua. Paris also has copyrights for two of her pet expressions, "That's hot" and "That's huge." If she finds somebody using that exact verbiage on any products for sale, she can and will take legal action. Last year she was in Tokyo and she saw this mouse pad with her likeness on it. "I bought it and took it to my lawyer. I was like, 'It's not fair that they're selling mouse pads. I should be selling mouse pads.'"

After Connie died, his will was read. Everyone was shocked. The bulk of his estate was left to the Conrad N. Hilton Foundation, a charity he'd established in 1944. His middle son, Barron, contested the will and won. The sixth of Barron's eight children was Richard Howard "Rick" Hilton, Paris's dad. Rick has a degree in hotel and restaurant management from the University of Denver. When he was nineteen he met the fifteen-year-old child actress Kathleen Elizabeth Avanzino, a model and a cheerleader (Nicky resembles her), whose acting credits list *Bewitched*, *Family Affair*, and *Happy Days*. Together, Kathy and Rick have four children: Paris and Nicky, twenty-six, were followed by Barron, twenty-one, and Conrad, who is sixteen. It was Conrad who inspired Paris to buy Princess Pigelette after he'd bought one himself from a special farm in Oregon.

Growing up in ritzy, secluded Bel Air, Paris says, "I was so sheltered. My parents were so strict. I wasn't allowed to go on a date, I wasn't allowed to wear makeup. They were really, really strict. When you're living in Bel Air in a house, you have no car, you're a teenager, you can't do anything. There's nowhere to walk. I was literally, like, stuck."

Paris friends were other "kids of"—Kidada Jones, daughter of Quincy; Brent Shapiro, son of Robert; Bijou Phillips, daughter of John. "Nicole Richie and I were best friends since we were babies. Our parents were best friends—Quincy was strict, too; we were only allowed to stay at one another's houses, not other people's."

When Paris was fifteen, the family moved to New York. "Nicky and I were like, *Yay!* Suddenly, we could take a taxi and go wherever we wanted. We could take the subway. I learned how to sneak out of the hotel by going down this stairwell where there were no security cameras." At first she attended the Professional Children's School with the likes of Macaulay Culkin and Christina Ricci. Later she transferred to Dwight, an exclusive private school on Central Park West, lampooned by some in Manhattan as "Dumb White Idiots Getting High Together." By most accounts, Paris didn't fit in well at either place. "She was different from everybody else," a Dwight classmate has said. "But she was always, like, really nice. Her parents were always traveling. She looked like a Barbie doll, and other kids didn't know how to react to it."

Before long, family friend Donald Trump made his overtures about Paris joining Trump Modeling Agency. "They said no, but then I heard about it. I just went to the agency without telling my parents."

In time, Paris fell in with the kids they called "the trustafarians," children of Sokoloffs, Radziwills, Steinbergs, Tisches, and various Saudi princes and other European royalty. They had a lot in common; they accepted one another for who they were. "My sister and I started getting invited to all these parties and all these socialite events, and we became, like, the Hilton Sisters, and everyone started photographing us."

The event that changed everything came in September 2000, when Paris was nineteen and *Vanity Fair* published the now-famous photos of the sisters by David LaChapelle. In one, Paris is lying on a dirty beach, legs akimbo, eyes closed, tankini top pulled down exposing one breast. In another shot she is wearing a mesh shirt with nothing underneath, flipping the bird. In another, with Nicky, Paris stands outside a colorful but sleazy motel, wearing tiny hot pants and a gold necklace that says: RICH.

"Those pictures were so, like, crazy," Paris says, drinking alternately from a soda can and a bottle of water. Her voice has the sober tone of a twenty-nine-year-old woman, looking back on her naive youth: "We didn't even know it was for *Vanity Fair*. I met him and everyone was like, 'Oh my god, he's like the Andy Warhol of our time.' David was like, 'Paris, you're my Edie.' He would take pictures of me all the time. Then we did this whole shoot in L.A. They flew Nicky out from New York—we didn't even tell my parents we were doing a photo shoot. We thought it was just a normal photo shoot, and then all the sudden, David's like, 'Oh, by the way, we're doing a whole story for *Vanity Fair*.' And I was like, *What?* It was really scary because, you know, they were pretty *artsy* pictures. I didn't really want my parents seeing them."

At nighttime the master bedroom is cold and breezy, probably in the low 50s, same as outside. Crossing the threshold feels a little like passing the invisible line in a department store that marks the perfume department; a mélange of sweet and musky scents prevails. A pair of floor fans are whirring. The doors to the papal-like balcony, overlooking the pool and the canyon beyond, are flung open wide—there is a bit of a wind tunnel effect, which causes the flames of all of the scented candles around the room to flicker and dance. Down below, you can see the San Fernando Valley, illuminated by the constellations of singular light bulbs that make suburbia.

The room is rendered lushly in black with white accents—even the ceiling is black. In her last house, her bedroom was pink. This time, "I wanted to make it better for resale value. When a man comes and buys a house, he doesn't want to see a pink bedroom. I think black is just more mature." There is plenty of faux fur and velvet and mirrored furniture, including a mirrored, four-poster bed. Everywhere the eye falls there is stuff; the room has the feel of an expensive antique store for little girls—dozens of Barbies still in boxes; a random pink feather boa; two large, lighted glass cases full of "my tiaras and shiny things and crystally stuff." And of course more pictures. "My man. My sister and Nicole. Me and Doug. Me. Us. Me. My BFFs from London. Me and Nicky and her babies. Pamela, Britney, Fergie, me, me, me, my girls. My love and my girls and my sister—that's who's in here with me," she says.

She is wearing a camouflage sweat suit with a matching cammo wifebeater. It has been a long day. There was a meeting with her record people, a meeting with her TV people, several hours of interviews, a lunch at the Ivy, a bunch of stuff I wasn't allowed to see, even a paparazzi chase through Beverly Hills: She set her jaw, blared Madonna's *Like a Virgin*, and gunned the throaty blue Bentley convertible (she also has a pink Bentley with customized Swarovski-crystal-bejeweled interior, but that one's *waay* too obvious), weaving through traffic, making it into a little game. At no time was there any anger evident; it was more like sport. She does not seem to be one of those celebs who complains about the very system that got her here in the first place—though she could do without the helicopters hovering over her place when she's trying to sunbathe at her own pool. At times, her celebrity is frightening even to her. Like when she landed in Istanbul, and her party emerged from the plane, only to set off a huge melee among the hundreds of reporters who'd gathered to meet her at the airport. "One guy busted this other guy's nose open, he was bleeding everywhere. And then a whole fight broke out. They all just went nuts." At a signing for her fragrance at a mall in Mexico, "There was like a stampede—like four people broke their arms and legs!"

Earlier tonight we had our "serious interview." I sense that she has chosen to wear the cammo outfit to convey her mood. In the interest of setting a new course in her life, she agreed to talk about *whatever*:

*The sex tape that surfaced two weeks before the premiere of her very first season of *The Simple Life*, distributed by a young man who'd been her boyfriend for three years. He said he was in love with her. ("I was humiliated. There were people who actually thought I released it myself. I was only seventeen, eighteen when it was shot.")

*The jail time that traumatized her and made her the butt of national jokes. Is it really possible that the whole episode could be traced to a mix-up by her lawyer, a silk-stockings guy who wasn't used to handling traffic cases? He told her it was okay for her to drive.

*The notion that she's famous for being famous. "Like, what do you think I've been doing all day? You don't think there's any skill to being me? You try it."

She seems determined to set the record straight, even offering to put me in touch with her gynecologist, who could confirm that those ugly rumors about her having herpes were untrue. And as for the whole sordid no-panties affair: Oh. My. God. *Totally doctored.* "I see it and there's like this disgusting Photoshopped *thing*," she explained. "And I'm like, 'Great, those are the nastiest private parts you can imagine and everyone in the world thinks it's *me*.' It was so embarrassing. *Ewww.* I always wear underwear. So that's fake. That picture was from St. Patrick's Day. I remember exactly. I was wearing *green* panties to celebrate."

Paris moves distractedly about the windy room, opening and closing drawers, looking through piles of stuff on the floor. There is a fragile quality to her movements, an awkward shakiness. A specific DVD needs to be found. She says she wants me to see it for background. But it feels very much like she needs to see it. Like we can't move forward with the last bits of our interview until that piece of very important business comes to pass.

Marilyn Monroe, the dog, is flitting around the room. Prince Baby Bear is sniffing after her. Princess Annabelle is observing from her perch on the black bedspread, absently licking herself. As Paris digs through a bedside drawer, Doug is on his hands and knees, rooting though stacks of DVDs kept in various credenzas and shelving units in the seating area of the room. Paris is a near-obsessive scrapbooker, collagemaker, and keeper of personal records. One of her product lines offers materials for scrapbooking and other crafts. Another day, when we go to an appearance on *Hell's Kitchen*, she'll take with her a large tote bag full of cameras and high-tech accessories. She will sit on the bottom step of her dramatic stairwell, in five-inch heels, fiddling with batteries and memory cards and sticks. Like a faithful historian, she is constantly documenting her life. Somehow, like her stream-of-consciousness business and marketing ideas—on the way to lunch, her manager and her PR woman in the backseat: "I think we should do my new music video with a Marilyn theme to go with my new perfume"—all of her primary source materials get funneled downward and through the flow chart of her organization, which is managed at the top (beneath Paris and Rick, of course) by an ambitious young guy with spiky hair named Jamie Freed, who came up through the bowels of the Hollywood talent agency UTA. His mission: "creating a superior digital platform and a community allowing fans and enthusiasts to engage with the release of Paris' new entertainment properties, all aspects of her business, and most importantly, with Paris directly."

Now Doug pauses in his search, sitting up on his haunches and straightening his back: "The last time I saw it, you had it in that DVD case."

"What's that, babe?" she asks distractedly, shuffling through a pile of DVDs.

"What happened to that special DVD case?" Doug asks.

"There's a million DVDs here," she pouts. This time she uses the little-girl voice.

"I'll look under the bed," Doug says fondly.

"You need a warehouse," I comment.

Doug laughs. "You should see the *garage*."

"When I have kids one day I want to show them *everything*," Paris says, undefensively.

Doug shuffles through a random fistful of DVDs: "*TRL, MTV, Extra, Access Hollywood, Entertainment Tonight.* She's got *everything* here." He sounds a little awed.

There is more rummaging. It is getting late. The PR lady is getting annoyed. Clearly Paris has gone off book.

Then Doug finds the disc! He raises it exaltedly, like the last out in the World Series.

"I love you!" Paris exclaims. She throws her long arms around his neck and kisses him on the lips.

The DVD goes in. The big screen comes to life. Paris and I sit side by side on the velvet love seat. Our backs are resting on a set of black-and-white throw pillows emblazoned with Paris's eerie, idealized face. Doug takes a knee behind, his meaty forearm resting casually between us.

The DVD turns out to be a compendium of their vacations together over the past year. In one scene, Paris goads Doug into sky diving. It is her third time, his first. "I couldn't let my girlfriend be tougher than me," Doug says. In another, Paris catches a silvery needle fish. "A *wiener* fish!" she exclaims in her baby voice, cracking up Doug and the native guide.

In the finale, Doug rents an entire island in Fiji for a week. There is nobody there but the staff. Doug catches a fish with his bare hands; they both get certified for scuba. One night, under a million stars, they drink kava with the natives and their faces go numb. "I miss those guys," Paris says wistfully. "I never wanna go back to the Maui Four Seasons again. I used to do that my whole life. Fiji makes Maui look like a joke. It was so *gorgeous*."

"We'll go back," Doug assures her.

Cut to:

Doug being interviewed. He looks earnestly into the camera. He resembles Mark Wahlberg; when you see him in pictures with Paris, he looks stiff as a board next to her always-polished pose. "She's very caring, very loving, very nurturing," he tells the camera. As he's speaking, Paris drinks him in with her purply blue eyes. Her lacquered fingernails tickle the hair on his arm. "She's a great cook. She travels all over the world, and she's my best friend, and we have a great time together. I couldn't ask for anything more. She's the best. And I know she has my back 'cause this one time I got into a scuffle, and she jumped on some dude's back, took off her headband, and was *whipping* him with it. So I know she has my back."

Doug laughs. "Of course, I just made that part up," he explains to me.

"It's fun to see how many places we've been," Paris says, rising from the love seat, seemingly fortified, the shakiness gone. It's as if, having watched it for herself, she knows once again who she is: a girl in love doing pretty well for herself. Like it says on the plaque over the doorbell out front, she is Princess Paris. She issues her toothy smile, the one reserved for family and friends. "Do you want any food?" she asks her prince, for the third time tonight. "I can bring you a plate."

He takes her by the shoulders and kisses her sweetly on the forehead. "Remember?" he says. "I told you, I already ate."

(2010)

The Someone You're Not

Ray Towler was sentenced to life in prison for raping an eleven-year-old girl. Even among murderers and felons he was considered the lowest form of scum. There was only one problem: He didn't do it. How one man lived through twenty-nine years of hell, only to be saved by a new wrinkle in DNA science. And how he emerged from his ordeal a better person.

A little girl sitting in a big chair, the witness stand in Courtroom 15-B, overlooking the lake in downtown Cleveland.

It is a Monday morning in September 1981. The girl is eleven. Her name is Brittany. She's in sixth grade, weighs eighty-nine pounds. She lives with her mom and her eighteen-year-old brother. Frequently she stays overnight at her aunt's house. Her cousin is named Jack. He is a year older, in the same grade at the same school. They spend a lot of time together.

Late in the afternoon on the Saturday of Memorial Day weekend, Brit (the names of the children have been changed) rode her bike unsupervised from her house to Jack's. The area where they live, the west side of Cleveland, is predominantly white. It is considered the safe part of town.

Upon waking the next morning—Sunday, May 24, 1981—Brit and Jack got the idea to go on a picnic in the park, something they'd done many times before. They went to a local market and bought provisions, returned home to pack lunch. As they busied themselves in the kitchen, Brit mentioned this cool fallen log she and her girlfriend had found two weeks earlier; you could climb out onto the end and dangle your toes in the river. She really wanted to show it to Jack. He was psyched. Every good outing needs a mission. This would be theirs.

With mom's permission, off they went the short distance, Brit on her ten-speed, Jack on his Huffy. Down Wagar Road to Detroit Avenue, into the entrance. The park was officially named the Rocky River

Reservation, but everybody called it the Valley—one link in a chain of lush metro parks that followed the meandering Rocky River south from Lake Erie and on past the airport. There were massive shale cliffs, bountiful forests, nature trails; a riding stable, three golf courses.

It was hot and humid, just past noon. They entered at the Scenic Park Marina, headed south along the All Purpose Trail. The thirteen-mile path was shaded and nicely paved; there was the usual sparse but steady flow of joggers and bike riders.

At some point along the way, the kids stopped to eat. Afterward, they resumed their journey southward until they reached the first golf course—two miles as the crow flies from where they started but probably twice that far in actual distance given the serpentine trail. From there they returned north, looking for Brit's special log.

They dismounted their bikes and began walking, Jack on point, Brit following. A black man approached from out of the woods. He was wearing sunglasses and had a stubble of beard. He was carrying a rolled up article of clothing beneath one arm. Two eye witnesses— a young secretary on roller skates and a tool-and-die maker who volunteered info to the police after being stopped with an open beer—would later testify that he was the only black person either of them saw that day in the park.

"I found a deer and I think it has a broken leg," the black man told the kids. "Could you come and help me?"

Without hesitation, Jack said yes.

Brit wasn't so sure.

"*Jack*," she implored.

Jack didn't catch her drift. There was a new adventure at hand. He set his bike against a tree and followed the man into the woods. Brit did the same.

A few hundred feet into the forest, the man turned and produced a gun from the rolled-up article of clothing—a wood-handled police-type revolver. Jack was shoved against a tree, ordered to kiss the dirt. Brit was dragged by one arm a few feet away from her cousin.

The man pulled down his pants, untied Brit's yellow jumper. He pulled down her underpants.

"And then what did he say?" the assistant prosecutor asks. His name is Allan Levenberg.

"He said, 'Lift your legs,'" Brit testifies.

"Did he do or say anything else at that time?"

"Yes."

"What was that?"

"He said, 'Is it in?' and I said, 'I think so.'"

A stunned, horrible silence falls upon the courtroom. Levenberg continues gingerly, speaking as much to the jury as to Brit, in the manner that trial lawyers have. He makes sure the words *penis*, *entered*, and *vagina* are added to the public record.

Then he asks: "This black male you have been telling us about ... the one you followed into the woods to look for this phantom deer. Do you see him in the courtroom today?"

"He is over there," she says. She points a small finger. "He has a blue shirt on and blue pants."

Raymond Daniel Towler is sitting at the defense table. He is a big guy, twenty-four years old, with a full puffy beard and a quick smile; his burnished ebony skin is a shade darker than the rich wood paneling in the courtroom. By most accounts he is a gentle, talented, thoughtful man who studied art in community college. He earns a living working temp jobs and lending his Jimi Hendrix-inspired guitar stylings to various rock bands around town. At the time of his arrest, he was collecting unemployment, thinking about reenlisting in the Army. He was living with his mother and little sister in a modest house on the west side, three miles from the Valley, a place he's been going with relatives and friends his entire life.

Ray Towler does not claim to be the best man on the planet. He's really just a regular guy. Though he doesn't drink, he does enjoy the occasional doobie—it is 1981, after all, and he is a musician. He has yet to find a regular civilian job. You could say he's always been a little bit adrift—a black kid in a white school who wanted to be an engineer or an astronaut but who was counseled toward shop classes and the assembly line; a volunteer soldier who was told he could learn how to work on missiles but ended up assigned to the infantry; a veteran with an honorable discharge who served overseas and then came back home to. . . the same old shit he was trying to escape.

One thing he is absolutely sure of: He is no child molester.

No fucking way.

And yet, inexplicably, he is here.

On trial for rape, kidnapping, and felonious assault.

Facing a life sentence.

Which is really a death sentence—a long, slow, lingering death behind bars.

Sitting in the hard courtroom chair, Towler feels weirdly detached, like he's here but he's not. He studies the little girl and the judge and the prosecutor. He's trying to listen, he knows he *should* be listening so he can make some sense of what's going on, so he can try to figure out what the hell has happened, how this huge mistake got made. It's hard to concentrate. He thinks about all the stuff black folks have endured throughout history. He thinks about Dr. King and lynching parties and white hoods. It's like he's entered the *Twilight Zone*—the worst horror movie you could ever imagine. In court they keep talking about this man. They keep asking the witnesses, "Did *he* do this?" and "Did *he* do that?" Evil, perverted, unconscionable things.

And every time they say the words Did *he*, they mean *him*: Ray Towler.

He wonders about the little girl in the big chair, about the prosecutors, about God. *Why are you doing this to me?* He has never before in his life seen these children. *Why are you accusing me of something I didn't do? Are you covering up for someone else who hurt you? How could these people really think it was me to do something like this?*

Towler looks to his lawyer, an old white guy with mismatched socks. His name is Jerome Silver. He is holding a pen poised above a legal pad. His hand is shaking. *Every one of his objections has been overruled!*

Towler's head throbs. He wants to cry. He wants to throw up. His whole family is sitting behind him in the courtroom listening. *This is how it's going to be. For the rest of my life, I'm going to be thought of as a person who does this kind of stuff to little kids.*

He feels like somebody is holding him down and beating him in the back of the head with a baseball bat.

Early the next morning, before the trial starts for the day, Towler and his lawyer are called into the judge's chambers for a meeting.

The Honorable Roy F. McMahon is semiretired but still hearing cases. Levenberg, the assistant prosecutor, is also present.

The judge asks Towler if he'll take a plea bargain.

"Maybe I'd consider if you tell me what you're putting on the table," Towler says.

The judge addresses Towler's lawyer. "If you don't mind, Mr. Silver, I'm going to talk to Mr. Towler alone."

When Silver objects, he is once again overruled. From day one of the trial, it has seemed to Towler that the judge's attitude has been, *Okay, we already know how this is going to end, let's just get it over with.*

Towler watches his lawyer's back recede. *Walkin' out the room with your tail between your legs,* he thinks derisively. *What kind of a lawyer can't even save an innocent man?*

At the time of the crime—approximately 1:00 p.m. on Sunday May 24 —Ray Towler swears he was in his bedroom at home, coolin' it and listening to music after a late party at his mom's house the night before.

It had been the usual family gathering: Moms grilling, people bringing covered dishes, gin and juice. Towler went to bed early, around 1:00 a.m. The low-key festivities lasted until four—even the kids stayed up until the wee hours.

The next morning, the day of the rape, Towler's nine-year-old niece, Tiffany Settles, woke up at 7:30. His moms, Josephine Drake— for years a data programmer; the daughter of a registered nurse and a construction worker—rose to supervise and fix breakfast. Towler came downstairs at about 12:30 or 1:00 to use the only bathroom. His moms and Tiff were watching a *Ma and Pa Kettle* movie on Channel 61. His ten-year-old sister, Priscilla Drake, was still asleep.

Towler went back up to his room. It was a close house, probably no more than thirteen hundred square feet over two floors. For the next few hours, his radio and his footfalls could be heard, but he was not actually seen. At 3:00 or 3:30, Towler reemerged from his room, clomped down the steps, passed through the living room to get a drink of cold water from the fridge. Then he took a shower and went back upstairs to get dressed. In about an hour, with a summer downpour threatening, he would sweep out the garage so the girls could roller-skate in there without getting wet.

By that time, having concluded a rape exam at a local hospital, little Brit was being questioned by authorities, according to the testimony at the trial.

Thirteen days after the rape, on the afternoon of June 6, Towler drove the three miles to the Valley in his green Monte Carlo, a clunker with the door and trunk locks punched out. He'd bought it recently for $700, the amount he'd gotten for selling his pro-quality reel-to-reel tape recorder.

Even though Towler went to the Valley occasionally, he never stayed down there very long. When he was little his moms used to take him all the time—picnics, baseball, hide-and-seek. Later, as a teen, he would usually go in a group; the rangers always wanted to stop and hassle them. Cleveland might not be the South, but the history of race relations here is as tortured as anywhere in the nation. Suffice it to say that while Ray Towler felt an inalienable right to be in the Valley, he wasn't 100 percent comfortable whenever he was actually there.

As he was leaving the Valley, Towler was pulled over for rolling though a stop sign—which was weird because he was sure he *hadn't* rolled though no stop sign. He was a very careful driver. Especially when he was in the park, or anywhere else on the west side. Driving While Black. It didn't have a name back in 1981—nobody really talked about it openly until Rodney King had his run-in with the Los Angeles police a decade later. But every black man in America knew the concept well.

The ranger issued Towler a ticket, but he seemed much more interested in bringing him back to the station house and taking his photograph. . . .

Which in turn would be selected from an array of eleven photos by the four witnesses: Brity, Jack, the skater girl, and the open-beer-can informant.

On June 19, they took Towler away from his mom's house.

Now it is September and the weather is changing. Towler is well into his trial. Judge McMahon is tall and skinny with a long face. He makes Towler think of a skeleton in a black robe. He's just asked Towler if he wants to make a deal. Towler has asked the terms.

Plead guilty, the judge tells him, according to Towler, and "we'll take care of you."

In the movies, when someone in power "takes care" of somebody else, it doesn't usually end very well for that person. Towler doesn't know what to say, so he says nothing.

The judge looks annoyed. "Do me a favor," he tells Towler. "Get up from that chair and stretch your legs a bit, check out the view from the windows."

From where they are situated, somewhere high up in the highest tower at the judicial-center complex, facing north, Ray can see the blue sky meeting the blue waters of Lake Erie, a seemingly infinite view. The shallowest of all the Great Lakes, carved by glaciers, the lake that drains and replenishes itself the most often ... how many times had they taught him those fun facts during his school years? In the foreground he can see a little airport. In the middle distance a few sailboats. Beyond that is Canada, he supposes.

"Get a good look at that view," Judge McMahon says. "If you don't take this deal, you'll never see that lake again."

Instead of making Towler feel defeated, the judge's remark makes him mad.

If they gonna railroad me, he tells himself, *they gonna have to do it all the way*.

Towler takes the stand in his own defense. He swears he has never before seen the little girl or the little boy. He was at home during the time the crime was committed. What more can he say? He didn't do it.

His mom, his little sister, and his little niece confirm his alibi. His lawyer drives home the point that Towler—now, for a long time, and in the photo taken of him that day—has a *full* beard, not a stubble, as described by the victims. His argument that Towler did not own a pair of sunglasses was less convincing.

The trial lasts seven days—the first three consumed by motions, impaneling the jury, and a field trip down to the Valley and to the scene of the crime; the last one and a half dedicated to impassioned summations, followed by a seemingly endless jury charge.

After one morning of deliberation, a verdict is returned.

Ray Towler is found guilty of rape, kidnapping, and felonious assault.

Judge McMahon sentences Towler to life for his crimes against Brit. For those against Jack, he receives an additional twelve to forty years. In addition, Towler is ordered to pay court costs of $1,951.95, due within sixty days, subject to interest charges thereafter.

Assistant Prosecutor Levenberg tells the press: "Anyone who preys on children should be put away and the key lost. This man, an animal, got what he deserved — life!"

Towler is transferred from the county lockup at the Justice Center to orientation at the Ohio Penitentiary (broken windows, pigeons flying around the tiers) to the maximum-security facility at Lucasville (an inmate population composed mostly of lifers).

Attorney Silver handles the appeal.

Denied.

Ray becomes his own jailhouse lawyer, pro se. He asks the governor of Ohio for a commutation. He petitions the federal district court for a writ of habeas corpus. He applies to the sentencing judge for early release.

Denied. Denied. Denied.

After seven years he is moved to lower-security facilities at the Marion Correctional Institution.

At the twelve-year mark, he sees the parole board in person.

Denied.

Two years later he is moved to a minimum-security prison at Grafton, Ohio, and eight years after that he moves to the Grafton Farm. Most of the inmates at the farm are allowed to work outside. Some can even drive into town themselves. As a convicted child molester, Ray cannot leave the facility. He has a similar problem with the mandatory courses he's supposed to take: Because he refuses to stand up in group and admit he is a child molester, he is not allowed to participate.

Years pass. He sees a couple guys have heart attacks. He sees a few guys get killed—they're lying there bleeding, you know, you just keep moving. He sees beat-downs, beefs, hassles, rapes. He watches a cellie die slowly of a heart blockage—a decent older man who'd shot a guy for messing with his daughter. Towler is locked down in solitary twice. The first, a ninety-day stint, follows a routine shakedown: His cellie has a shiv fashioned from a spoon he bullied Towler into bringing back from the kitchen. The second stint follows the death of his mother, in 1984. He is allowed to go to the funeral; he wears shackles. When he returns, he asks to be put in solitary—he just wants to be alone. Over the years, all of the prisons in which he is housed are far from home—one is on the border with Kentucky. After the funeral, the only relative who visits is his sister, Deborah.

From the very beginning, he draws portraits of guys, amazingly realistic likenesses with a number-2 pencil, on the back of an envelope or on a sheet of plain paper, something very special an inmate can send to his mom, his woman, his kids. Ray sells the portraits for cash or other valuables. His talent grants him a certain respect within the prison community, despite the mark of his despicable crime, which is written at the very top of his file and all of his paperwork, along with his prison number, 164681. His offense follows him everywhere. There is no escape. He feels like the actor Chuck Connors in that old TV show, *Branded*. The theme song plays over and over in his head: *What do you do when you're branded, and you know you're a man?*

That he is almost six feet tall and weighs three hundred pounds also helps keep him safe. His worst moment comes one afternoon at Lucasville when three would-be assailants corner him in the dish-washing area of the kitchen. Luckily he's been warned; only by mentioning some special words given to him by his cellie does he avoid becoming their bitch. (He still doesn't understand exactly what he was telling them. He thinks maybe he was saying he was already taken.)

He carries himself upright. He doesn't complain and moan. He doesn't gossip. He does his own time. He maintains his maintain. Never for one minute does he ever let himself think he is destined to spend the rest of his life behind bars—he knows he might, but he never thinks he will ... so he doesn't live like that, like an animal in a cage. He tries to live like he's at home. He tries to respect himself and others. He acts in a way that makes others respect him. His Zenlike demeanor, a calm he's possessed since childhood, when he used to sit for hours and draw on the data-entry cards his moms brought home for that purpose, fits well to his circumstances. He has the patience of an artist—to render a face with a million tiny strokes. At Lucasville he does wall murals in the cafeteria (using scavenged house paint and car paint and spray paint) in exchange for better food. By the time he gets to Grafton he has the coveted job of overseeing the rec department. There is an art studio with a nice airbrush and plenty of supplies, four hours a day of uninterrupted time to paint. Each of his canvasses takes a week to complete. Over the years, he makes more than four hundred large pieces, and many more small ones. The top price is $250. Even the assistant warden buys a portrait. With the earnings Ray buys a television and other comforts. All the inmates have the same model TV, the body fabricated of see-through plastic. He learns to measure the seasons by the calendar of televised sports. Somehow, the haplessness of Cleveland's franchises fits his predicament. It doesn't matter if they win or lose, as long as they eat up time.

He takes the courses he's allowed to take. Through Shawnee State University, he studies English comp, literature, and accounting. He retakes his GED exam because the Army can't find the paperwork. He receives his associate of arts degree. He wants to go further but the budget gets cut. He works in a furniture factory and learns woodworking. He takes electronics classes and learns how to fix amplifiers and other appliances. He takes a class in home electrical wiring—to become a licensed electrician on the outside, all he would need to do is take a written test. For his guitar playing, he studies the jazz masters, people like Wes Montgomery and George Benson, going all the way back to the crossroads, the blues. He forms a bunch of different bands and singing groups—part of his rec-department job includes overseeing the musical equipment. He contributes two songs to a state-financed album of children's lullabies—he writes, arranges, plays all the instruments, directs the singers, records and mixes it himself. (To his supreme embarrassment, a furor breaks out in the local press when the CD comes out and his status as a sex offender is discovered.) To enrich his skills as a painter, he studies the Old Masters. DiVinci, Vermeer, and Rembrandt are his favorites; he likes the way they always have something real shiny in the picture that makes it stand out with the dark backgrounds. He also likes Salvador Dalí, whose absurdist abstract realism seems to fit his situation perfectly.

Towler does his best to watch his diet and stay healthy. They give you a lot of starch at every meal; he tries to stick to the proteins. His favorite fare is canned salmon mixed with contraband salad and vegetables. You can get almost anything in prison, except good fruit. (What little there is—apples, oranges, the occasional hard pears— quickly becomes custody of the resident hooch makers.) He loves playing basketball. He plays pretty much every day until he gets up in age, around forty-five. He is the guy driving to the hole, a power forward like Charles Barkley—don't get in his way. There are leagues; every game devolves at some point into a scuffle. One year in Lucas- ville his team wins the championship. He joins a football team, too. It is kind of like *The Longest Yard*, except they won't let them play the corrections officers or leave the front gate. The COs are pretty much what you'd expect. Some racist shits and some good human beings. Some of the females are nice, too. They have their pick of the inmates. You'd be surprised how much nookie goes on.

Incredibly, he is never seriously ill or injured. He pulls a muscle in his left calf. He chips a tooth on somebody's head playing basketball; the state dentist gives him a crown. He has a few colds, but never any food poisoning. A lot of guys cook stuff in their cells and try to save the leftovers; the place is crawling with germs. When he thinks about it, he is living in a bathroom, literally. His bunk is in the same room as his toilet/sink combination. The ventilation is bad. The reek can be powerful and lingering.

Over the years there are literally hundreds of cellies. They live with him for one night. A month. Two years. They go home, they are transferred to another prison, they go to the hole and never return. He tries not to keep track, neither of the faces nor of the time. He is not a maker of hash marks. His sentence is infinite, there is no purpose in mocking himself this way.

His all-time worst cellie is called Chicken Saw. Don't ask how he got that name. He's a bully. He's shorter than Ray, but he's a muscle freak—does push-ups, sit-ups, jumping jacks in the cell all day and all night long, grunting and sweating and stinking. He's the one who gets caught with the shiv.

The all-time best cellie is the guy who dies. His name is Jackson. He was a welder on the outside. He is diagnosed with a 90 percent heart blockage. He is given thirty days to live but lasts almost three months. Towler teaches him how to paint. The last time Towler sees Jackson, they are bringing him out of the cell on a stretcher, loading him onto the back of one of the golf carts they use for an ambulance. He has a look on his face, this strange scared look. He asks Ray, "Am I going to be alright?"

"Either you're going to see Jesus or you're going to be back here," Towler tells him. They'd talked about this many times. "We both know which is better."

That was a tough day, one of many tough days. Many, many tough days. Pretty much all of them endured without the comforting touch of another human being; all of them endured without the feeling that there is someone squarely on your side—no one to love and no one to love you. Towler is alone in there. And everyone thinks he is someone he is not.

You look in his file, he knows the first impression you get. But he can never let himself believe that somebody can just look at him and say: "He's a rapist." Of course, guys always ask. They're like, "What are you in for?" If he tell them, they frown at him like he's a scumbag.

He thinks about escaping. How many times does he look at that fence, that gate, that barbed wire and think, *Shit, man, I can get over that no problem. I can find a way to escape. I'm a pretty smart guy.*

But he always puts those thoughts away. *If I choose to run, nobody will believe I'm innocent. Once you leave, you're marked. People are like, "If you're innocent, why did you run? If you're innocent, you would have stayed and fought."*

In 1993, after he is turned down for parole, Towler is visited by a dream. It will follow him from Marion to Grafton to the farm, across the years, though the dark prison nights.

He's in a long corridor— splendid and regal, like a castle or something, a palace fit for a king.

He is walking and walking.

There is nowhere to rest. There is nowhere to sit down. He feels like he must be going somewhere but he doesn't know where.

Finally he comes to a door.

He pulls the golden handle. He steps through.

Into another long corridor.
Walking and walking.
Endlessly walking.

In 1995, everybody in Grafton was glued to their identical, prison-approved, see through television sets, watching the O.J. Simpson murder trial.

One part of the proceedings had Towler and his fellows riveted.

DNA: Deoxyribonucleic acid. The unique genetic fingerprint that distinguishes each human from every other. Given the proper sample, a person could be identified with nearly 100 percent accuracy.

In 2001, following DNA tests on old evidence, a fellow inmate at Grafton, a convicted rapist, is exonerated by a judge and set free. Towler redoubles his efforts to sell paintings, hoping to build a legal fund.

In 2003, the Ohio legislature passes a bill allowing qualified prisoners to request state-paid DNA testing. Most cases are denied or indefinitely delayed. Incredibly, Cuyahoga County Common Pleas Court Judge Eileen A. Gallagher takes an interest in Towler's case. She appoints a lawyer free of charge.

In 2004, after consulting the Ohio Innocence Project—newly founded by Mark Godsey, a former federal prosecutor turned University of Cincinnati law professor—Towler's attorney gets the state to agree to send the evidence from Towler's twenty-three-year-old case to a lab for DNA testing. Three envelopes are shipped: One contains two pubic hairs recovered from the victim's pelvic region; one contains scrapings from under her fingernails; one contains the panties she was wearing beneath her yellow jumper.

When the evidence arrives at the lab, two of the envelopes are empty.

Because Towler's lawyer did not take Professor Godsey's advice, the test he chooses turns out not to be sophisticated enough to detect any evidence of male DNA in the panties. The lawyer is notified of all of these findings in writing, as are all the other parties to the case. . . .

Except Towler.

He doesn't know what the heck's going on. He's at the Grafton farm. Mentally, he's rubbing his hands together: *Okay, It's only a matter of time.*

Two weeks pass.

Two months. No word.

He starts to get worried. He tries to call the lawyer but he can't connect.

More months pass.

Now Towler's all tore up. He's pissed. *Why can't this fuckin' guy call me back?* One day on the phone, he's venting to his niece, Tiffany. She volunteers to go in person to the lawyer's office, where she learns the truth.

Towler feels like that scene in the movie *Full Metal Jacket*, where all the guys in the barracks put bars of soap in their towels and beat the crap out of Vincent D'Onofrio.

Four more years pass.

Towler writes letters to judges, senators, congressmen, anyone he can think of. He writes a letter to the home office of the Innocence Project in New York, founded by the well-known legal activists Barry Scheck and Peter Neufeld. They refer him to the Ohio branch.

Professor Godsey sees Towler's letter. Towler doesn't know it, but he is already uppermost in Godsey's mind as Godsey works with the *Columbus Dispatch* on a newspaper series exposing the flaws in Ohio's DNA testing system. Together with reporters from the paper, Godsey's volunteers, most of them law students, identify more than 300 cases that could be fruitful to investigate. Thirty inmates are short-listed as strong candidates for DNA exoneration; Towler is at the top.

Towler formally reapplies to the court for further testing. In late 2008, with the benefit of rapidly advancing technology, a lab comes back with results showing that he was almost certainly not the rapist.

The prosecution is not satisfied. The assistant prosecutor assigned to the case (prosecutor Levenberg, attorney Silver, and Judge McMahon have all since died) has a reputation as a hardass who fights for the sake of fighting.

By 2010, the technology has again improved. The DNA in the victim's panties is proven conclusively by the lab to be the product of a different man, not Raymond Daniel Towler. Towler is "excluded as the contributor of the sperm-cell DNA sample in this case," according to the findings of the Orchid Cellmark Forensics Laboratory, one of the nation's leaders in DNA testing.

Meanwhile, Towler waits. He has no idea what is going on. The whole thing is eating him up.

One night after lockdown, he finally gives up hope.

I can't take this no more, man, he tells himself. *This is all I can think of. I wake up and wait for it—are they going to call today? Are they going to say I'm free? Or is it going to be like every other time: Sorry, we lost your samples. Sorry, we used the wrong test. Sorry, the prosecutor is a total bitch. Sorry, sorry, sorry!*

And he tells himself: *I'm done. I can't worry about this no more. It's out of my hands.*

At that moment a great weight lifts.

Ray Towler feels like he can breathe again.

Wow, he tells himself. *Maybe I should've done this a long time ago.*

Four days later, his attorney gets the word. Towler still has no clue. He's in his cell when the shift sergeant approaches, acting all friendly: "You have a call," he says.

Towler is suspicious. Usually this dude is a butthole. "What's going on?"

"I ain't supposed to tell you this. . . but you're getting out tomorrow."

Towler doesn't believe him. It's the kind of mean thing this guy always does.

Towler is sitting beside a long table in Courtroom 23-A, over-looking the lake in downtown Cleveland. It looks exactly like the last courtroom he was in. It sort of gives him the creeps.

Towler is wearing a black sweater, a white shirt, and black dress pants. His shoes pinch. He hasn't worn civvies since. . . probably since his moms's funeral, back in '84. Today is May 5, 2010. Someone tells him it's Cinco de Mayo, a Mexican holiday that celebrates a hard-fought military victory. *I can go with that,* Towler tells himself.

Judge Gallagher asks Towler for his patience as she summarizes the case for the public record. He can't focus on what she's saying. It feels like the longest speech in human history.

"Raymond Towler was a wrongfully imprisoned individual," she declares for all to hear.

After bestowing upon him an Irish blessing (May the road rise up to meet you. May the wind always be at your back. . .), Gallagher steps down from her high bench and approaches Towler with extended hands. She fights back tears.

"Mr. Towler, you are free to go."

They lead him out of the courtroom, a celebratory whirlwind gathering family and well-wishers as it goes. There is a press conference. People shout questions.

He hasn't slept a wink. His mind is so full of stuff, it feels empty, the way all the brilliant colors of the rainbow, mixed together, make black.

Twenty-eight years and eight months.

He doesn't know what to say.

All he can think about is pizza.

Towler spends his first night of freedom with his brother in their mom's old house. He can't even shut his eyes. He has so much to do. *My lists have lists.* He needs a Social Security card, a driver's license, a photo ID, a bank account, all the stuff people have. There are appointments with lawyers—there is a settlement due; more than forty grand per year of incarceration is guaranteed. If he wants more, he'll have to fight the state over lost wages, pain and suffering, the usual. He will fight. There will be money, probably a couple of million, but not yet. Another item on the list: Find a job.

He rises at dawn his first morning, as he is accustomed. Everyone else in the house is still asleep. Birds are chirping. It is nice and cool. He sticks his head out the front door of the house, sniffs the suburban air ... but he can make himself go no further. It's like there is an invisible barrier.

On the fourth morning, he musters the courage to walk to the corner store. A container of orange juice never tasted so good.

He is like a new person, starting all over from where he left off. He's hoping to get in twenty more years. He tries not to think of all the time he spent behind bars as "lost." Instead, he tries to focus on the positive. Sometimes he finds himself standing for a few moments in the bathroom, sort of marveling. For three decades he lived in his bathroom. Now, after living with his cousin Carole for a few months, he lives in his own apartment (another of his life's belated firsts). No longer must he shit where he eats and sleeps.

Driving around the city, his new license in his pocket, Towler notices all the changes everywhere. There are fancy new street signs and crosswalks; a zillion new buildings downtown. He's still timid about nosing into traffic; he'll sit forever at a left turn, letting everyone in front of him. Frequently he finds himself lost. Somebody gives him a GPS but he doesn't know how to use it. Somebody else gives him a BlackBerry; he's pretty good with that. He doesn't have a computer yet, but he manages to gather a guitar, a sax, an easel, an amplifier (he has to fix it himself using his prison-learned skills), and a bass guitar, for which he shells out $400 because the band at the church needs a bass player.

Another thing Towler notices is the number of nonwhite faces everywhere. When he gets his job in the mail room at a big health-insurance company downtown, he is pleasantly shocked. There are coworkers of every hue; it almost feels like race doesn't exist in the same way anymore. His immediate supervisor is a big and pretty white lady. He could swear she's kind of flirting with him.

That's another thing: women. It's tripping him out the way they so aggressive today. Before, a gal would just kind of wait around, and you would make your move, and she would make her answer known. Now they come straight up to him and it's like, "I think we should date, Raymond." Women are more bossy now, too. He is at this art festival with this one gal, and she's telling him, "You need to do this," and "You need to do that." Finally Towler smiles real big and says, "Really? Do I really have to do all of this? Is that, like, an order?"

In restaurants he feels responsible to read every word of the menu. He calls the tortillas "little pancakes." He marvels over this wonderful offering called a western omelet; he thanks the waitress profusely for taking the time to list the ingredients. While he's eating at a chain steak house on the outskirts of a mall parking lot, a guy in a suit comes to the table and asks how dinner is going. Ray wonders politely who he is to be asking. . .and is flattered to learn he is the manager of the entire place! When his favorite lawyer comes to town—she was on the conference call in the sergeant's office—he tries to take her to a nice Mexican restaurant to show his gratitude but ends up taking her to a taco stand by mistake.

Wherever he goes, everything is computerized. The gas station, the convenience store, the hardware store: Swipe this, enter that code, do it yourself. Automated supermarket checkout? You wonder why people are crying about needing jobs. It used to be anybody could get a job in a grocery store, from teenagers on up. Likewise cars: He used to be able to fix anything. Now he'd have to go to school all over again to learn fuel injection and the other computer-driven stuff.

So many choices. Which car insurance. Which cereal. Which deodorant, toothpaste, toothbrush, soap, shampoo. Rows and rows of products. Varieties, sizes, colors. Which is cheaper? Which is better? What's the best buy? Which gum to chew? When he went into prison there were, like, two kinds of chewing gum. Now there are a zillion. One of the small gifts he gives himself is trying all the gums. *I can spoil myself a little as long as I stay within my means.* Papaya Juice! Kiwi and strawberry nectar! Green tea! Arnold Palmer—he was a golfer when Towler went down. Now he is a drink, sweet and so incredibly thirst quenching.

He loves work. He came home May 5 and started working June 21. *Hell, I've been vacationing for thirty years.* He wears a smock and pushes a mail cart. He stops at all the cubicles, greets everyone with his friendly smile. Ray even loves commuting to work, especially now, in his new car, a black Ford Focus. He's like a sixteen-year-old who can finally drive himself to school. It costs almost the same to park as it does to take the train.

One day before he gets his car, he is sitting on the train with his commuting buddy, this German girl he met. They're stopped; a cop gets on the train, this big white guy. He stands for a minute kind of looking around—he keeps looking down the aisle, but then his eyes keep returning to Towler. Then the cop says, "I want to check everybody's ticket."

Towler's like, *What the fuck?* He kind of has a flashback almost, like, *What: You gonna try to pat me down or something, man?* Luckily the German girl notices the look on Towler's face. He has told her his story. That's one great thing. Everywhere he goes people recognize him from the news. Or if they don't recognize him, they've heard of him—this guy whose life was stolen by the state. Everyone feels bad for him. And when Towler shows he doesn't feel bad for himself, that he's not going to be a resentful complainer, everyone wishes him well. . . he is an easy guy to like.

Of course, the cop on the train doesn't know all this.

Towler's eyes bulge. The German girl leans over and whispers, "He's just doing his job, Ray, don't worry."

The moment passes.

At eleven o'clock one evening Towler is feeling hungry. He gathers up the keys to his car and drives off into the dark, in search of a three-piece chicken dinner.

It's the first time he's driven anywhere at this time of night by himself. He is careful to drive the speed limit. The windows are down, the air is humid and smells of tree pollen, the sounds of summer filter past. For three decades they locked him down without fail at 9:00 p.m. Unless there was a fire drill, he never got to see the night.

He drives down Loraine Avenue, past some restaurants and clubs. He looks at all the people, just checking things out. As usual, he kind of knows where he's going but he kind of doesn't.

He makes a wrong turn. Maybe two. He finds himself. . .

Down in the Valley, in the Rocky River Reservation.

His heart begins to pound. *Dang, man, it's kinda dark.* It's like the shark theme from *Jaws* is playing in his skull. *You need to get up outta here fast.*

Towler pulls it together and finds his way out. He kind of laughs at himself, at his momentary freak-out. *Why should I be worried? I'm an American. I got my rights. I ain't doing nothing wrong.*

All his life, he tried to be a stand-up guy. He was a dutiful son, a good relative. He respected the law. He did all the things he was supposed to do.

His reward: three decades in prison.

Since he's been out, everybody asks the same question. "Are you mad for what they did to you?"

And the answer is: "You know, I kind of am. But it's over now. I have to look ahead."

On 117th Street, Towler finally comes across the place he's been hunting. He orders his three-piece fried with a biscuit.

Then he drives back to Cousin Carole's.

He takes his food into the backyard. He chews and watches the stars. He listens to the crickets and the night birds. *This is one thing I always wanted to do,* he tells himself.

And so he does.

(2011)

Bobby Jindal, All American

Piyush "Bobby" Jindal is the first Indian-American governor in U.S. history—and the first nonwhite governor in Louisiana since Reconstruction. A week in the life of the man who has been called, variously, a "wonderkind technocrat," "the next Ronald Reagan," "a cool guy to hang out with," "an Indian Barack Obama," and a "scary, ultraconservative religious fanatic." He's been mentioned for vice president. Will he run for president?

Bobby Jindal, the thirty-seven-year-old Republican governor of Louisiana, walked across the set of *The Tonight Show* with the bashful aplomb of a newly-crowned spelling-bee champion. The longish, spidery fingers of his right hand, often seen ticking off the points of a complex answer or multipart plan, were extended in anticipation of his first televised handshake with Jay Leno. Jindal's left hand was buried instinctively in the pants pocket of his navy-blue suit, waist 28, one size up from the boy's department, a delicate physiognomy inherited, along with his elfin ears and prominent nose, from his mother, Raj Gupta Jindal, a native of Punjab in northern India.

Raj was the daughter of a bank manager. She first came to America on a scholarship to study for her doctorate in nuclear physics at Louisiana State University. She brought along her husband, a love match named Amar Jindal, the son of a shopkeep from the *bania* caste, the only one of nine children in his family to attend school past fifth grade. At the time the couple immigrated, Raj was three months pregnant with their first son, Piyush. Though the university health plan denied coverage for the birth (it was ruled a "preexisting condition"), a one-month paid maternity leave was awarded as promised — that was the perk that had tipped the scales for Amar, who'd been hesitant to leave home, having worked his way up through the ranks to the respected position of assistant professor of engineering at Punjab University in Chandigarh, the newly dedicated capital city of their home state. At the age of four, according to family lore, precocious little Piyush Jindal would announce to his teacher and all of his friends in school in Baton Rouge—a town of politics and industry on the banks of the muddy Mississippi River—that he would heretofore be known as Bobby, after his favorite character on television's hit sitcom *The Brady Bunch*.

Illuminated by a bright follow-spot, accompanied by The *Tonight* Show band's funky rendition of Sly Stone's *Everyday People*, the young governor made his way toward Leno. Jindal (pronounced *Gin*-dul) was nearing his one hundredth day as the first nonwhite governor of Louisiana since Reconstruction—the first-ever Asian Indian governor of any state. (That's the U.S. Census term for the 2.7 million descendants of the Indian subcontinent living in this country; those who were born in America call themselves South Asians or, more familiarly, *desis*.) After a mercurial first decade in public service, spent mostly beneath the radar—secretary of the Louisiana Department of Health and Hospitals at age twenty-four, high-level George W. Bush appointee at twenty-nine, U.S. congressman and House assistant majority whip at thirty-three—Jindal had lately been cast as a Republican answer to Democratic presidential hopeful Barack Obama. Dark skinned, highly intelligent, a harbinger of change, Jindal had just been mentioned as a possible running mate for Republican presidential candidate John McCain—the reason for this invitation visit to *The Tonight Show*. America wanted to meet the new man.

Known variously as a "wunderkind technocrat," a "speed-talking policy wonk," a "problem solver, not a politician," a "credit to all South Asian-Americans," "the next Ronald Reagan" (Rush Limbaugh), a "guy who looks in the mirror and sees a white man," and a "scary, ultraconservative religious fanatic in cahoots with the Christian Right," Jindal's first act as governor was to call two special sessions of Louisiana's part-time legislature. During those three heady weeks, Jindal fulfilled many of his campaign promises by pushing through dozens of new bills, including an overhaul of ethics laws, tax breaks designed to make the hurricane-ravaged state more attractive to businesses and an income tax deduction for parents whose children attend private schools. Crowed an editorial in the New Orleans Times-Picayune: He is "a youthful rising star who generates genuine excitement in a party that's been feeling awfully old and tired lately."

His left hand still in his pocket, making his shoulders slouch, Jindal shook hands warmly with Leno and then issued to the audience the fey little wave customary to politics. His rubbery lips formed a crooked smile, exposing his slightly buck teeth, which seemed brilliant against the contrast of his skin. To use the argot of the Old South, Jindal's complexion is darker than a brown paper bag. Riding along with him in his SUV on the way to New Orleans to tout his new mental-healthcare-initiative, or in his helicopter, Pelican One, on the way to Shreveport to tout a new workforce-training initiative, or sitting with him in his office in the breathtaking state capitol building—a thirty-four-story art deco monument built by Jindal's distant predecessor, Huey Long, the great populist and iconic corrupt politician whose body lies buried beneath a tall statue of himself in the gardens opposite the Mayan-temple-like entrance—I could have sworn that Jindal was wearing some kind of cover-up or cosmetic to soften his razor shadow, which is very dark, as if an artist had rendered his stubble in charcoals.

Oddly, tonight on Leno, that did not seem to be the case. It was as if Jindal had, for some reason, refused the customary television cosmetics, lending to his countenance a somewhat unfortunate Nixonesque swarthiness. Jindal's press secretary, Melissa Sellers, twenty-five, a blond-streaked journalism major from the University of Texas, denied that Jindal uses cover-up. A solid woman in high heels, quick on the draw with both her smile and her middle finger, Sellers had been recently derided by reporters for blocking access to her boss—literally—having performed a sort of perfectly executed moving pick that put the kibosh on any chance for spontaneous questions about the veep talk.

As it was, the state and local media had been complaining about lack of access ever since Jindal took office. For a time, the Baton Rouge Advocate was keeping a printed tally of the number of its requests for interviews he'd turned down (meanwhile, he'd granted audiences to the New York Times, the Wall Street Journal and Esquire). The honeymoon with the legislature was also waning. With term limits in effect in Louisiana—folks used to joke that "half the state is under water, half is under indictment"— the 105-member House had 59 new members; the Senate had four new faces out of 39, plus eighteen more serving their first term. In the past, Louisiana governors had been more than accessible. That's how it worked in Baton Rouge, a town of hidden staircases and secret tunnels built by a politician who once boasted that he bought other pols like sacks of potatoes. The part-time legislators—who can often be seen dressed unironically in seersucker suits—are housed together for the duration of the session in a historic, pentagon-shaped barracks; as you would expect, the cookouts in the courtyard are legend. (There are actually only four sides to the Pentagon Barracks, built in the early 1800s. The fifth had to be torn down due to construction flaws attributed by some to graft.) Two recent elected officials, former governor Edwin Edwards and former state representative David Duke (who also served Grand Wizard of the KKK), served time in Federal prisons—Edwards for extorting payoffs from riverboat casino applicants, and Duke for mail fraud and lying on his tax return.

Though Jindal had courted the legislators with ardor during the special sessions, once the regular session started, in late March, he'd stopped answering calls. If you wanted him, you could find him on the news: Speaking at the National Press Club in Washington, D.C., and at the National Rifle Association's Celebration of American Values Banquet in Louisville, Kentucky. Dining at Commander's Palace in New Orleans with President Bush and LSU football coach Les Miles. Visiting McCain's Sedona ranch with the other vice-presidential hopefuls and their wives. Bobby's wife, Supriya Jolly Jindal, was born in India. They went to the same high school for a period; initially, she turned him down for a date. She has an undergraduate degree in chemical engineering and an MBA from Tulane; she has also completed all the coursework for a Ph.D in marketing from LSU. For fun, she said in an interview in the mansion, she does calculus problems. They have three children—Selia, six, Shaan, four, and Slade, two. (Shaan was born with a heart defect and had surgery as an infant. Slade was born precipitously at home in 2006; Bobby delivered the eight-pound, 2.5-ounce boy himself before the EMTs could arrive, with a nurse assisting by telephone.)

Now he was here on *The Tonight Show* with Jay Leno, the glad-handing Mayor of America. "Tell us about your background," Leno said. "First-generation American, correct?"

"Born and raised in Baton Rouge," Jindal said with a distinct drawl. He launched into the story of his parents' journey to LSU. "[My dad] walked uphill going to school...and coming back from school," Jindal joked.

"So your parents have an accent?" Leno asked.

The young governor winced, like a bookish kid who'd just realized he'd wandered into the wrong area of playground. He looked down into his spidery hands—the palms light, the backsides dark, arranged at the moment as if they were holding an invisible bowl. He looked into the bowl as if searching there for an answer to Leno's question.

"My dad more than my mom," Jindal said of the accent. "But my dad, you know...none of his brothers or sisters got past the fifth grade...He went all the way to college. That's pretty amazing."

"When you were born...did your dad say—" here Leno bobbled his large head, playing to the studio audience. He put on a corny, over-the-top, Apu-from-*The Simpsons* accent: "We will name him *Bob-by!*"

The studio audience roared.

Jindal protested, faint but distinct, "*Nooooo.*" His chin drooped to his chest; he was clearly mortified. The first time he ran for governor, in 2003—his very first attempt at public office of any kind—Jindal lost in a runoff to Kathleen Blanco (the governor during Hurricane Katrina, which hit in 2005). Four days before the runoff, polls showed Jindal with a comfortable 10-point lead. Then Blanco's campaign started running a television ad featuring a picture of a young, very dark-appearing Jindal with his hair disheveled and sticking up. "Wake up, Louisiana! Before it's too late!" viewers were urged.

By Election Day, Jindal was trailing Blanco by three points. He did especially poorly in what they call Bubba Country, the northern part of the state, usually a Republican stronghold. Over the course of the next four years—during which time he successfully ran for a seat in the House of Representatives, raising so much money in the process that he was able to donate to other GOP candidates around the country, insuring his election as president of the incoming freshman class of congressmen—Jindal visited northern Louisiana, by his own count, more than seventy-seven times. Many of those visits took place on Sundays at small evangelical churches, where he gave testimony about his conversion from Hindu to Roman Catholic. Some churchgoers noted that they had never before heard a *Roman* testify in quite the way Jindal did, casting his own experience in terms similar to that of a born-again fundamentalist. Reporters noted that Jindal had taken to wearing cowboy boots.

In 2007, running in the primary against twelve other candidates (Blanco did not seek reelection), Jindal won with 54 percent of the vote—the first candidate to win an open gubernatorial seat outright since Louisiana adopted its nonpartisan primary system in 1975. This time Jindal carried Bubba Country by a considerable margin. There was even a group called Bubbas for Bobby. A photo of the diminutive brown man with some of his Bubbas was widely distributed on the web.

Now, with a huge, embarrassed smile plastered across his face, Jindal bravely told the story Leno wanted—how he'd taken his name from the youngest of television's three Brady brothers, who lived in a blended family with three blond stepsisters in the idealized and lilly-white suburbs of the American seventies. "It could have been worse," Jindal said, hamming it up, making the best of things. "At the time, if you remember, The *Brady Bunch* came on right before *Gilligan's Island*."

"You could have been known as Little Buddy!" Leno quipped.

"There would have been *no* future for me in politics," Bobby said.

"How *did* you even get interested in politics?" Leno asked. "Dad wants you to be a doctor. And then you go and do the sleaziest profession of all."

"Well, that and *Hollywood*," Jindal said, not missing a beat, the bookish kid who'd just corrected the asshole teacher.

Bobby Jindal's father, Amar Jindal, grew up in northern India during the chaotic years that followed the partitioning of India and Pakistan.

The family lived in a remote farming community that was backward even by Indian standards—the main source of fuel for cooking and heat was dried cow dung. Amar's mother was illiterate. His father was educated to the fifth grade. Several of his five sisters told a visiting reporter from the *New Orleans Times Picayune* stories of a boy who practically raised himself, waking before dawn to bike five miles to school, riding home for dinner, returning afterwards to study—he found the family's house, with its eleven occupants, too chaotic. "Amar was self-centered, not interacting with other people much," said Pushpa Bansal, who herself attended school until third grade, the only of the sisters to be educated. "He used to feel bad that other members of his family...were not as literate." In high school, Amar once collapsed from exhaustion; when consumed with his work, he often forgot to eat.

In time, Amar graduated with a degree in civil engineering from Punjab University. He married a classmate's sister, Raj; she had a master's degree. As luck would have it, Raj and Amar's families are both bania, members of the same caste of businessmen, tradesmen and educators. Coincidentally, they are also from the same sub-class, known as *agarwal*. Though Amar was clearly marrying up, there were no misgivings on either side.

The Jindals settled into graduate-student housing near LSU—home of a much different sort of tiger than they were used to seeing, this one purple and gold. In the eyes of an immigrant, Louisiana in 1971 was paradise on earth. There were abundant oil and gas reserves, thriving industry, major ports, multiple railroads, jobs aplenty, the guarantee of schooling for all. Amar got a good job with one of the railroads; Raj switched from nuclear physics to the budding field of computer science and was hired by the state of the Louisiana as one of its very first IT people. (Thirty years later, she is still working in the same department. Technically, Bobby is her boss.)

Jindal remembers his parents always working hard. For a time the family had no car; they rode the bus everywhere. A friend's car broke down on the way to Bobby's birth, the story goes. In the second chapter, the doctor allows them to pay for the delivery on an installment plan. There is a family joke about Amar stopping payments to see if Bobby would be repossessed.

As his son grew, Amar took great pains to be home at night to read to him before bed, something Bobby now tries to do with his own children. (Supriya complains that Bobby's version of monster hide-and-seek gets the kids riled up at bedtime. All three children sleep together in one room, right next door to the master suite in the governor's mansion. You get the picture of a little family camped out in only a few rooms upstairs in a scary old mansion.) After his own bus rides home from work, Amar didn't have quite so much energy. Frequently, it would be he who fell asleep during story time. Bobby would pad out and dutifully report to his mother: Dad's asleep. "I think I felt it was my job to put my father to bed," Bobby Jindal recalls with a smile.

Jindal remembers his father being disappointed with mere A's—it had to be A-pluses. As a youngster, Bobby competed in tennis tournaments. Later he would turn entrepreneurial, starting a computer newsletter, a retail candy business, and a mail-order software company. He also worked the concessions at LSU football games; rooting for the Tigers remains a passion to this day. Jindal has said that when he was growing up, there were "several" other Asian Indian families in the Baton Rouge area and that he was raised in a "strong Hindu culture." Because there was no temple in town, the Jindals worshipped at the homes of friends. Jindal has spoken of attending weekly *pujas*, reading the Vedic scriptures, and making trips back to India to visit relatives. At the same time, he said recently, during a conversation in the back of his SUV as he was driven through Baton Rouge, "my parents, and my mom especially, were adamant that, 'Look, we made the decision to come to America, our kids are Americans, they should grow up fully American.' If you look at our childhood, it was pretty typical of a whole lot of other children's childhoods."

The Jindals lived in a series of apartments for nearly seven years, until the birth of Bobby's younger brother, Nikesh. Today, Nikesh Jindal is a thirty-year-old lawyer in Washington. He went to Dartmouth and Yale—"Quite a shock for a southern boy," he said on the phone recently with a chuckle. Unlike Bobby, he has no southern accent. Nikesh remembers fondly the family's one-story, three-bedroom house in a "small little neighborhood where you knew all the people on the street." There was a swing set in the back, a basketball hoop in the driveway, plenty of football and bike riding with the neighborhood kids, trick-or-treating every Halloween without need for parental supervision. Bobby was a good older brother, though Nikesh doesn't recall ever beating him in any sport or game. He does remember fondly their long football catches, and driveway hoops with their dad. Amar, it turned out, loved to ball. He'd drop everything to play with his boys. One time, when both parents were busy, Bobby volunteered to drive Nikesh to see the movie *Transformers*. "All the other kids my age were with their parents," Nikesh recalled. "And here I was with my older brother. I thought this was the coolest thing in the world."

When asked if his family ever got together with other Hindu families to worship during holidays, Nikesh, who has never before been interviewed, became flustered. "I'll have to think about it and get back to you on that," he said. (Requests for an interview with Amar and Raj Jindal were declined.)

Bobby Jindal entered Baton Rouge Magnet High School at age thirteen. At the time, the school system in the city was under a controversial desegregation order; while the LSU community lent some diversity, Baton Rouge was still very much a part of the Old South. Jindal said he never once experienced prejudice as a youth. "Before I went to college, I didn't realize not everybody grew up the way we do in south Louisiana." (The postings on popular desi Web sites often seem at odds with Jindal's experience, especially for those raised in the South.)

The magnet school attracted the best students, and Jindal was one of the stars. He was president of several of the clubs in which he took part—his participation demonstrates a wide range of interests: science, math, foreign languages, leadership, technology and law. He also worked behind the scenes as a campaign manager for a friend's run at student government office. "He always had his eye on, first of all, where he wanted to go, and second, how he was going to get there," said Fred Aldrich, a former teacher. "He was very—I don't want to use the word *clever*, because that's a cheap word. I think he was very good at analyzing what will work and then going out and doing it."

Around this time, Jindal began questioning his faith. It began when his best friend, Kent, a born-again Baptist, gave him a Bible with his name embossed on the front in gold letters. The two buddies would often engage in lively and serious religious debate; Jindal delved into both the Bible and the Bhagavad Gita, arming himself with scriptural ammo. At the end of his sophomore year, Jindal's maternal grandfather died. Pitaji Gupta was his idol. "I almost could not believe that his wealth could not save him from his mortality," Jindal wrote years later, in one of a series of essays on his religious awakening, in the *New Oxford Review*. Shaken to the very foundations of his faith, the straight A student tackled the problem like he always did, setting out to make a study of life's eternal questions. (Later he would write an intellectual treatise on the stages of change one passes through as he makes the decision to convert from one religion to another. See "The Gospel Trumps Multiculturalism," Oct 1995, *New Oxford Review*.)

Soon Jindal began dating a girl named Kathy. Cute and blond, she was Catholic. According to Jindal's writings, their relationship began on the top floor of a downtown hotel after a high school dance. That night, in between their attempts to toss quarters into the large ornamental fountain twenty-two stories below, Kathy told Bobby that "she wanted to be a lawyer so she could serve on the Supreme Court and stop the country from killing babies." With Kathy, Jindal attended his first Roman Catholic mass. "I was probably the first teenager who ever told his parents he was going to a party so that he could sneak off to church," he wrote later, in the *New Oxford Review*. A teacher who knew both students in high school remembers that the couple's relationship ended badly due to parental concern on both sides about the differences in their cultures and religions.

By the end of high school, Kent's simple fundamentalism had won out over the saints and rituals of the Romans. The exact moment can be traced to the intermission of a religious musical Jindal attended. The youth minister showed a "crude black-and-white film" depicting the crucifixion. "Suddenly, God was tangible," Jindal wrote. "Seeing Christ's sacrifice convicted me of my sinfulness and my need for a savior...I asked seriously who was I that my Lord should suffer for my sake."

Because he feared the "inevitable confrontation with my very unsympathetic Hindu parents," Bobby simply didn't tell them. He found refuge in his closet, where he studied the Bible by flashlight.

In his writings, he would later compare his situation to that of the earliest Christians, worshiping in caves, "hiding from government persecution."

Bobby Jindal settled into his place in the prayer circle on the floor of a classroom at Brown University. It was finals week, the Spring of 1990. An urgent call had gone out to the membership of the UCF—the University Christian Fellowship, an ecumenical group that embraced all denominations, from Pentecostal to Papist. Jindal was carrying a double concentration in biology and public policy: the bio for his dad, who wanted him to be a doctor, the policy for himself—work that could save thousands or millions, he believed, instead of one at a time.

Though he was offered scholarships at other universities, Jindal went to Brown on his parents' dime, primarily because he was accepted into the school's unique Program in Liberal Medical Education, which guaranteed an undergraduate freshman a place in Brown's medical school. "I didn't have a car. We didn't go on vacations. I remember my father and my brother fighting over a hundred-dollar pair of Girbaud jeans. But when it came to college, my parents' attitude was, 'You just find the best school and we'll make sure you can go," Jindal said one morning as we drove in his SUV toward a press conference in Lake Charles, where he was touting a new statewide computerized prescription program. Because Bobby felt beholden to his father, Jindal did the double major, twenty hours a semester. He eventually forfeited his place in the PLME program, feeling it wasn't fair to tie up a coveted slot when he was ambivalent. Nevertheless, he would still be accepted into medical school *and* law school at Harvard *and* Yale. He'd turn down both to accept a Rhodes scholarship, where he'd study public health policy.

At Brown, Jindal was known to his classmates as an affable, somewhat nerdy guy with a brilliant mind who liked to talk policy. ("The kind of person who had three- or five- or ten-point plan for everything," recalled one friend.) He had recently converted to Roman Catholicism—the high-church ceremony had been held in Providence in the fall of 1989, his sophomore year. His parents hadn't yet been informed. Though people around Baton Rouge say today that Jindal "looks in the mirror and sees a white guy," many of his college acquaintances had names like Choi, Chan, Rivera, and Kalhan. Given his double concentrations (Brown lexicon for major), people mostly remember Jindal for studying a lot. He also spent a good deal of time resurrecting and leading the College Republicans—an uphill battle at liberal Brown. Having come of age in the Reagan-Bush era, in a state where the GOP was seen as the party of reform, Jindal embraced his new political identity as wholeheartedly as he had his religious one. Most likely, the conservative beliefs of his spiritual peers and mentors were an influence. So too the traditional American values embraced by his grateful immigrant parents.

On this evening during finals week, the UCF members were gathering to pray for a girl named Susan. For more than a year, Bobby and Susan had enjoyed "an intimate friendship; indeed our relationship mystified observers, who insisted on finding a romantic component where none existed," he wrote in a remarkably personal essay for the *New Oxford Review*.

In time, he and Susan "succumbed to pressure from our friends and decided we should not be so emotionally interdependent without a deeper commitment. To be honest, my fears of a relationship and the constraints of a commitment had kept us apart." (Looking back, Jindal told me, it was around this time, hurting from a past breakup, that he first saw what is today his favorite movie, *Casablanca*. "Here's a movie where the good guy did the right thing and he *didn't* get the girl at the end," he said. "I thought that was great, because that's how real life goes.")

Time passed. Jindal and Susan continued to attend UCF gatherings, albeit separately. One day, Susan seemed particularly down. Jindal invited her to come along with some friends to a Christian a capella concert being held on campus. Throughout the evening, Susan seemed composed. Then, in the middle of a song, she abruptly left. At a friend's urging, Jindal ran after her.

He found her sobbing uncontrollably outside the auditorium. "Since we had been very careful to avoid any form of physical contact in our friendship, I was not sure how to respond," Jindal wrote. He walked her back to her dorm room. Susan confided that she was awaiting the results of a biopsy on her scalp. The doctor feared it was skin cancer, she told him. She was scared to death.

Jindal reached out from his place in the chair across from her bed and took her hand. He "promised to stand by her forever, to be the rock against which she could lean, to accompany her to the doctor's office and the operating room," he wrote.

As the night went on, "tears vanished as suddenly as they appeared several times." After getting her some milk "to ease the gastric pains caused by her anxiety," Jindal sat on the bed next to her. "We were both startled to find my arm around her shoulder, but she asked that I continue to hold her for just a few minutes longer. I happily complied and we embraced her problems away...the simple gesture of a hug was enough to bring peace to Susan's heart for one night."

The next day, perhaps "scared of her own feelings and dependence on me," Susan avoided Bobby. Several uncomfortable weeks passed. Finally, there was a rapprochement. The pair discussed their "true feelings for each other and Susan's upcoming operation," Jindal wrote. Then the subject steered to a different path. Susan was a charismatic Christian. She'd talked before to Jindal about speaking in tongues. Now she began telling Jindal of recent "visions" she'd been having. She described, "various odors (which others would later ascribe to the sulfur that supposedly accompanies the devil), sounds, and appearances that both she and her roommate had witnessed," he would later write.

Overwhelmed, a bit freaked out, Jindal left the room "on some flimsy pretense, made the sign of the cross in desperation, and pleaded with God for Divine assistance."

When he returned, recomposed, Susan "angrily lashed out at me, telling me she never wanted to talk with me again, since I did not love her...I had a vague sense that her anger and tears involved both my inability to care for her and also my inability to understand her recent experiences."

The next day, Susan's older sister flew into town; the prayer meeting was hastily arranged. Despite their hectic finals schedule, many of the sober young Christians made their way to the classroom. Susan was brought in by her sister. She refused to acknowledge Jindal's presence.

Songs and prayers and silent meditations were offered. "Suddenly, Susan emitted some strange guttural sounds and fell to the floor. She started thrashing about, as if in some sort of seizure.

Susan's sister must have recognized what was happening, for she ordered us to gather around and place our hands on Susan's prostrate body," Jindal wrote.

Jindal tentatively approached. He "placed the edge of my fingertip on her shoulder, as if afraid of becoming infected with the disease that was ravaging her body."

And then, "in a voice I had never heard before or since," Susan yelled out, referring to herself in third person: "Bobby, you cannot even love Susan."

Jindal withdrew his fingertip, recoiled from the group. The strange voice coming out of Susan launched into a tirade, attacking every member of the UCF by name.

Susan's sister began to chant, "Satan, I command you to leave this woman." The others followed her lead. "Demons leave in the name of Christ," they chanted.

Jindal huddled against a wall, apart from the group, watching the proceedings. He "desperately wanted it all to end, but could not leave," he wrote. He felt completely stunned, unable even to pray.

Time passed in furious prayer. Other campus Christians were consulted. One pastor refused to come; he thought Susan should see a doctor. Then the leader of a "rival" group of campus Christians arrived with a crucifix that had been blessed by the Pope. It seemed to have a calming effect. Susan's sister began reading biblical passages. Susan responded with curses and profanities. "Mixed in with her vile attacks were short and desperate pleas for help. In the same breath that she attacked Christ, the Bible's authenticity, and everyone assembled in prayer, Susan would suddenly urge us to rescue her. It appeared as if we were observing a tremendous battle between the Susan we knew and loved and some strange evil force."

At last, "the momentum shifted and we now sensed that victory was at hand....With an almost comical smile, Susan looked up as if awakening from a deep sleep and asked, 'Has something happened?' She did not remember any of the past few hours and was startled to find her friends breaking out in cheers and laughter, overwhelmed by sudden joy and relief."

Jindal wrote: "I eventually left the room in a stupor. As I was leaving, Susan's sister...called my name and asked that I 'commit my nightlife to prayer.' I hardly understood what she meant and was startled that others continued to single me out for attention. I nodded and looked gently at Susan, who thanked me for coming."

Beneath a threatening sky, the Black Hawk assault helicopter touched down in a wheat field in Morganza, in Pointe Coupee Parish, the prop wash setting off a blizzard of Styrofoam meal boxes that had been stacked on the tailgates of pickup trucks where neighbors were offering lunch—gumbo and corn bread, beans and dirty rice; come hell or high water, you always eat well in Louisiana.

Governor Jindal, the commander in chief of the state's Air and Army National Guard, stepped into the doorway of the chopper and issued his customary wave. He wore a blue shirt with a button-down collar but no tie; his lips were molded into a thoughtful arrangement, at once friendly and concerned, like a minister on a house call. His coal-black hair was disheveled and sticking up; he was sporting his cowboy boots. He hopped down into the churned earth; following closely behind was Major General Bennett Landreneau, the commander of the Guard. The two men have been acquainted since they served together under Governor Mike Foster, when Jindal was the boy-wonder secretary of the Department of Health and Hospitals. (During his tenure, Jindal became well-known for trimming $400 million in Medicaid expenses; from there, he was named director of a bipartisan Medicare-reform commission in Washington, then head of the statewide University of Louisiana system, and then assistant secretary in the Department of Health and Human Services under the younger Bush.)

During the bumpy, thirty-five-mile chopper ride northwest from Baton Rouge, General Landreneau had brought Jindal up to speed on the operations at Morganza, his voice crackling through the headset intercoms we wore. With the rains and flooding up north in Missouri and Ohio, the Mississippi River had risen past flood stage and was still rising. For the past thirty-six hours, a crew of fifty laborers—local farmers, flood-district employees, inmates from the Avoyelles Correctional Center, and National Guard troops—had worked side by side, using backhoes to fill and position hundreds of bags donated by a seed company. As it happened, this wasn't the first time the guard had been called out to help Morganza, population seven hundred. Twenty-five years earlier they'd come on a similar mission. Some of the farmers on site today were there the last time, too, the general added.

He further explained that the four-by-four-by-four, cube-shaped sandbags being used in the operation—originally intended to transport large quantities of seed—were much larger and more effective than the traditional kind. And they were made locally, the general added. They'd even been used in Iraq. A real key to preparedness.

The sandcubes were being placed in two courses along a two-mile section of earthen berm, known locally as the Potato Levee, that separates the swollen river from five thousand acres of rich Delta farmland. If the river were to spill over, this low patch of land would be lost to crops for at least a year—ruinous to the families affected. The higher the water rose, the softer the ground on the other side of the levee was becoming. According to the Army Corps of Engineers, the workers needed to be out within twenty-four hours or the back-hoes would become mired in the muddy liquefied soil. Complicating matters was the forecast: Rain was on the way.

Jindal climbed to the top of the levee where a crowd was milling about. It was nearing lunchtime; you could smell the food, mixing in the air with the smells of earth, river, mold, and diesel fuel. Jindal had not yet eaten today. His only liquid had been a mini-can of Diet Coke. Jindal rarely eats lunch, or much of anything else, according to his staff, a wholesome group of twentysomethings, some Christian, some South Asian, some blond. Nor does Jindal ever seem to have to urinate. Finding a chance to stop sometimes becomes a problem for his brawny security guards, who are older than he and less stout of bladder.

A fortish man from one of the farm families was introduced to Jindal. He wore a baseball cap; his jeans were tucked into his cowboy boots. "We appreciate all your support," the farmer said.

"What are you growing out here?" Jindal asked, nodding in the direction of the fields.

"We run 50,000 bushels of soybeans, 100,000 bushels of wheat, 280,000 pounds of cotton."

"I hear it's supposed to be a real good year— if we can stop the water," Jindal said.

"We couldn't do it without ya'll's help," the farmer's friend said. He was dressed the same as the first, but he was overweight, most of it in the gut.

"There was no hesitation," Jindal said modestly. "They say there are some folks out here that remember twenty-five years ago when this happened before."

"I was here then," the first farmer said, pleased that the governor remembered. "We were on the crew," the second farmer said proudly. "The National Guard was here and with us every step of the way"

"We'll do better this time," Jindal said, taking the tone of a grad student, his hands forming the familiar bowl, his brown eyes searching in there for the right words. "Part of the problem was that last time, they didn't have the size bags we got today. These four-by-four-by-fours are *amazing*."

The two immense farmers looked down at their small governor with the sort of expression you might see on a couple of neighbor men when a third of their number, a brainiac with hairy forearms and a utilitarian watch, drives home one evening in an enviable new truck. This guy gets it, their ruddy faces seemed to say. Two more Bubbas for Bobby.

Jindal put his hands on his narrow hips and twisted around some to survey the swiftly flowing river. The waterline had risen twenty-five feet since yesterday, he'd been told. Bringing a hand up to shade his eyes, he panned toward the land side of the levee—the fertile earth, the backhoes, the several half-filled four-by-four-by-fours, the pickup trucks serving tailgate lunch, the panoply of uniforms and prison jumpsuits and baseball caps and ponytails. "All this brings out the best in the state, it really does," the young governor said wistfully.

"To see people helpin' one another," agreed the first farmer.

Just then, the wind picked up. Jindal squinted ominously toward the darkening sky. "Let's just hope this is the worst thing we have to deal with," he said, combing his flyaway hair back into place with his spidery fingers. "Pray for a quiet hurricane season."

"Yes, *sir*," the farmers chanted in unison.

On Father's Day Bobby Jindal took time away from his family to appear remotely on *Face the Nation*. Sitting in for host Bob Schieffer was CBS congressional correspondent Chip Reid, a handsome news-Ken in a blue and white patterned tie. Jindal appeared on split screen, wearing a red repp tie; as always, the knot was a little loose, exposing the top button.

Five months into his term, Jindal was continuing his lap though the public arena. After his two effective special sessions, an unusually aggressive regular session of the state legislature had come to an end. Among the bills that passed: A requirement that employers allow workers to bring guns onto company parking lots. An authorization to perform chemical castrations on convicted sex offenders. A renaming and restructuring of the labor department (part of Jindal's workforce-improvement plan). A "Teacher's Bill of Rights," guaranteeing a safe environment in the schools (more Jindal; teachers had been leaving the state in droves). A voucher plan that allocated $10 million to pay the tuitions for inner-city children to attend private and parochial schools.

It also included a 123 percent pay raise for legislators—a bit of self-dealing that Jindal, reluctant to start a pissing match with the legislature, had promised not to veto; a week later, after a public outcry, he would reverse course and kill the raise, calling his original promise "a mistake."

And then there was the "Science Education Act." Critics said the bill, passed by both houses, opened the door for teaching creationism and intelligent design in Louisiana public schools. Jindal said he would sign it when it reached his desk.

And so it was that Jindal was facing the nation. Chip Reid gave him a glowing introduction. "Republicans say you are the future of the Republican party," Reid said.

For the next seven minutes, in response to a series of softball questions, Jindal spoke fluently in his rat-a-tat style, sounding *exactly* like the kind of young, brilliant, and energetic person you wish was running the city, the state, the country, the entire planet. As he does whenever he speaks, Jindal gave the impression that he could accomplish all the great stuff he was suggesting, no problem, and still get home in time to play Monster/Daddy hide-and-seek with his kids.

He rejected as divisive the notion of "identity politics." It doesn't matter what color or gender you are, he said; it matters what kind of job you do. He called Barack Obama the best speaker he has heard since Ronald Reagan. He said the Republican party had gotten away from its traditional strengths, that it had become a victim of its own success: Wholesale change was needed. Luckily, he was proud to say, America has the choice of two great candidates for president. While he himself was supporting McCain, he said, he urged the American people to go to the polls in November and "vote *for* one without voting *against* the other."

Then Reid turned ominous. "Let me make a sharp turn here to a different issue, an issue that has raised some controversy," he said.

Jindal's lips molded themselves into a berm of grim determination. He knew what was coming.

"You were a biology major in college," Reid said. "And you support the teaching of intelligent design in schools. Do you have doubts about the theory of evolution?"

Since the beginning of his public career, Jindal has spoken openly of his faith and his socially conservative views. He is against abortion, even in cases of rape and incest. He is against stem-cell research, for private- and parochial- school vouchers, for teaching intelligent design. Like his closest advisor and chief of staff, Timmy Teepell, Bobby and Supriya Jindal have a covenant marriage. Teepell, thirty-two, is a product of home schooling. He never went to college. For most of his life, Teepell has been a foot soldier for the conservative movement, working his way up to deputy political director for the Republican National Committee before throwing in with Jindal, after Bobby's first gubernatorial loss. Teepell wouldn't take the job with Jindal without first having his wife meet Bobby. They made it a foursome for lunch and have been close ever since.

Jindal forged ahead without hesitation. You couldn't see his fingers but you knew he was ticking them off. "One, I don't think this is something the federal or state government should be imposing its views on local school districts...Secondly, I don't think students learn by us withholding information from them."

"But how about you *personally*," Reid pressed. "Where do you stand *personally* on the issue?"

"I personally think that life, human life and the world we live in, wasn't created accidentally," Jindal said matter-of-factly. "I do think that there's a creator. I'm a Christian. I do think that God played a role in creating not only earth but mankind...."

So it went for the next seven minutes, Jindal explaining in some detail his true and honest feelings about his faith.

"O-*kaay*," Reid said, closing out the governor somewhat abruptly, heading toward a commercial. His dubious tone was reminiscent of the comedian David Spade, as if to say: *Time to go, nut job.* Clearly, he'd heard a little more about God this morning than he felt comfortable with.

Jindal stared into the camera, unblinking. The man who may well be the most accomplished young political figure in the country looked like someone who'd just survived a rollover in the family SUV. He seemed to take stock for a moment—yup, all limbs were still operational.

Then he managed a spastic half smile. You could tell what he was thinking:

I'll be back here again.

(2009)

The Boss

Dana White is the heart and soul of the Ultimate Fighting Championship league—equal parts Don King, Oliver Twist, and South Boston gym rat. Thanks mostly to White, mixed martial arts, once banned in all fifty states and labeled "human cockfighting" by a U.S. Senator, has all but replaced boxing in the public's heart. Experience the fast times and hi-jinks inside the Escalade with this unlikely millionaire and his real-life entourage.

B eneath a big tent hastily erected on a roof behind the Staples Center in downtown Los Angeles, a collection of modern gladiators gathers behind a portable stage, twenty-two sets of broken noses and cauliflower ears standing in a reverent semicircle around a familiar pug—the former bar bouncer, hotel bellhop, and personal fitness trainer who has, over the past decade, helped to turn the Ultimate Fighting Championship into a $1 billion dollar business with fans across the globe.

They are a fearsome-looking bunch—from six-eleven Dutch submission expert Stefan Struve to five-seven crowd favorite Joe "Daddy" Stevenson—all of them having just stripped to their skivvies for the prefight weigh-in, witnessed by three thousand raucous and mesmerized superfans from the coveted eighteen-to-forty-nine demographic, males and females both. There will be eleven bouts tomorrow night in the Octagon, the distinctive eight-sided ring with its black, chain-link fence to contain the mayhem. Six of the fights will play free on Spike TV—part of UFC's fan-friendly marketing approach. The remaining five will be seen exclusively on pay-per-view, including the main event, a light-heavyweight championship bout between Mauricio "Shogun" Rua and reigning champ Lyoto "The Dragon" Machida—two prime-time Brazilians with matinee-idol looks and savage fighting styles.

Sixteen thousand will attend the Saturday-night event, styled UFC 104; ticket prices run from $50 to $600. There can be no value placed on a seat in the celebrity section, where Demi Moore and Ashton Kutcher will rub shoulders with Anthony Keidis, Everlast, Will.I.am, Jamie Pressly, David Spade, much of the entire cast of *Dancing with the Stars*, and even Janet Jackson, who will spend the hours before the fight overseeing an effort, in a big parking lot nearby, to break the world record of people dancing the "Thriller" choreography at the same time. In fact, Michael Jackson was a huge UFC fan. He once attended a match in a wheelchair, disguised as an old man.

The guy at the center is Dana White. Equal parts Don King, Oliver Twist, and South Boston gym rat, he is the heart and soul of the UFC—a man who is living his adolescent dreams. He is forty years old, five-eleven, 205; his strength as an amateur boxer, he says, was his ability to take a punch. He still benches 325, though the six-pack is a memory. He wears a T-shirt and ripped jeans, a colorful pair of low-top Pumas. His head is stubble-shaved, as are his meaty forearms—to prevent the sting of hair burn when grappling, which he still does as part of his workout routine.

Fifteen years ago, White was riding his bike through the slushy winter streets of Boston with eighty pounds of equipment in a hockey bag on his back, going from gym to gym to train his fitness clients. A little more than ten years ago, mixed martial arts was labeled "human cockfighting" by Senator John McCain. It was banned by athletic commissions in every state.

Today MMA fighting is legal in forty-eight states, soon to be fifty. There is a UFC Magazine, a best-selling UFC video game, UFC action figures and trading cards. Nine UFC Gyms will be opened in 2010 in partnership with the founder of 24 Hour Fitness. White flies around in one of several company jets, stays in palatial suites at luxury hotels. In the parking garage beneath the company offices in Las Vegas he keeps a stable of exotic cars. His thoughts on Twitter are followed by more than 800,000 people; another 250,000 follow his madcap video blogs; millions more see him on *The Ultimate Fighter*, a reality show on Spike TV. Scores of news outlets, from Yahoo! Sports and ESPN to the more esoteric FiveKnuckles.com, follow his every move. His partners, the Fertitta brothers, whom he has known since before he was kicked out of Las Vegas's Bishop Gorman High School (for accidentally hitting a nun with his shoe, which had flown off his foot when he kicked the classroom door open), are the billionaire owners of seventeen properties in Vegas. According to the dispute-resolution clause in their contract, disagreements between Frank and Lorenzo Fertitta are to be resolved via "a Sport jiu jitsu match ... three five-minute rounds, refereed by White and decided by submission or points."

"I wanna welcome you guys," White says warmly to the gathered. Along with his partner Lorenzo and his matchmaker, Joe Silva, White has helped to engineer every one of the upcoming fights. In the early days of UFC fighting, the matchup idea was style versus style: How would a boxer fair against a wrestler? Today, all of the fighters practice mixed martial arts—a little bit of everything, from muay Thai to wrasslin'. Unlike boxers, they fight every few weeks. White estimates that eighteen of his ultimate fighters earn in the millions per annum. Many others earn in the hundreds of thousands. New guys make fifty to seventy-five, "depending where you are in the pecking order."

"Here's how it works," White says—he speaks with the tough-guy inflection of a blue-collar know-it-all. "There's gonna be a lot of people there tomorrow and they wanna see you guys *fight*. So fight. Let it go. Fight to fuckin' *win*. Bonuses are sixty grand. I'll give $60,000 each to the two guys involved in the best fight of the night. I'll give sixty K for the best knockout. And sixty thousand for the best submission. You can win both. Double bonus. You can be involved in the best fight of the night and also win the knockout or submission."

Claps and whistles of approval. The men look around at each other approvingly.

"Didn't that happen last time?" Joe Daddy asks.

"That's right," White says. When he smiles, his mouth sags slightly on the lower right side—the result, he says, of a fight in his youth with a pair of neighbor twins. He had one of them pinned on the ground when the other hit him in the face with a shovel.

Joe Silva mentions the name of the last fighter who won the double bonus— Rick "Horror" Story, a former national-guard officer and all-American wrestler at Southern Oregon University. "You call that a good day," he says.

"He was making five and five," White says, meaning $5,000 to show up and $5,000 to win.

"And he ended up walking with $130,000," Silva says.

Hoots and applause.

"Wow, Dana, have you been lifting weights?" This is Joe Daddy again. A short guy with veiny arms and swollen, stick-out ears, he brings to mind a cinnamon-colored Hulk. His sweet smile and raspy, childlike voice don't match at all. "You look huge," he tells the boss.

"There's no drug testing for promoters," Silva laughs.

"No brownnosing," White admonishes. He flexes his biceps—more hoots and jeers. There are deep sweat stains under his arms, sweat streams down his head; he is fighting a losing battle with the flu.

Now Silva steps forward. A small man with a thin moustache, he's the one who finalizes the details of the fights. He looks around the semicircle ominously. "The absolute worst part of my job is having to cut people," he says. "I have to cut people after every show; that's just how it goes. But I don't judge you on wins and losses. What I do care about is a great fight. If you fight your ass off, if you go out there and go to *war*, I'm gonna give you another shot. If you go out there and your fight sucks, you're probably not coming back. So please fight hard."

A hush falls over the group.

White nods approval to his minion ... and then he aims his face toward his fighters and rolls his eyes—*Gawd, can you believe this pencil-neck geek?*

"On a better note—" White sings sardonically, breaking the tension, causing everyone to laugh— "have a great night you guys. Go eat and drink, rest and relax. We'll see you tomorrow."

A black Escalade with oversize rims arrives to collect White and his entourage. The cobbled driveway of the Montage Beverly Hills is crowded with exotic horsepower. It is Saturday, late morning. The fight is tonight. Like fans undertaking a road trip, they pack the back compartment with dress clothes and a cooler full of refreshments.

Riding shotgun is Tom Page, head of security, an affable retired Las Vegas cop with a thick white pompadour. White sits behind the driver; behind him is Bob Moore, forty-three, a Southie and former training client. At one time Moorzo, as he is called, may or may not have had dealings with the Mob. As he says, "Back in the old neighborhood, you either swim with the sharks or you're fuckin' bait."

Next to him, at a perfect vantage point to capture White's every move and snippet of commentary is Elliott Raymond, thirty. He showed up a few years ago to shoot some photos of White for a car magazine and basically never left. Like his boss, Raymond is the son of a single mom who worked in health care to support her only son. (Raymond's mom was an EMT, White's was a nurse.) Like his boss, Raymond had an absentee dad. (Raymond's was a state trooper; White's was a fire-fighter with a penchant for drink). And like his boss, who hails from Ware, Massachusetts, Raymond has come a long way from his roots, in his case a small town in northwest New Mexico.

Because they fly ungodly distances every year producing shows and spreading the word, the guys have about them the going-nowhere-fast air of professional travelers. A second cooler, stored in the passenger space, holds fluids and flu medications. Raymond pours a tube of raspberry Emergen-C into a bottle of Smartwater and hands it to White. The schedule is packed with interviews other pre-fight obligations, but first there will be lunch at the Peninsula hotel. White needs a big bowl of the chicken soup—the best in town, he says, taking another swig of his pink-tinted water.

There is a lull in the cabin while everyone checks their phones. White has three—an old flip phone, a BlackBerry, and a $10,000 TAG Heuer that he is ready to throw out the window for lack of reception—he only bought it because everyone was giving him shit for having such a cheap flip phone. (A 10 percent owner of UFC, he's worth something like $200 million.) White gives out his telephone number to everyone. He answers everyone's texts, from the actor Lee Majors, who used to play the Six Million Dollar Man, to Jesus Castillo, UFC fan from the Inland Empire.

"Can you believe I lost ten pounds?" White says, looking up from one of his devices. "How do you keep a virus? I'm not taking any more medicine, man. I'm gonna try and keep this thing as long as I can and lose some weight."

"You can start licking people's palms," Elliot suggests.

"Nasty!" Moorzo says.

Everybody cracks up.

"I fuckin' lost ten pounds after I went in that Porta-Potty yesterday," White says, recalling the portable facility he visited behind the big top after his talk with the fighters. "I seriously thought I was gonna puke."

"You have to wonder," says Raymond, the artsy-philosophical one in the bunch. "who takes a shit in a Porta-Potty?"

"I have no problem dumping in a Porta-Potty," Moorzo says unequivocally in his thick Southie drawl.

"After that $1,200 room-service bill, do you doubt it?" White asks.

It's a running joke—Moorzo's $1,200 room-service bill at the Peninsula hotel in New York. ("It didn't even include the breakfasts, lunches, and dinners he ate with everybody else," White says.) Moorzo was one of White's first clients, twenty dollars an hour to train at his gym in South Boston, a nonprofit where street kids were taught to box. The personal fitness clients kept the place afloat. Moorzo eventually lost a hundred pounds. These days he's down to a steady 210.

"I've gone home with dye stained on my underwear from back-splash," Moorzo offers.

White makes a disgusted face.

"TMI, dude," Raymond says.

"Depth charge!" Moorzo calls.

"Never mind lunch," White groans, only half joking. "Let's go straight to the venue."

After a meal, there must be Pinkberry.

White orders his regular: a large cup of original flavor topped with Fruity Pebbles.

Moorzo orders his regular: a taste.

"How come you never fuckin' get your own serving?" White asks every time.

"I'm on a fuckin' diet," Moorzo explains every time.

"Order some more room service," White suggests.

Fans approach. White talks to them with his mouth full, sends them to Tom the cop for free tickets. Tom pulls the stack from the back right pocket of his blue jeans like a greaser going for his comb. "What do you need?" he asks. "Two together? Three?" He fans out the tickets like a deck of golden cards, looking for just the right seats.

The Boss | 153

Raymond shoots everything. The results are edited and posted late at night, comic minimovies about White's life, viewed by hundreds of thousands.

Often, when there is a big fight upcoming, White likes to Twitter where he'll be so people can meet him and win free tickets. So far this weekend, he and the boys have given out thirty-three hundred free tickets. All of the recipients are grateful and overwhelmed. To meet such a huge media celebrity! And he's so *normal*. Bro! Dude! "You seem just like a regular person," one girl tells him as he signs her T-shirt. Another guy chokes up telling White about losing his job: "These tickets are the best thing that's happened to me in two years." White doesn't know what to say to that. He gives the guy a strong soul shake, followed by a hug.

Now he lifts a spoonful of his Pinkberry to his mouth, savoring the tangy taste. "Lemme tell you when I started goofing around with Twitter," he says. "Lemme fuckin' lay this out for you.

"I'm in New York City. It's 10:30 on a Monday night in midtown Manhattan. It's raining. And it's a Jewish holiday, okay? As you know, I'm a Pinkberry freak. I like to have my Pinkberry. I have this one store in midtown Manhattan that will stay open for me late. I just have to call and let them know, and after I have dinner I always go there and eat Pinkberry, right? So this one time I'm like, 'Let's just fuck around here and try something.' I Twitter my people. I say, 'Meet me at Pinkberry in midtown Manhattan. I got tickets to the fight if you guys want to go.'

"So you've been to New York enough, right? People don't give a fuck about anything in New York. I've never seen a city where people just don't fucking care—Brad Pitt and Angelina Jolie can be walking down the street holding hands and people could care less, you know? They take shit in stride.

"I'm twenty minutes late showing up to Pinkberry. The fucking place is packed. There's people everywhere. I get out of the car and everybody starts cheering and going crazy. I look at the police and I'm like, 'Are you guys mad?' And they're like, 'We didn't believe you were coming.' I get out, I sign autographs, take pictures. We hand out like a zillion tickets. We're there for two hours.

"And this is the craziest fucking thing about this whole story: Not only is it Monday night, raining, in midtown Manhattan on a

Jewish holiday. I'm giving away tickets to a fight in fucking Los Angeles."

He shakes his head abashedly—*Shit, man, I can't believe it either.* "Look at my arm," he says, offering up his big, stubbled salami of a forearm. "I get chills just talking about this."

A swirling, carnal, hypnotic atmosphere prevails inside the Staples Center. Huge screens run footage and interviews, beautifully produced in-house by the UFC's parent company, Zuffa, an Italian word meaning "melee." Music pounds at shattering volume from special high-power speakers overhead, a mix of rock and hip-hop that readjusts the rhythm of your heart. Celebrities laugh and preen inside the velvet ropes; fans from all strata strut the concourse between matches, seeing and being seen; the alcohol and nachos flow. Down in the Octagon, the fighters come two by two, carved and thickly muscled. There is much kicking and punching, much grappling on the mat. Pounding fists, spurting blood, flying sweat, arms and legs twisted in the wrong directions; the sickening rolled-back eyeballs of a man being choked, followed by the frantic tapping hand, the tap out, a cry of uncle to stop the match. White patrols the territory ringside in a Tom Ford suit, welcoming VIPs, signing autographs, putting out fires. At the start of each round, he returns to his place at a table where there is a monitor and headset so he can listen to the live broadcast. He watches his fighters raptly, grimacing with each elbow and roundhouse like everyone else in the joint. Like a kid in his room with a boxful of action figures, he has willed this spectacle into reality.

As it happened, we're here tonight because White, a lifelong boxing fan, had become fascinated with jiu jitsu—an ancient form of combat developed around the principle of using an attacker's energy against him, rather than directly opposing it. One night at the Hard Rock Hotel in Vegas White met an MMA fighter who specialized in the discipline. In short order White had himself and both Fertitta brothers signed up for lessons. "We got fucking psychotic about it," White recalls. "We started training three, four days a week. And then we started to learn shit on our own that the other guys didn't learn, so that when we trained, we could tap each other out."

Traveling around the country to attend UFC fights as spectators, White and the brothers would sit in the audience and brainstorm—*We could do this so much fuckin' better!* White branched out to managing and training some MMA fighters himself, including Chuck Liddell and another former champ, Tito Ortiz. During negations for one of his fighters, White discovered that the then-two-year-old UFC was in trouble. MMA fighting was banned almost everywhere; pay-per-view wouldn't touch it, either. White and the brothers ended up buying the league in 2001 for $2 million.

Lorenzo Fertitta had recently stepped down as the senior vice-chairman on the Nevada State Athletic Commission. Using Fertitta's contacts and general know-how, the partners set about changing the rules of UFC fighting (e.g., no head butts), cleaning it up, making it more palatable in statehouses around the nation. At one point the league was $44 million in debt. There was a decision to stay the course. At the eleventh hour, White and company somehow convinced testosterone-rich Spike TV to air a UFC show, The Ultimate Fighter. (That first season, to sweeten the pot, the partners even paid the production costs.) Today, it is the network's biggest franchise. In 2008, *Forbes* estimated the UFC's worth at $1 billion. Even in 2009, despite the awful economy, UFC says its revenues grew by 20 percent over 2008.

UFC 104 goes off without a hitch—until the title bout.

The reigning champion, Lyoto Machida, thirty-one, is an ethnic Japanese trained by his father in a special form of karate. In the days leading up to the fight, White raved about him: "He can throw his feet as fast as other guys throw their hands," he told the press. "He's only a couple fights away from being called, pound-for-pound, the best MMA fighter in the world."

Mauricio "Shogun" Rua, twenty-eight, was in the middle of a comeback, a former star of the Pride Fighting Championships, a popular Japanese MMA league where he picked up his nickname. Two years ago people were calling him the best fighter in the world. He beat Liddell, he beat everybody. And then he had two knee surgeries back-to-back; he was out for a little over a year. "He's back to his former self," White declared.

In person at various press stops during the week, Shogun and Machida had been perfect gentlemen, each safely enfolded within his own entourage. One person in each camp spoke English. (Machida's father, a distinguished little mop-haired man, wearing a denim karate gig and Japanese-style sandals, brought to mind the *Star Wars* character Yoda.) "These are arguably two of the best strikers in the world," White told the press—the language barrier meant that he had to carry the lion's share of prefight publicity himself. "They both have great kicks, knees, elbows, punches. It's going to be a war."

The fight is slated to be five rounds, five minutes each. (Non-title bouts are three rounds.) Shogun takes the offensive from the opening bell, pounding Machida's outer and inner thighs with kick after kick, a tactic designed to rob the champ of his legs. Machida gives his best, but without his secret weapon, feet like hands, he seems unable to do much beyond surviving the repeated savage blows from his opponent. Toward the end of the match, Machida's lip is split and bleeds copiously. Later it will require stitches.

When the decision is announced, Machida is the surprise winner, three rounds to two. The champ retains his belt—fourteen pounds of sterling silver and twenty-four-karat-gold plate.

There is a smattering of boos—the music is so loud it is hard to be sure.

Visibly angry with the decision—"Who cares what I think? I'm only the fuckin' promoter!"—White retreats with his entourage to his private dressing room, where he is joined by two financial officers from Zuffa. Together with Lorenzo Fertitta and Silva, White decides who should win the bonus money for best submission and the rest. Paychecks for all the fighters are written out by hand. When they get to Shogun's check, White orders the accountants to "pay the taxes." Meaning, essentially, that he wants Shogun's previously contracted payday to be doubled.

With a check for $250,000 in hand, White goes off looking for Shogun.

When the defeated challenger sees the boss entering his dressing room he rises shame-facedly from his bench—his body language says defendant about to be sentenced. His manager stands stolidly at his left elbow; his entourage surrounds him in a semicircle. They all wear T-shirts emblazoned with an artsy logo of Shogun's dark and mysterious eyes.

White hands Shogun his check. He points to the amount. "Tell him that's the *real number*," White instructs the manager.

"Thank you, thank you very much," Shogun says, in heavily accented English. Back home in Curitiba, Brazil, his wife is expecting their first child. He looks appreciative—if not exactly satisfied.

"We paid the *taxes*," White reiterates. *Maybe he didn't understand?* He points to the check again. "That's the *real* number there. That's take-home pay."

Shogun listens to the translation. He ratchets his proud, chiseled jaw one crank higher. "Okay thank you," he says. "Thank you very much."

"I know it doesn't erase what happened."

Resigned: "No, no problem."

"But it's gotta make you feel a little better." White elbows the fighter playfully in the triceps—*I just gave you an extra 125 grand, dude, lighten up!*

Shogun breaks down and smiles for real. White regards him appraisingly. "Do you want a rematch?"

No translation is necessary.

The corner men clap and cheer and hug one another. They pound their fighter on the back. He winces.

"He will do it if Machida will do it," the manager says, not to be disincluded.

"Thank you very much," Shogun says. This time you can tell he really means it.

"No, thank *you*," White says. "Great fight. Really great fight." He also means it. "But listen. Next time? Be more aggressive at the end. When there's thirty seconds left, go for it, steal the round, you know what I mean?"

"I know I know I know," Shogun says. Coming into that last round, he'd thought he had it won. The expression on his face is universal.

Back in the Escalade, headed west toward Beverly Hills, there is a sated, overtired feeling among the occupants, reminiscent of a ride back to the hotel with relatives after a wedding. Extending the image are the extra bodies stuffed into the vehicle. Lorenzo Fertitta is wedged between Moorzo and Raymond in the far back. Craig Borsari, a Zuffa executive in charge of operations, is sitting on top of the medicine cooler, next to White in the second row. (White's wife—a natural stunner—has wisely opted to take a separate car back to the hotel. Together they have three children under age nine. The two boys train with daddy in MMA.)

Raymond hands White another bottle of pink-tinted Smartwater. The boss is still sweaty and congested. His shirt is unbuttoned to the abdomen. Everyone fusses with their various phones.

"I have so many fucking texts." White says to nobody in particular. He scrolls down, reads randomly: "'Shogun got fucked.' 'That's a fucking rematch if I ever saw one.' 'Maybe the worst decision in Zuffa-UFC History.'"

"No way!" Fertitta protests from his seat in the back.

"Truthfully," White says, "I had Shogun winning the fight."

"It was close," Fertitta says diplomatically. "But to say it was the worst decision in fuckin' history?..." His voice trails off in real disappointment.

"This fight was very calculated," allows Borsari.

"How about that flurry from Machida in the third round?" Raymond enthuses.

"How about Shogun dancing in the fourth?" Moorzo says. "He looked like Ali up there."

"Some of those kicks were brutal."

"Do you know how bad it hurts when you get kicked like that?" White asks. "That shit will fold you."

"It looked like Machida broke a rib," Raymond observes, ever the caretaker.

"Machida's beat up, man," White says. "He sat there at the end of the press conference because he didn't want to limp off the stage in front of everybody. He can't even fucking walk."

"You know how bad they must feel in the morning?" Borsari muses.

White groans. "How do you think they feel on the flight back to fucking Brazil?"

"I'd just stay here for a week first," Borsari says.

"Or go to a spa for four days," Raymond suggests.

"So what's a good place to eat late in L.A.?" White asks, changing the subject. He hasn't had a thing since the chicken-noodle soup.

"How about Mr. Chow's?"

"Mel's Diner?"

"Spago?"

White succumbs to a coughing fit. He hocks up a loogie; Raymond hands him a napkin. "Actually, I still feel like shit," White concludes. "There's good room service at the hotel."

"*Great* room service," Moorzo enthuses.

Everybody cracks up.

(2010)

Vetville

More than two million Americans have served in the Afghanistan and Iraq Wars. Many returned wounded, thousands have committed suicide—nearly twenty-five percent suffer from PTSD or major depression with little hope of relief. On one small farm in the mountains of Tennessee, Alan Beaty and his rag-tag squad of marine vets have found a modest solution—taking care of each other.

Alan Beaty navigates a rutted road, once again a man on a mission. His eyes track grimly side to side, scanning for irregularities along this dusty and familiar route in the Cumberland Mountains of Tennessee. Gravel ricochets off the undercarriage of his battered red Honda CR-V, the springs squeak and complain. The half-assed mini-crossover van is a remnant of his former life, when he was a postmaster and a husband, a full-time father; he'd found it parked outside his empty house upon his return from his third tour in Iraq. The odometer has already run around twice. It will have to do. There is no room in the budget for a car payment—inevitably he finds himself finishing out the month on pimento cheese, Wonder Bread, and moonshine, brewed in a 150-year-old still rescued from the family homestead, awarded to his great-great-great-great-grandfather for his service in the Revolutionary War, at the Battle of Kings Mountain.

Andrew Beaty walked hundreds of miles in 1780 to lend his long rifle to this pivotal victory in the fight for American independence; history records him as one of the original Overmountain Men, the first wave of the storied Tennessee Volunteers. The Beaty family has continued the tradition in successive generations. Alan's father, Keith, endured some of the thickest fighting in Vietnam. Alan himself did four different stints, the last as a U.S.-government-employed mercenary commanding Ugandan and Bosnian security forces. Like their ancestor, bitten by a rattlesnake during the final assault on the British loyalists at Kings Mountain, none of the Beatys returned home from their service unscathed. Alan's wife is gone. He has no hearing in one ear, a constant ringing. Veterans Affairs gave him one of those sound-effects radios to help him sleep— and also a ton of prescription pills. The ghosts of his past are constantly a swirl. They come to him in dreams, they come to him awake: Staff Sergeant Anthony Goodwin, beloved platoon leader, a Marine's Marine—shot in the face and killed instantly; Staff Sergeant Kendall Ivy, Goodwin's battlefield replacement—killed two days later, he remembers, by a small piece of shrapnel that entered just below his ass cheek and nicked an artery, causing him to bleed out; the men in Ivy's AAV, a large armored troop carrier with tank-like tracks—burned to a crisp, their bodies had to be peeled from the wreckage.

Beaty and Ivy were good friends. After a mission, they'd hang in Beaty's can at Al Asad air base in western Iraq and have a shot or two of whiskey—regular shipments from Beaty's dad came masquerading as Listerine mouthwash. Ivy's wife was pregnant. The night before he was killed, he and Beaty were watching a DVD of The Alamo, starring Billy Bob Thornton, talking all kinds of shit about going back in a time machine to kick some Mexican ass—*Gotta get us a coonskin cap!* They were U.S. Marines. Brothers in combat. Men trained to hunger for a fight, even as they were recovering from the last, even as they dreaded the next. Now Beaty keeps Ivy's shot glass in a cabinet in his dining room. One thing that wasn't lost.

After Goodwin, after Ivy, the operational leadership of the 2nd Marine Expeditionary Force's RCT-2 Jump Platoon—a bodyguarding element assigned to an impossibly tall and fearless colonel whose mission was to pacify the largely Sunni western Iraq province of Al Anbar—had fallen to Sergeant Alan Beaty, thirty-one.

Upon receipt of his promotion, at the cost of his best friend's life, Beaty retreated to his can, which is what they call the pre-fab barracks. He'd put his face in his hands and cried like a little boy. *If there's anything you can do to take me out of this, Lord, please do it now. I don't want the responsibility of these Marines on my hands.*

That was 2005, more than six years—and two more deployments—ago. He still can't drive past a dead dog or a bag of garbage lying by the side of a road. The smell of burning trash. The smell of diesel fuel. The loud report of a firearm in the hollow. A rubber hose stretched across a street to count traffic. A line of slow, stupid, complaining motherfuckers at the checkout line at the Walmart. . .*anything* can set him off. The way people look at him. The way his family tried to treat him with kid gloves, like some cripple. The way he couldn't even bond with his own kids.

The VA awarded him 100 percent disability: post-traumatic stress disorder. Social Security told him to get a job. It's like he's home but he's not. Like part of him was left behind. Maybe that's why he kept going back.

One year ago, Beaty rode his favorite horse eighteen miles out from his farm into the wilderness, a .40-cal pistol hanging from the pommel horn of his saddle. He was broke and depressed. He felt a little bit guilty about some of the stuff that was done overseas, and angry about other stuff. As part of a post-Blackwater crackdown on contract mercenaries, he'd been arrested and jailed on inflated charges involving an assault committed by a man under his command. The charges were finally dropped; thankfully, his dad had borne the financial burden of his defense. Home again on US soil, faced with building a life... well, he didn't know who he was. He'd felt useless and unproductive and off, you know? Just off. Like nothing was ever quite right. And so goddam tired. What he would do for some sleep.

He was FUBAR, as they say in the corps.

Fucked-Up Beyond All Repair.

He just couldn't handle it no more.

He planned carefully. Thought it through. It became kind of an obsession, getting all the details slotted. Something to keep him busy, to keep him slogging forward, one foot in front of the other. He considered slitting his wrists in the bathtub, taking an overdose of his prescription drugs. He decided he didn't want anybody he knew to find him dead.

At last he settled on Leonides—half-Arabian, half saddlebred. Leo knows his way all over the mountain. He is famously ground tied—you can drop the reins and he'll stand for six hours in one place till you get back. Alan had figured Leo would stand over his body awhile, wondering in his loyal equine pea brain what to do next. But eventually he'd get hungry and come back to the barn. They'd send out a search party. Let the professionals deal with such things...

Now, driving the Honda along the rutted road, Beaty worries his goatee. Up before dawn, he is nearing the end of a six-hour round-trip drive to the Nashville airport. Of course, he would have driven six days. *One of my Marines is in trouble.* He glances to his right, checking the welfare of his passenger. His name is Pat Myers. As far as Beaty is concerned, what happened to Myers is on him.

I was extremely uncomfortable with the new platoon sergeant who was succeeding me. He wasn't the guy for the job. He was scared to go outside the wire. He didn't know how to run a convoy. He'd never get in a lead vehicle, because that's the one that always got hit. He didn't know how to do any of that crap and he didn't want to learn.

And then I leave him alone for twelve hours, not even that, and he's done wounded three of my Marines.

Beaty spotted Myers right away at the farthest bay of the baggage claim. He saw the wheelchair, recognized the tattoo on the back of his right arm, a big cross that covers his whole triceps. They served together for nearly a year, ran eighty-four documented mobile combat patrols, always in vehicle two of the convoy. Beaty rode in the passenger seat. Lance Corporal Pat Myers sat right behind. Though he was rated as a radio operator, Myers never once touched the comms—instead he carried a 12-gauge shotgun, the door breacher. Myers was known in the platoon as the guy who could always make everyone laugh with his irreverent humor. No matter how dark things got, he always had some smart-ass quip to lighten the mood. He saved Beaty's ass on Route Uranium, between the city of Hit and Al Asad, when he noticed their Humvee was parked directly on top of a thin green wire connected to three 120mm rockets buried in the sand. Seeing his tattoo across the airport concourse, it occurred to Beaty how many times he had followed that cross straight into the asshole of the unknown.

The last time Beaty had seen Myers was five years earlier, on the Marine Corps birthday, November 10, 2005. Elsewhere in the world, Marines in dress blues were attending formal balls to honor their beloved branch. Lance Corporal Myers, twenty-two, was mounting up for patrol, his first in nearly two months.

For all his joking around, Myers was clearly a troubled kid. His father had been career Army, medical discharge. His mother was a nurse. The family moved around a lot—Indiana, Alaska, Texas. "My dad was an ass," Myers would later say. "He just expected way too much of me. When I was a teenager, I went to church. I played nearly every sport. I was even in band. He never came to one concert, one game, nothing. He was one of those guys, no matter how hard I tried to please him it was never enough. I could never get it right with him. I always made these standards for myself, and they never, ever met his."

Three years after high school, Myers was working in a grocery store. He met a local recruiter. "My dad told me I wasn't man enough to be a Marine," Myers recalled. "That's the main reason I joined."

Natural athlete that he was, Myers flew through basic training and the School of Infantry. Eventually he was assigned to the jump platoon. He thought he'd found his place. Until he encountered an unexpected complication: He fell in love with a female Marine.

Beaty had seen this kind of thing before. He preached to the kid; of course he wouldn't listen—never mind that now. Everyone who has ever been around Marines knows this: They do love the same way they do war. They went on a $7,000 cruise together. After two seemingly blissful weeks, on the gangplank exiting, she told him she'd found somebody else.

When he returned to Al Asad, Myers was a train wreck. He'd come over to Beaty's can and cry—Beaty actually gave him two weeks off to get his shit together, unofficial time away from duty. During this time, Myers didn't shave, didn't shower, didn't do shit but mope around and act demented. One day he was walking across the base wearing civvies, sporting a full beard. As it happened, he passed Colonel Stephen W. Davis, the regimental commander he was being paid by the Marine Corps to protect.

Colonel Davis did a double take. "Are you okay, Myers?"

"What's up?" Myers called. He issued a goofy wave and kept on strolling.

Within three minutes Beaty's radio was blowing up. The sergeant major chewed his ass. Myers was pulled from the jump, given gate guard duty—six hours on, six hours off.

Six long weeks. Whenever the jump convoy would return from a mission, Myers would be waving them into the gate. *And us throwing bottles at him and stuff. Giving him a ton of shit. Ha ha, look at you, gate guard.*

Finally Myers could take no more. He begged with tears in his eyes, "Please let me get back on the jump."

Beaty talked to the sergeant major, went to the mat for the kid. Myers got the thumbs-up.

There was only one problem: Beaty wouldn't be there to supervise. His deployment was over. He was one wake-up from going home.

Myers reported for duty the next morning. He'd shaved . . . everything except his moustache. Of course, the sergeant major went batshit. *As soon as we get back you're gonna shave your fuckin' face, Marine!*

Then the new platoon sergeant informed Myers that someone else now carried the 12-gauge. Myers would be driving vehicle five, the caboose. He'd driven only once before. That time, his Humvee was hit by a roadside bomb; he'd narrowly escaped death; he'd vowed never to drive again.

Not that anybody gave two shits what he'd vowed.

All he remembers is a huge explosion. It was like the ground came up to meet him; then everything went black.

He woke up clear of the wreckage. He knew he was fucked: The tough-as-nails sergeant major was holding his hand like somebody's mommy. "I guess this means I don't have to shave," Myers said, and everybody laughed.

In the Nashville airport, what was left of Lance Cpl Pat Myers pivoted his chair to face Beaty, each hand working a wheel in opposition.

Beaty couldn't believe what he was seeing. Both of Myers legs were gone above the knee, a couple of fingers were missing. He was heavier then Beaty remembered; his jug-eared face wore signs of successive generations of fights. He looked like shit, really, like he just didn't care no more, didn't have nothing in the world to look forward to. The other night in Ft. Worth, he'd gotten so fucked-up he'd left his wheelchair in the parking lot of a roadhouse. He'd driven home fine, but then he had to crawl up the driveway to his house.

The next morning, after a call from a concerned friend, a Marine gunnery sergeant, assigned his case by the corps's Wounded Warriors Regiment, let herself into Myers's house with a key he'd given her for these kinds of occasions, which were becoming too numerous to count. Myers was already facing a DUI. He seemed to have hit rock bottom.

After rousing him the best she could, Gunny Teresa Grandinetti pulled out her cell phone and dialed a number. She handed it to Myers.

"Who is this?" Myers demanded insolently.

The Tennessee twang was unmistakable: "This is Sergeant Beaty."

Myers got real quiet. "Sarge, I'm really fucked-up." He burst into tears.

"You wanna come out here and stay with me a while?"

"Can I come tonight?"

As it happened, Gunny Grandinetti's husband is an employee of Southwest Airlines; he finagled Myers a free ticket. They had him on a plane the next day.

The GPS signal cuts out about a mile from the house, at the clearing by an antique whitewashed church where the congregants are said to handle snakes. The cell phone dies a few hundred yards later—the Honda is picked up instead by a pack of abandoned dogs Beaty has adopted, barking and yipping and running alongside like a welcoming committee. (His old blind dog waits behind. You can kick a deflated soccer ball anywhere in the field and he'll find it and bring it back. . . eventually.)

As Beaty pulls up in the gravel before his modest cracker-box house, he fights a twinge of doubt. *Holy shit*, he tells himself, *now we got another mouth to feed.* And then he tells himself: *Who knows where he'd have ended up if I didn't come get him.*

Maybe like Keith Hull, living under a bridge before he came to crash with Beaty. Or Jason Delong. He was in the turret of a truck when they hit a double-stacked antitank mine; he flew in from California just to spend two days at the farm, 260 acres of cleared fields and forest and untended walnut trees deep in a hollow near Oneida, Tennessee, a hamlet of thirty-eight hundred in the far north central part of the state, just across the border from Kentucky. Or Adam Hand, another turret gunner, living hand-to-mouth in Washington, D.C. He stayed for a few weeks. Now he's a mall cop; he's thinking of coming back down. Or Spencer Pellecer, still on active duty at the School of Infantry at Camp Lejeune, who finds his way every holiday to Beaty's copious and embracing leather couch—Pellecer's mother calls Beaty for updates on her own son. Or the score of other Marines who have found work, camaraderie and refuge at Beaty's farm since June of 2008, a sort of do-it-yourself halfway house for Marines broken by war. Some stay for a week; some stay for months; one guy is working on year number two. Though Beaty has been asked informally by the Marines to help out from time to time, he has up to now gotten no formal support or guidance from them or the government; lately he's been thinking about applying for grants, soliciting contributions— something to help make his idea more serviceable than the sets of bunk beds in his kids' room. For now, it's a jerry-rigged operation. Whatever it takes, they make it work.

If only there was room for all of them.

Horses graze in the field behind the house; mountains rise in the middle distance. A small rickety porch with three steps frames the doorway. Off to one side is a pile of fresh lumber, two-bys and four-bys and such.

The engine hiccupps to a stop. "Look Devil Dog, I ain't lifting your fat ass up into the house," Beaty says, a tone of command once again swelling the barrel of his chest. He gestures toward the lumber pile. "You're gonna have to build your own ramp."

Hungover, fucked-up, possibly suicidal, Myers stares at his former platoon leader. It is hot as hell, the sun was beating down, fat bees were buzzing everywhere. He is twenty-five years old. He's been blown up and bled out. His lungs collapsed, his heart stopped three times. When he finally awoke from his medically induced coma, he found himself in a hospital in Washington, D.C. The first person he saw was his mother. *I asked her if my junk was still there.* After that he spent two years in an army hospital in San Antonio.

Beaty climbs out of the truck and shuts his door, heading for the house. "When you get the ramp built," he tells Myers, "you can roll yourself inside and I'll pour you a drink of whiskey and we'll talk about the war."

On a somnolent afternoon at Beaty's farm six months later, rain drums relentlessly on the tin roof overhanging the back porch; dense fog looms, obscuring the thickly forested mountains. A war flick plays at low volume on the big screen in the living room— King Leonidas is leading his elite Spartans into battle against a vastly superior force. The sounds of children's laughter and video games drift out from one of the bedrooms, Beaty's three kids in residence for the weekend.

Four men sprawl on sofas around a big old wood-burning stove, sipping beer and moonshine. His first night in the house alone, Beaty slept on the wall-to-wall carpet by the stove, too heavy for his wife to move, he supposes. Now there's a hardwood floor. After he built the ramp, Myers put in the floor. (Of course, Beaty worked by his side. . . as he'd ended up doing with the ramp.)

Myers has been gone four months. He's back in Fort Worth, has a girlfriend and a baby; he and a partner are working on a plan to train vets as mechanics. He still visits from time to time—you should have seen him driving the hay wagon with broom handles duct-taped to his stumps so he could work the pedals. Later they duct-taped him onto a smooth-gaited Tennessee walking horse and took him for a ride up the mountain. Obviously his time with Beaty, and the camaraderie of the Marines who are always coming and going from the place, helped turn him around. The truth is, you come home and nobody understands. While you've been out killing and trying to survive, they've been shopping for groceries, ordering wine in fancy restaurants, attending to math homework. (It helped also that Guny Grandinetti finally got the military to send Myers a pair of prosthetic legs.)

More recently, Myers's room at the farm has been occupied by Keith Hull. Skeleton thin with dreadlocks, the former sergeant is wearing his usual surfer shorts and rubber flip-flops despite the cold. Hull was raised in private schools, the rebellious son of a successful insurance man. He tried high-rise steel construction before joining the corps in 1998. Following 9/11, he was assigned to Task Force 58, the first Marines on the deck in Afghanistan; they pushed straight through to Kandahar. After mustering out, Hull attempted college for several years. When he was recalled by the Marines in 2004, he was assigned to Beaty's jump platoon as a turret gunner. "The best platoon the Marine Corps has ever made up," he says.

"Everybody was experienced," Hull remembers. "Everybody had a different MOS. It was like a James Bond platoon: No matter what situation we were in—say there was a tank to be moved, or a piece of equipment that needed to be fixed, what have you—there was always somebody who knew how." Out of twenty-three in the platoon during his deployment, two were killed, four wounded. The psychic toll is yet untallied. Several months after his return, the sergeant who replaced Beaty was thrown from his motorcycle after driving off a road. There were a lot of rumors about a suicide note in his back pocket. Only the family knows for sure.

According to a recent federal-appeals-court ruling that took the VA to task for failing to care for veterans suffering from PTSD, an average of eighteen vets (from all eras) commit suicide every day.

Of 1.6 million Iraq/Afghan war vets, according to a 2008 Rand Corporation study cited by the U.S. 9th Circuit Court of Appeals, 300,000 suffer from PTSD or major depression. As of 2011, the number of vets from those wars surpassed two million.

By the time Hull came to Beaty's farm, he'd spiraled into homelessness. A proud and intelligent man with a gift for cleverly bending a truth, he'll tell you he was "stealth camping" while working as a bar bouncer, getting paid off the books in drugs and alcohol. That he ended up sleeping under bridges, he explains, was inspired by a Web site he came across. Admittedly he was a sorry case. His apartment was gone; he'd donated all his furniture to needy neighbors. His girlfriend was gone and so was most of the contents of his bank account. (He'd have given her the money if she'd only asked.) He'd lost his job as a janitor in a small restaurant—he worked the night shift because he couldn't stand to be around so many people; a can of beans would fall off a shelf and he'd dive for cover. He was drunk or high all the time. He'd gotten to the point where he'd asked his father to lock up his guns. "I was ready to go the way of the dodo," he says.

Now Hull is chillin' in Beaty's living room, where he's pretty much been part of the furniture for the last nine months. At the moment, he's helping to play host to the dignitary who's just come limping up the new front ramp. (At least he's not in the bedroom staring at the popcorn ceiling. In the beginning, that's all he did. It was Beaty who finally dragged him to the VA to start him on treatment.)

Lieutenant Colonel Tim Maxwell, forty-six, is one of the highest ranking Marines to be seriously wounded in Iraq. While in the hospital recovering from traumatic brain and other injuries sustained on his sixth overseas tour, he began ministering to wounded Devil Dogs, going from bed to bed in his bathrobe. Eventually he saw to fruition his dream of creating a Wounded Warriors Regiment, a unit to keep account of Marines after they'd been injured—a series of barracks and facilities and social services where the wounded can begin their recovery in the embrace of their fellows. The first such barracks, at Camp Lejeune in North Carolina, was named in his honor.

Like many wounded vets, Maxwell has discovered that what's broken can never really be fixed. There are ongoing complications, constant tinkerings with meds, weird side effects, oddly unexplainable medical breakdowns, revisionary surgeries. In 2008, Maxwell had an operation to remove the remaining shrapnel from his brain— originally the doctors thought it was embedded too deep to risk extracting. As it turned out, the toxins leaching from the metal were cooking his noodle—*How do you like that?* He had reached the point where he was losing more function every day.

The surgery, following a long and tortured rehab, eased some of Maxwell's speech, behavioral, and cognitive problems. But it also left the strapping former triathlete without use of his right arm, with tenuous balance, and with a greatly reduced field of vision on his right side. More recently he needed further surgery on his rebuilt left elbow—all the metal had attracted a horrendous infection. "The doc wanted to put me in a cast for six weeks. I said, 'You're talking about me having to have somebody wipe my butt again. I'm not okay with that,'" Maxwell will later recall over dinner, having opted for lasagna at the best steakhouse in Oneida because he couldn't cut the meat with one hand, and because he was too proud to let somebody do it for him.

A few months ago, Maxwell flew from his home in northern Virginia to the Marine base at Camp Pendleton, north of San Diego to try out for a Wounded Warriors Paralympics team. Despite his balance problems, he managed to ride his bike one-armed for eighteen miles without crashing. Swimming proved more difficult. Sank like a stone. A guy he met wants to teach him how to swim with one arm. Maxwell doesn't want to learn. Neither does he want to learn to write with his left hand. He is convinced he can rehab the damn right limb if he just keeps working. Already he can make his fingers move a little.

Having heard a lot of talk about Beaty's farm, Maxwell has driven his specially equipped camper van (licence plate BUMR) nearly six hundred miles from Camp Lejeune, where he was attending the dedication of a brand-new Wounded Warriors barracks. After Maxwell founded the first barracks in 2007, an entire Wounded Warrior Regiment was formed. There's a command center at Quantico, Virginia, now a second barracks at Camp Pendleton, and satellite offices around the country. Since its inception, Maxwell's regiment has helped nearly twenty-seven thousand wounded Marines. But the program benefits primarily Marines still on active duty. For those who have left the service, help is hard to find.

Retired now from the corps, Maxwell runs SemperMax.Com, a nonprofit support group for wounded Marines, both active and vets. He has a Web site and a zillion contacts. (As does his wife, Shannon, also active in helping wounded families. She has recently authored a children's book, *Our Daddy is Invincible!*, aimed at helping kids cope when their parents suffer injuries at war.) Each day brings Maxwell a different project, a different hard-luck tale, another wounded Marine with a problem to solve—which means that each day Maxwell has something important to do. He would have arrived at Beaty's place sooner, but he couldn't drive straight through; he doesn't see very well in the dark anymore, either.

Of course, he drove some distance in the dark anyway.

"After six and a half years, the doctors are starting to tell me they don't know what to do for me," Maxwell is telling the others. Though his speech is slurred and he likes to play himself off as a humble, brain-damaged crip, Maxwell's mind is sharp, his ideas run well before the wind, his gruff irreverence is intact. "Doctors never say 'I don't know.' Those three words: They're frickin' *restricted* from saying that."

"They might lose their status as gods," Hull quips.

"The most irritating thing to me is the doctors grouping PTSD and traumatic brain injuries together because they know so little about the damn brain. They're saying we got the same problems, me and you. Well, hello? Our problems are *totally* different. They both suck. But they suck different. Like with my injury, my brain is wacked. Shrapnel is what got me, not the *kaboom*."

"There's an actual physical injury," Beaty says.

"Exactly," says Hull.

"I know I'm supposed to be a dumbass grunt, but even I can tell the difference between who's got what," Maxwell says. Though he was born in Ohio, he has a southern accent that showed up after the initial injury, the result of an enemy mortar round that landed serendipitously within the sandbagged doorway of his tent inside a command base. "When I was in the Wounded Warriors barracks, you'd see the PTSD guys up talking to each other at 2 a.m. None of them could sleep. What about you?"

Hull shrugs. *Who gives a shit.*

"You're kind of new at it—you have to learn how to fight the fight," Maxwell says.

"That's the thing that's so jacked up about PTSD," Hull says. "It's a mental degradation that you can't describe. If you hurt your arm, you have a mark. But if you hurt your mind. . . it's like, *Whatthefuck*, you know? I'm like, *I've been through some bad shit before, much worse shit than this. Why can't I fix myself now?*"

"I think everybody who goes through combat has PTSD," Maxwell says.

"The experts say it's like 20 percent," Beaty offers.

Maxwell screws up his face like he's smelled something bad. "That's 'cause when you go to treatment, they ask the wrong questions. The first thing they should ask is: Did you experience combat? Did you have to return fire? Then they should ask: Did you ever lose a friend? 'Cause when you see a dude get wacked, a friend of yours, a stranger, it don't matter—it always fucks you up."

"What person in combat ain't lost a friend?" Hull asks.

"Exactly," says Beaty.

"You spend the rest of your life lying awake at night thinking: If I didn't do such and such then Tommy Smith wouldn't be dead," Maxwell says. "It's always: my fault, my fault, my fault. I should've been on the left side of the Hummer. I should have been on the right. I should have gone first through the door. There's no way around it."

"The problem is getting guys into treatment," Beaty says. "My dad was a Marine in Vietnam. A Suicide Charlie guy. Served in 1968. Purple Heart. He's had PTSD his whole life—but he only just started to get treatment when I did. He's been gutting it out for like thirty, forty years. Bad dreams, cold sweats, the whole nine. And he never told a soul."

"It's damn embarrassing," Maxwell says. "You've got to convince a guy he's got PTSD. You gotta be like: 'Don't feel like a wuss. It's a real injury.'"

Hull: "The docs are like, 'Tell me about your issues.' But it's hard to explain. Because sometimes I don't even have words to express how it makes me feel. And the docs are like, 'Well, you gotta come up with something.' And I'm just like, Fuck, you know? It feels like something's trying to come out of my chest. Like in *Alien*? That's how I think of it—it feels like something is trying to rip through my chest. It's like: I don't understand it either, motherfucker! I just know I'm fucked-up and I need help. I'm just really at the point where I want to fucking get my shit together and move on."

"Are you taking your meds?"

"I take something for my rage issues—so I know that works. And then I only take my other ones when I have panic attacks. Those pills are weird. It's like they make my insides calm down but it doesn't make my brain stop working. You know what I'm saying? It's like my brain is still going *What the fuck? What the fuck? What the fuck?*"

Maxwell takes a swig of his beer. "I have days where I just sit there and. . . " his voice trails off. The lamp light catches the jagged scar on the side of his head, just below the hedge line of his high-and-tight military fade.

Beaty and Maxwell judder back down the rutted road on the way to town for an early dinner. Hull has volunteered to stay home with the kids, the eldest of whom is now fifteen. The sky has cleared and the moon has risen, presiding over the twilight and bare trees. With the windows down, you can hear the water in Stanley Creek, more of a rush than a babble.

Beaty points out his barn, a circa-1960s corncrib renovated by Marines, and his locust fence posts—harvested, hauled down the mountain, and set in place by Marines. "And see right here on the left? Keith Hull cleared that entire field. It was nothing but woods when he started. He disked it up and sowed it and did everything by himself." Most of the fields were cleared by Marines.

"It's not me asking them to come work," Beaty tells the retired colonel. "That's the funny thing. They just show up because they want a place to go." He shakes his head, the way a person does when he feels both blessed and perplexed. "Sometimes it gets a little bit crowded."

"I'm sure there's plenty of work to be done," Maxwell says.

"There's camaraderie," Beaty says. "There's people here that understand 'em, other combat Marines. We sit around at night, and I'm not gonna lie, we sit around and have a drink or three and talk about the war. It's huge for them. This is their home."

"It's hard to feel comfortable anywhere else," Maxwell says.

Beaty scratches his head, resets his trucker cap. "When they teach you to be a Marine, they teach you to focus, because you can't be emotional in combat. You learn to be able to put things out of your mind. You learn to build walls. We've been trained to just keep functioning, to operate without emotion, without conscience. That's what you need in war.

"But once you get back to society," Beaty continues, "the walls are still up. It's hard to have an emotional attachment to people. Because in your mind, you've been trained to know that this right here could be your last day on earth. So why allow myself to be connected to this woman? Why allow myself to be connected to my children? Lucky I got an amazing woman therapist now at the VA. It's only in the last few months that I'm learning how to take the walls down."

"The main strength of the Marine Corps is also the main weakness," Maxwell says matter-of-factly. "We're *too* well trained."

"They make 'em Marines, but nobody ever turns them back into civilians," Beaty says. "Even prisoners get halfway houses. Druggies get sober living."

Maxwell looks out the window. Crisscrossing the country, he's heard it all a million times before. He grinds his jaw, the wheels turn.

"Let's just estimate," Maxwell says at last. "What if we got a hundred grand? You'd be amazed with what we could do in this place with 100k. We make a campsite. When each kid comes in, we give him some lumber and we let him build his own cabin. We could have ten, twelve cabins, a rec hall—"

"I could sure put 'em to work," Beaty says. "Right now the only thing we're taking off the farm is hay. I thought about turning it into a tomato farm. And I got enough walnut trees to fill fifteen dump trucks with walnuts. But it's too labor-intensive. Right now I just have to let shit rot."

"It's like that movie. With that actor, you know? He builds the whatchacallit behind his—" Maxwell knits his brow, searching for the proper noun. People, places, things. It's called aphasia. It's part of the brain injury; there's no escaping it.

"*Field of Dreams?*" Beaty offers gingerly.

"If you build it, they will come," Maxwell says, pleased to remember the damn quote.

Yes! Yes! Yes! Beaty is thinking.

Turning his farm into a heaven for Marines—it's one of the reasons he decided to ride his horse back down the mountain that fateful day.

Seventy miles south of Alan Beaty's farm, John Cybula is sitting at a picnic table on the back deck of a house belonging to his girlfriend's mom. His stealth-black, Hi-Point 9mm semiautomatic pistol is broken down on the table; we've just finished emptying a few mags of hollow points into an assortment of car-stereo amps and tree stumps and other unfortunate objects that live for that purpose in the backyard. In a little while he'll demonstrate how fast he can put it back together with his eyes shut. Like he says, "Gotta stay sharp."

Cybula is twenty-five. He brings to mind Elvis Presley in his thirties, a handsome devil gone a little bit puffy, a certain darkness around the eyes, his hair carefully gelled and spiked. Chelsea is by his side; they share a pack of cigs. She is twenty-one, sweet as can be, taking the semester off from community college—she's thinking either forestry or nursing. She's got blue eyes and a trim little bod, an asymmetrical haircut with a pink swath dyed into the back, about as fashionista as it gets around Madisonville, Tennessee, a town so small that you can be shopping for a toothbrush at 2 a.m. at the local Walmart and be spotted by the local cop, who is aware that you are wanted for a probation violation. (He let Cybula kiss his girl good-night and took him to jail without cuffs.)

Cybula followed his granddad into the Marine Corps at seventeen, another boy from another family of Tennessee Volunteers—a high school quarterback who majored in cheerleaders, who wanted payback for 9/11. When we first met, in the summer of 2007, he was twenty-one. He'd been wounded in Fallujah, caught a bullet in the hip. The impact knocked him off a roof; he fell three stories and broke his pelvis. Young and gung ho, not wanting to be the weak link in the chain, he tried to rejoin his unit before the bones had properly healed. He ended up at the Wounded Warriors barracks at Camp Lejeune, eating a fistful of meds every day.

The sky is blue, the sun is unseasonably warm, a dog sleeps at his feet. "When I first got out, I was really lost," Cybula says. "I didn't know what to do. I was on all those pain meds. It hurt to stand or sit or lie down. The only thing I was trained to do since I was seventeen was how to kill somebody. But it's not really a marketable skill. It kind of works against you, even.

"Like, I got in a fight with my stepdad. He came at me with a baseball bat. He swung and I caught it and I jerked it away from him. And you should have seen the look in his face. He knew he'd done the wrong thing. I just destroyed him. He had some messed-up vertebras in his neck. I broke his jaw, his eye socket, a couple of his ribs.

"When the police came I explained it to them—he came at me with a baseball bat, you know? Self-defense. But they arrested me for aggravated assault, assault with a deadly weapon, because of my Marine Corps training.

"After that I started abusing drugs bad again—I ain't going to lie to you, I started shooting up OxyContin and crap like that. I was on drugs so bad like I had to pawn my TV, my car, everything I had. It's just like, I don't know. I went to war, I did this, I did that. I have lots of feelings inside my head; I try to tuck them away—but they always come out. I don't know how to deal with these feelings. You can ask her: Sometimes I'll just flip out and like our dog will do the littlest thing and like, what was it? What did Roxy-dog do that one night where I was wanting to take her out back and like just like blow her head off?"

Chelsea: "I don't remember what she did."

"She did something to me and I was just so pissed that I was like—"

"The one thing we fight about is the dogs," Chelsea says, "There's a difference between discipline and beating them, you know?"

"I don't like hurting her," Cybula says. He looks down the barrel of his weapon, making sure the chamber is clean. "I'm going to the VA now. They put me on Xanax so I'm more chill."

"He still has the worse dreams," Chelsea says.

"Tell him about the time you got up without telling me. Remember I grabbed you?"

"He sometimes just starts crying. And like, at first, I didn't want to wake him up, you know? I was afraid or whatever. So I finally asked him, I was like, 'If you have a bad dream, do you want me to wake you up?' And he was like, 'I feel like such a pussy for crying.'"

"And then I've also sleepwalked," Cybula says. "Like I woke up in my boxers standing out in the woods here behind the house. And I was like, *What am I doing outside?* It was crazy. Sometimes I can be so happy. Like, alive? And then all of the sudden I'll just be like, my head is down. And she'll be like, 'What's wrong?' And I'll just be like, 'Nothin,' and then I'll cry or something. And then sometimes I'll just be really, really *mad*. And she'll go, 'What's wrong, honey?' And I'll just be like 'Don't talk to me.' That's why I got this pistol. Believe it or not, I don't want to hurt nobody. It's like an outlet, you know? Like when I get pissed I'll come outside and shoot it. That's what we did in the Marine Corps. We let off steam by shooting guns and stuff like that."

Chelsea takes two cigarettes from the pack, hands one to her man. Gallantly he lights hers first; she smiles at him adoringly. They don't know it yet, but she's pregnant.

(2011)

If Someone Shot You In The Face And Left You For Dead, Would You Try To Save His Life?

Ten days after the terrorist attacks of 9/11, Rais Bhuiyan, a Muslim immigrant from Bangladesh living outside Dallas, was shot in the face by a white supremacist determined to kill some "A-rabs" for revenge. Ten years later, after a harrowing recovery, Bhuiyan mounted an international crusade against hate. His first cause: attempting to win a stay of execution for the man who'd attacked him.

A small brown man with one good eye is driving through his Texas-sized apartment development in northeastern Dallas, on the way to dinner. It is September, nearly a week after the tenth anniversary of 9/11. He's chosen to take his second car, easier on gas than his BMW, a five-year old Toyota Matrix he was stuck with after cosigning a loan for a friend, a seemingly small act of Muslim charity gone puzzlingly awry, another jarring cultural lesson to add to the many he's learned since coming to America.

The night is dark, with hard rain and gusting winds, an epic cloudburst to wash away temporarily the summer's lingering triple-digit heat wave. In truth the man is a bit agitated. Thirty-eight years old, a native of Bangladesh— a former elite-military-academy cadet, Air Force pilot trainee, minimart clerk, telephone solicitor, waiter, and computer-programming student—he has been working around the clock, holding down the equivalent of two jobs. His time is at a premium. With nobody to clean or cook for him, he sometimes forgets to eat. There are phone calls to make, memos to write, an organization to create, a Web site to manage...and so many interviews to do, more and more lately, which doesn't actually bother him, because at the time of his shooting he was pretty much ignored. Over the last few months he's lost twenty pounds.

In one of his roles, Rais Bhuiyan (pronounced *Race Boo-yon*) is a six-figure-a-year supervisor of global IT for a travel company, responsible for teams of systems engineers in India, the Philippines, and England. He lives in a planned community called the Village Apartments. There are jogging paths and soccer fields, cooking classes, even a country club. Most afternoons he strolls beside a man-made lake with its central fountain, taking in the utopian panoply. The ducks like corn. The squirrels like sunflower seeds. They eat out of his hands. For the fish he brings a piece of bread; no creature unconsidered.

The other cap he wears is newer and a little less well-defined. As the founder of an organization called World Without Hate, he's dedicated himself to an international crusade against hate crime—spreading the word, offering education, trying to build a fund to assist victims, working to make his adopted country, in the words of a visiting speaker earlier this afternoon at his mosque in Richardson, Texas, "a Judeo/Christian/Muslim land where all people can live together in peace."

It's proving to be a little more difficult than he'd imagined.

In 2001, ten days after the attacks on the Pentagon and the World Trade Center towers, Bhuiyan suffered a terrorist attack of his own.

He'd been living in Dallas only four months, having moved from Manhattan, seeking a more affordable lifestyle. A year earlier, he'd experienced impossible good luck—being one of the thousands of winners among the millions who'd applied to the U.S.A.'s national green-card lottery of 2000. Even though he'd been cautioned by his friends in the immigrant community that the natives in Texas could be somewhat hostile, Bhuiyan had his heart set on bringing over his fiancée and starting a family as soon as he could. Given the promise by a friend of a job and a place to live, and with plenty of opportunities for continued education, it seemed like a perfect fit. He was already twenty-seven. He was ready to start his life.

Just after noon on September 21, Bhuiyan was working an extra shift at a Texaco station—subbing for a friend— when a twenty-one-year old meth addict and father of four with a shaved head, a long criminal record, and an array of racist tats did what he said "millions of Americans wanted to do" after 9/11—he walked into the minimart where Bhuiyan was standing behind the counter and, from a distance of about four feet, took his revenge with a sawed-off shotgun.

Mark Stroman would later tell police he was hunting Arabs. His claim to have a sister who died in one of the Twin Towers was never confirmed. Bhuiyan was one of three victims. The others were immigrants from Pakistan and India. Neither was Arab. Neither survived. Between them they left behind two wives and six children.

Stroman was tried for the murder of the Indian, a forty-nine-year-old Hindu named Vasudev Patel. That shooting, also in a convenience store, at close range with a .44-caliber pistol, was caught on tape. Bhuiyan's place of work, in a bad part of Dallas called Buckner, had no security monitoring. After reading in the newspaper about the murder of the forty-six year old Pakistani, Waqar Hasan, in a grocery store he owned, Bhuiyan dreamed for three successive nights that he'd be killed in similar fashion. He pleaded with his boss/friend/roommate to reinstate the cameras—or at the very least to hire a security guard.

On the fourth morning, Stroman entered the Buckner Food Mart wearing a baseball cap, sunglasses, and a red bandana tied around his lower face like an outlaw in an old cowboy movie, the kind Bhuiyan and his seven brothers and sisters used to watch with subtitles in their comfortable middle-class household in Dhaka, the capital of Bangladesh, in the years after George Harrison's landmark aid concert. (Bhuiyan's father was a government telecommunications engineer who spent much of his year working in the United Arab Emirates.)

When Stroman entered the store carrying his sawed-off, double-barreled shotgun, Bhuiyan figured he was about to experience his second robbery. The first time, he thought the robber was trying to sell him a handgun—locals were always trying to sell him TVs and watches and other stolen merch.

Bhuiyan asked, "How much?"

The man cocked the hammer.

This time, Bhuiyan was prepared. He did the sensible thing and immediately emptied the cash register. Per his boss's instructions, there was only about $150 in the drawer. "Sir, here's the money," Bhuiyan said. "Please don't shoot me."

Then Stroman asked, "Where are you from?"

Oddly, it was not an unusual question in the days after September 11. Just the day before, in fact, Bhuiyan had been talking about Islam and geography with a couple of friendly police officers who always stopped by for sodas and snacks—they were interested to learn that the religion was practiced by people who weren't even Arab.

Bhuiyan heard an explosion. At first it seemed far away; one of the random gunshots typical of the neighborhood. Then his body was jerked back and he felt "a million bee stings" on his face. He looked down and saw blood pouring as if from an open faucet from his right side, and he thought, *Maybe my brain is going to come out pretty soon; I have to keep it from spilling out.* He applied both palms to his slippery head. He wondered, *Am I dying today?*

Then he hit the deck.

Stroman showed no remorse at trial. In 2002 he was found guilty and sentenced to death for the shooting of Patel. His was one of the first such cases to be tried under the state's new hate-crime statutes, created partly in response to the death of James Byrd Jr., an African-American man from Texas who was beaten, urinated upon, bound by his ankles with a heavy logging chain, and dragged behind a pickup truck for three miles, causing decapitation.

Bhuiyan survived with thirty-eight pellets embedded in his face, scalp, and eye. Because he had no health insurance and no one to drive him consistently to treatment, he lost the sight in his right eye—he now sees only blobs of light. The pellets irritate the nerves under his skin. He doesn't sleep on his right side. Getting a haircut can be agony if the barber isn't careful.

Since the shooting, he has had two of the most bothersome pellets removed—a process that involved much yanking, like an old-fashioned dentist pulling a tooth, and copious amounts of blood. The worst piece was embedded in the center of his forehead. A devout Muslim, he prays five times a day. Every time his head touched the floor, the pain was excruciating. The lead sphere was flattened into the shape of a pancake by the impact against his skull. His mother always told him he was hardheaded. Now he knew for sure. He chose not to keep the souvenir.

After Stroman was remanded to death row, Bhuiyan got on with his life the best he could. He had no car, no money, tens of thousands of dollars in medical bills, and no place to live—the friend and employer who had brought him here made him feel like a burden. Even so, Bhuiyan was too proud to go home. He'd given up his future in Bangladesh's more elite circles to try his hand at the American dream. He'd promised success to his beloved mother and father, who'd backed his decisions and happily financed his whim. Meanwhile, his fiancée had moved along; she could no longer wait. There was nothing left for him.

Bhuiyan stayed in Dallas, living on couches. For a long time he was afraid to go outside. He probably suffered from post-traumatic stress but couldn't afford counseling. In 2003, after much prayer, he decided to seek employment as a waiter in a restaurant. What better way to reacclimate himself to people, right? He started at Olive Garden. Along the way, the Red Cross determined he was not eligible for payment from its 9/11 fund and could not give him anything but free food, which he adamantly declined. Later, with the help of a friendly doctor, Bhuiyan's medical bills were paid by a state-run victim's compensation fund. With most of his debt cleared, he was able to open a new bank account, rent an apartment, apply for credit, buy a car.

By November of 2009, after attending for free a computer school owned by a member of his mosque (and starting a company to promote the restaurant software he designed with his teacher), Bhuiyan felt strong and flush enough to keep what he'd thought was a deathbed promise to Allah: to make the *hajj* to Mecca.

Because his father had already been three times, he took his mother, who had never made the sacred pilgrimage, one of the five pillars of Islam. The pair stayed an entire month, praying among the millions of faithful.

Bhuiyan returned to Dallas a different man. "I could feel that I'm not worried about myself anymore," he would later explain. "Instead, I started thinking about this guy, Mark Stroman, who is waiting behind bars for the last nine years to die."

"He's a human being like me," Bhuiyan remembers thinking. "He made a mistake. Definitely it's a terrible mistake, no doubt about that. But in Koran it says very clearly that if you're in a situation like mine, either you can ask for justice, you can ask for financial compensation, or you can forgive. And once you forgive, that means he is forgiven; he is not supposed to go and serve time behind bars. Once I forgive him, what is the point of punishing him again? That is Islamic teaching. I suffered the worse I could. These two women who lost their husbands, and their children, they suffered, too. But there is nothing we can get now by killing Mark Stroman. He must be saved."

Polite and somewhat impish, with an endearingly bashful smile and a musical South Asian lilt, Bhuiyan set out to implement a public campaign for Stroman. He got busy on the Internet, doing research. He attended fundraising programs, listened to speakers, began to build a network. Finally he met a professor at Southern Methodist University, Rick Halperin, who had a long history of battle against the death penalty in Texas. Over the last decade, despite a dip in violent crime, the Lone Star State has averaged twenty-four executions per year, the highest rate in the modern history of the death penalty.

Halperin is the former chairman of the board of Amnesty International U.S.A. With his help, on May 16, 2011—about eighteen months after Bhuiyan's hajj and his pledge to save Stroman—an article was published in the *Dallas Morning News*: BANGLADESH IMMIGRANT SEEKS STAY OF EXECUTION FOR MAN WHO SHOT HIM IN 9/11 ATTACK.

In a longish op-ed piece that ran a few days later in the *Morning News*, Bhuiyan called for a reduction of Stroman's death sentence to life without parole.

"I forgave Stroman many years ago," Bhuiyan wrote. "I believe he was ignorant and not capable of distinguishing between right and wrong; otherwise, he wouldn't have done what he did.... I believe that by sparing Stroman's life, we will give him a chance to realize, through time and maturity, that hate doesn't bring a peaceful solution to any situation. Perhaps, if given the opportunity, it might generate such a positive influence on him that he may want to become a spokesman against hate crimes."

There was only one problem: Stroman was due to be executed in exactly two months. The date was set: July 20, 2011.

Overnight, Rais Bhuiyan became internationally known—the subject of articles, TV interviews, blogs, and news reports. Yet, he got nowhere in his quest. With the clock ticking on Stroman's execution, Bhuiyan bounced back and forth between Stroman's lawyers and state officials. Mired in law and red tape, Bhuiyan finally found an attorney to take his case pro bono.

Together with a anti-death penalty group called GRACE, Khurrum Wahid pushed Bhuiyan's case through the state courts on grounds of victims' rights. But as it became clear that any thought of commutation in Governor Rick Perry's Texas was folly, Bhuiyan's team sought at least to engineer a face-to face meeting with Stroman.

On the day of the scheduled execution, with eleventh-hour legal wrangling still proceeding in the courts, Bhuiyan made one last, unsuccessful attempt to call the prison in Huntsville and speak to Stroman.

Moments later he called an Israeli filmmaker who'd been following Stroman for years. Ilan Ziv was at the prison, talking with Stroman. Ziv said that Stroman was expressing remorse for his crimes, his racist beliefs. He'd been especially touched by Bhuiyan's unselfish campaign to have his sentence commuted.

Ziv offered to facilitate a conversation via speakerphone. Bhuiyan accepted. Late that afternoon, his legal team gathered around. This is part of the their exchange, as taped by Ziv:

"Hey, man," Stroman said in his heavy southern accent. "Thank you for everything you've been trying to do for me. You are inspiring. Thank you from the heart, dude."

"Mark, you should know that I am praying to God, the most compassionate and gracious. I forgive you and I do not hate you. I never hated you—"

"Hey, Rais, they are telling me to hang up now. I will try to call in a minute."

The line went dead. Bhuiyan looked frustrated. "I never got the chance to tell him *why* I forgive him" he lamented. "That was the whole point, and I didn't get to say it." He looked out the window. "This is *not* what I wanted."

At 8:53 p.m., Mark Stroman was put to death by lethal injection.

Rain drums the roof of Bhuiyan's Toyota hatchback as he maneuvers through his vast apartment complex. It is three days before the tenth anniversary of his shooting, which he has since recognized as one of those blessings from Allah that sometimes come wrapped in the cloak of misfortune.

After a long and emotional final interview, Bhuiyan and I have set out for dinner. He drives past the lake. Headlights glare off slick asphalt, wipers drag and screech across the windshield. Since Stroman's execution, and on through the run-up to the 9/11 anniversary, Bhuiyan's career as a spokesperson has taken off. Each week brings more inquiries and interviews. Nearly every weekend he is jetting somewhere to give a speech. Recently, he participated in a march and interfaith service in a Jewish temple in Washington, D.C. In November he will speak at two different Amnesty International conferences.

His paying work aside, with the attendant complications and office politics, he has a million plates in the air: Helping Stroman's down-on-her-luck twenty-something daughter and grandchild. Helping Stroman's son when he gets out of prison, where he is serving time for aggravated robbery. Helping the widows and children of Stroman's other victims. Navigating the fraught world of donations and volunteers. Working with a lawyer to legally charter his organization. Answering tons of e-mail; working on a book; managing all the media requests ...

"I'm really confused right now," he is saying. His voice is troubled; his hands are at ten and two on the steering wheel. "I'm thinking, *What should I do?* I know my destiny is to move toward helping people full time. But is it the right time to quit my job? Because right now I have the energy. I'm single, I have time, the momentum is there. But I only have savings enough to last three months. Maybe it is smarter to wait for a year and save —"

As Bhuiyan speaks, a tow truck to our left pulls away abruptly from the curb with its payload. Jacked up high, with huge tires and lots of lights mounted on its gleaming chrome exoskeleton, it is heading directly for Bhuiyan's left front fender. Clearly the driver doesn't see us.

At the last moment, Bhuiyan sees him and swerves to his right, just out of the way. The driver lays on his horn. Bhuiyan waves feyly out the window—*so sorry, no worries*— and continues on.

A few hundred yards down the street, we stop at the complex's exit. We sit in silence, waiting for an ebb in the traffic on a large and busy avenue.

Suddenly the tow truck reappears. It pulls up to our left, beside Bhuiyan. The driver guns the engine. He trains a bright halogen light down into Bhuiyan's face and unleashes a fusillade of curses.

Bhuiyan immediately raises both palms. He apologizes profusely in a supplicating voice. "I am so sorry, I did not see!"

The curses continue.

"Turn off the light, *motherfucker!*" I holler.

"Yes!" Bhuiyan hollers, joining in. "Turn off the *damn* light!"

We bellow back and forth for a few long seconds. Then the driver yells, "You're a fucking jackass!" There is a certain finality in his tone. He rolls forward into traffic, pulling a smaller pickup behind him.

A man more experienced in the subtle ways of American culture might have known at this point that the altercation was pretty much over. Or maybe Bhuiyan did know but couldn't help himself. He might be five foot six, but he was trained in a military academy for much of his youth, after all. Or maybe he is only human.

In any case, as the tow truck begins pulling away, Rais Bhuiyan finally boils over. He sticks his head fully out the car window into the dark and stormy night and yells, in a loud but somehow still endearingly innocent-sounding voice: "YOU ARE THE JACKASS, TOO!!!!!"

For one long beat, Bhuiyan's words hang in the humid air.

Then the tow truck's brake lights turn angry red.

The back-up lights come on, white and bright.

The rig reverses direction.

"Go, go, go!" I yell.

And like the fighter pilot he once hoped to be, Bhuiyan punches the gas and the Toyota fishtails across several lanes of traffic.

"Dumb redneck Texans!" he hisses.

Bhuiyan eats his roll, chewing thoughtfully. "Now I feel bad that I raised my voice. I'm feeling guilty right now. I'm feeling pressure: Why I could not control myself. It's not me."

I remind him he's been through a lot. He tells me about hearing Stroman interviewed in Ziv's documentary footage. "Mark was telling that in this kind of situation he was taught to fight back and do worse to somebody than what they did to you. That was Mark Stroman's teaching."

He butters the last piece of his roll. "There's a lot of Mark Stroman on the street. In this country and also in the world there's a lot of hate. If you don't like my color or my faith or my accent, well, I cannot change because that is the way I was born. If you don't like me, that's okay. Just don't cause any pain or suffering.

"In this kind of situation I always feel scared that they are going to, you know, pull gun," he says. "It happened in Dallas a couple of times. People killed on the highway. One because he was driving too slow."

He doesn't mention the pellets in his own face.

"The low-hanging fruit is *Can I change myself?* It doesn't cost anything. Change your vision. Change your mentality. It's important to let people know not to hate each other because they're different. If you really want to hate something, hate that attitude."

(2011)

The Zen of Big Balls Pete

As unlikely as it seems, Pete Carroll is one of the winningest coaches in college football history—a Grateful Dead-loving, former undersized D-back from hippified Marin County who believes in Zen philosophy, tweets nonstop, and jogs everywhere he goes, even to the bathroom. Can he make it as a coach in the NFL?

Pete Carroll, the winningest active coach in college football, parted the crowd of six hundred alumni donors, many of them dressed in cardinal and gold, who were milling about the ballroom at the Hyatt Regency in Irvine, California, juggling cocktails, items to be autographed, and long strings of raffle tickets hawked by a multicultural array of leggy, spandex-clad Song Girls and ardent volunteers.

To the rousing strains of the University of Southern California's fight song—offered by a spirited if somewhat pudgy contingent of brass players and percussionists from the marching band, with their trademark Trojan helmets and sunglasses and spats—the silver-haired dynamo (seventy-nine wins in the last eighty-six games, two national championships, three Heisman Trophy winners, fifty-three NFL draft picks in eight years at the helm) trotted up the steps to the stage, joining USC basketball coach Tim Floyd, who himself was wearing a cardinal-and-gold repp tie. No one suspected that this would be Floyd's last appearance as a citizen of Troy. A couple of weeks later, from the safe haven of his native Mississippi, Floyd would submit his resignation, carefully not commenting on an alleged payola scandal involving basketball phenom O.J. Mayo, who had spent a year with the rejuvenated USC program (three NCAA tournament appearances in the last three years, a school record) on his way to the pros.

Carroll was wearing an expensive-looking dark suit and a crisp white shirt—his own tie was a shade of robin's-egg blue that appeared to be dangerously close to the shade worn by crosstown rival UCLA.

This was the first of seven scheduled tandem appearances, the annual Coaches Tour. With the shadow cast upon Floyd's program, there was an injured, expectant, wagons-circled feeling in the crowd, which ranged in age from freshman to geezer. Dragging along behind the Mayo story as B matter was the NCAA investigation of former USC running back Reggie Bush. Three years after allegations surfaced that the Heisman winner had accepted some $300,000 in cash and gifts from would-be sports marketers, the case was open but inactive; nothing had been proven.

Which meant, of course, that nothing had been *dis*proven, either, at least in the eyes of the media, which seemed determined to continue "dredging it up," in the words of one alum between sips of his gin and tonic.

Loitering at the back of the ballroom, under supervision of Trojan press aides, were two such agitators. One reporter was from the *Los Angeles Times*. He was all over the Mayo deal, a colorful case involving an alleged envelope full of hundred-dollar bills. I was there for Carroll, a product of northern California's laid-back Marin County, high school class of 1969; a frequent reveler at Grateful Dead shows at the Fillmore; a two-time All Pacific Coast Athletic Conference free safety; a coach known for his uncanny ability to influence young men and win college football games, which he has done at an 85.4 percent clip since arriving at USC. In the process of honing his craft and his philosophy, Carroll had begun to emerge as a regional pied piper, a man who, in his own words, has the "ability to convene people" in one of the world's most powerful cities. His Facebook page has maxed out his allotment of friends. Nearly fifty thousand souls follow his blog and his tweets on Twitter, which include inspirational messages ("Been thinking all morning about how you only got one life to live. . .so you better live it or it'll live you"), notes from the Lakers' victory party ("Watching Kobe and the mayor rock out to Lil Wayne —so insane!"), and songs of the day (everything from "Live Your Life," by T.I. and Rihanna, to "Add It Up," by the Violent Femmes). Carroll had already turned down my first request for an interview. An aide had suggested I drive the seventy miles to Irvine to press my case. "He has a hard time saying no in person," I'd been told.

As Carroll settled into his director's chair on the stage, a Saturday-afternoon-tailgate-party atmosphere prevailed. Servers began bringing the salad course, a prelude to the chicken with fennel sauce. Off to one side, a rowdy group of thirtyish guys began to chant:

"Big Balls Pete!" they hooted several times in succession, meanwhile playing their cupped palms up and down in front of themselves, symbolically measuring the weight of Carroll's giant *cojones*.

Imagine for a moment the historic Los Angeles Coliseum, filled to capacity with a USC football crowd of more than ninety-three thousand, the majority doing this same cupped-hand thing, *Big Balls Pete!*, a celebration of Carroll's confident tenacity, his tendency to *go for it*—on fourth down, in noontime pickup basketball games, at a fantasy-football camp for grown men...in every single endeavor he undertakes...from his efforts with ghetto youth (A Better LA) to his partnership with the new owners of the L.A. Marathon...to his recent enlistment, by the U.S. government, to help focus the training of small-group military units (a military squad of 12 men closely resembles a football side of eleven)... to the little competitions he is constantly playing against himself, like the one where he has to throw a football his age in yards every year on his birthday, fifty-eight this autumn, or the one where he stands in the middle of the practice field and tosses his wad of used bubble gum toward the sideline, trying to make it land on the fresh white paint.

The moderator for the evening was a man named John Jackson. A former NFL pro who'd played wide receiver at USC, he is now an ESPN radio announcer. His first question concerned spring football practice. With quarterback Mark Sanchez gone from the team a year early to the NFL—a move Carroll had privately and publically opposed—how was the 2009 season shaping up?

"There's something I want to say before we get rolling," Carroll said gravely, causing Jackson's pearly smile to wither. "We have members of the *media* here—" the emphasis his—"that we're *really* happy to have." He rolled his eyes theatrically, issued a large fake smile.

Big laugh from the crowd.

"So we have to be careful and respectful of all the issues that are about," he continued. "We want to respect the media... *and not tell them a thing!*"

Hoots and laughter.

"Let's introduce them," Coach Floyd said archly, warming to the game. In the grip of his viscous southern accent, the idea sounded ominous.

Everyone in the place turned around, looked toward the back of the room where I was standing with the *Times* guy. Two hacks caught in the headlights, we had no recourse but to acknowledge with a little wave.

"Honestly," Carroll said, addressing the crowd with all earnestness, "we can't talk about *everything*. So you can ask great questions. . . and we'll answer the ones we *like*."

"*Only* the ones we like," Floyd added, a dead man sitting in a director's chair. He seemed to sense it.

"As a matter of fact," Carroll said to the moderator Jackson, puffing himself up lampoonishly, "that first question you asked? I'm not *frickin'* answering it."

Huge laugh, followed by applause.

"Big Balls Pete!" chanted the rowdy guys in the back.

Carroll paced the cardinal-colored carpet at the front of Heritage Hall auditorium at USC, speaking in a confessional tone. Behind him was a giant aerial photo of the Trojan's home field, the Los Angeles Memorial Coliseum, and the adjacent campus. Sitting in the seats in front of him were thirty-six middle-aged professional men (and two women) who'd paid up to $3,000 to participate in this 2009 Trojan Chalk Talk, two days of intense exposure to Carroll and his program. The coaching staff lined the walls on either side of the room—offense to his right, defense to his left—all hands on deck.

As a character, Carroll seems perfectly cast. His granite jaw bespeaks his suborn streak of courage. His eyes perfectly match the blasphemous tie from the other night. His skin—pale, soft, and papery —is full of fine wrinkles; it seems much older than rest of him. His nose runs a zigzag pattern down the middle of his face, breaking first to the right and then to the left... a pass route the Trojan playbook calls Z-quick.

As always when he's talking football, his loopy, free-flowing, Bay Area cadence had morphed itself into a southern twang. He was wearing a cardinal-and-gold polo he'd just opened, fresh from the plastic bag—his office upstairs is awash in Nike swag, though the tennis shorts he was wearing would be recycled several times over the next week, memorable for the quarter-sized stain on the butt that he didn't seem to notice or care about.

We were just around the corner from the atrium entryway of Heritage Hall, the physical home of Trojan football, where a visitor is greeted by a line of seven Heismans (won, in order, by Mike Garrett, O.J. Simpson, Charles White, Marcus Allen, Carson Palmer, Matt Leinart, and Reggie Bush).). Larger than you'd expect, enshrined in huge glass cases, these and other keepsakes lend to the building the air of a museum. There are NCAA championship trophies, bronze medallions honoring Olympians, the 150-pound Gauntlet Trophy (awarded each year to either USC or UCLA for best overall athletic performance, looking like a giant's armored glove abandoned on a medieval battlefield). Even a bust of the actor John Wayne, who played football at USC in the 1920s under his real name, Marion Morrison. Every day football players from the current roster—on campus most of the summer to take one class and work out unofficially with trainers—tread unselfconsciously through this forest of hardware, through their own moments of history, toward the locker room. Later they will remember this room and revisit, perhaps bring children; right now they pay it no mind.

One week after our brief meeting in Irvine, I'd received an email summoning me to campus; the coach had changed his mind. I'd reported for duty yesterday. ESPN was filming one of those clever in-house commercials they do. Carroll played the straight man to college Game Day commentator Kirk Herbstreit, who would later come by Carroll's office and ask for a lesson on defending the spread offense. (Additionally the day would bring visits from high-powered coaches Nick Saban and Urban Meyer, who were also in town on ESPN's tab; the summer-quiet campus, normally an oasis of grass commons and purple flowering jacaranda trees, had been overrun with the network's people and equipment.) Though I was instructed that the coach wanted me "on his hip" during my visit, over the course of the next week I would know the frustration of a defensive back assigned single coverage on a fleet and stealthy wide-receiver. It didn't help that he literally trotted everywhere he went, inside or out. To an assistant coach's office. To the playing field. To the men's room. To his noon-time pickup basketball games. Dutifully I trotted after him.

Like any Carroll undertaking, this fantasy camp for adults had been carefully orchestrated. Prior to this kickoff lecture, the staff had been briefed at several typically raucous meetings around the oblong conference table upstairs in their suite of offices. At one gathering, Carroll had presided while wielding a baseball bat; at another, a Nerf football flew back and forth around the room for nearly an hour, punctuating the serious talk.

This morning had started as usual, with breakfast at this morning's 7:00 a.m. meeting. As he does every day, Carroll has treated his staff—a personal expense that runs him nearly $500 per week; one of the graduate assistants (GAs) picks it up from the food wagon that parks next door at the construction site for the new $175 million film-school addition, donated by George Lucas.

At all times, no matter where Carroll is—checking e-mails, watching film, mulling defensive schemes, holding a meeting, trading zippy e-mails with his buddy Will Ferrell— there is music playing at party volume, classic oldies like, Stevie Wonder's "Living for the City," War's "Low Rider," Santana's "Black Magic Woman." Carroll will absently sing a line or a chorus, dance a step or two; he and his assistant coaches will challenge one another to name that tune; they'll argue about who sang what song on what album during what year. Several different aides-de-camp maintain Carroll's iPod and his Mac; his secret shopping addiction, he says, is iTunes. Carroll is constantly playing drums on his thighs or on the table, air guitar on his baseball bat; he is one of those men of a certain age for whom music is definitive. Despite his gnarled right ring finger, bent south at an obtuse angle toward the pinkie, he plays a passable keyboard (and throws a tight spiral—on the field, he is almost always engaged in a game of catch). To benefit A Better LA, he sat in on an original song (and performed onstage at the Roxy on Sunset Boulevard), with the artist Kelley James. His daughter, Jaime, twenty-seven, a former USC volleyball player, sang on the track as well. His youngest son, Nate, is twenty-two, a senior at USC. His eldest, Brennan, thirty, is known as BC. He played tight end for Pitt. Now he's the tight-end coach and chief recruiter for the Trojans. At the conference table, BC is always the loudest and most boisterous. He always sits to Carroll's immediate right; he stopped calling him Dad some years ago. They have the same blazing blue eyes and granite jaw; they speak to each other like two parts of the same brain.

"We both have ADD," Brennan said. "We're weird. It probably helps more than it hurts, being a little off the wall. In this profession there probably aren't a whole lot of people who would pattern their styles after the way he is, and now I'm the junior version of that. Originally I hadn't planned on coaching, but it was more important to come back and be able to do something with him as opposed to going to do my own thing. If we were doing something else we'd probably be working together too. He just happened to be coaching ball and I needed a job. I got entrenched."

In person Carroll appears smaller than you might expect, and more crooked. Like that of many of his recruiting prospects, his reported height (six feet) seems exaggerated. Peter Clay Carroll, son of a liquor distributor and a fifties homemaker, was a late bloomer. Barely 110 pounds as an incoming freshman at Redwood High School, he was required to bring a special doctor's clearance in order to go out for football, a lack of size that eventually plagued his attempt at a professional career, which came to an end after a tryout with the Honolulu Hawaiians of the World Football League. His various official bios often note he was thwarted in his efforts by a shoulder injury in training camp; that explanation might be a bit convenient, Carroll allows today.

He is a man who has always been happiest and most comfortable with a ball in his hand. He was the fastest runner in his elementary school class, voted Athlete of the Year at Redwood High. Even today he is a guy who will spend an extra hour in the gym playing a dogged three-game match of one-on-one basketball against a six-five undergrad he'd played once before. After being down 6–2 in the final game, the rubber match, he came back to win. "I'm not gonna let this guy have this story, 'I beat the coach.'" Carroll said. "Instead it's: 'This old coach beat me. *Again.*'"

The cartilage is gone in his left knee, causing his lower leg to angle outward as he moves, adding a slight limp to his bumptious

gate. He says he has no spinal issues, but his neck seems perpetu-
ally stiff; to speak to someone next to him he'll turn his whole body
instead of just his head. The frozen tilt of his pelvis, the grabbing
hamstrings, the slow and painful rise from a chair, are reminiscent
of a man with a couple of bad discs. (After the one-on-one basketball death match with the kid, Carroll rose to diagram a play on the
whiteboard for ESPN's Herbstreit. The coach appeared so painfully
debilitated that the commentator let out a sympathetic groan.)

"Once you're a football player, you're a football player for life,"
Carroll will later say. You could substitute the world athlete just as
well. "You always think of yourself in terms of that. We all do. It's
hard to get rid of when you can't play anymore. I'm still pissed. I'm
still pissed. I still think I can play. I still want to, you know."

After washing out of the WFL, Carroll worked for a short time
as a roofing materials salesman. He got his first shot at coaching in
1974, as a graduate assistant coach for defensive backs and receivers
at his alma mater, the University of the Pacific in Stockton, where
he met his wife, Glena, a former standout volleyball player. Glena
Carroll does not speak to the press. Brennan, 6'4", allows that he got
his height from his mother's side. "My mother did a really good job
of keeping everyone sane," he said. "She's still always right. Dad's
like one of the kids. She pretty much runs the show."

To be a professional football coach is to belong to a large
fraternity. There is all kinds of nepotism and attention to legacy;
everyone seems to be separated by only one or two degrees. One of
Carroll's early mentors was legendary NFL defensive coach Monte
Kiffin. Carroll in turn would mentor Monte's boy Lane, the new
coach at Tennessee (And eventual coach at USC.) Carroll himself
got his first two assistant jobs (at Pacific and Arkansas) through a
U of P mentor. Later there were positions at Ohio State and North
Carolina State.

In 1984, Carroll jumped to the NFL as defensive-back coach
for the Buffalo Bills. The New York Jets gave him his first try at head
coach in 1994. The team finished 6–10. Carroll was fired after one
year. In 1997, he succeeded Bill Parcells as coach of the New England
Patriots. Tough shoes to fill, it turned out. Eventually, he was fired.
("In three years in New England we actually did better than most

people think," he'll later say, a justice-seeking look on his face. "We were 27–21, won the AFC division title, went to the playoffs twice.")

"One day after I was fired, I was home in my office," Carroll told the fantasy campers assembled in Heritage Auditorium, all of whom were swaddled in USC merch, free with registration. He'd been speaking for roughly ten minutes; this being a first time event, you got the feeling that he wasn't giving a canned speech; it felt like he was coming from the heart. Earlier, several of his staff had come up to the podium. They'd been moved to near-tears when speaking about Carroll and the program.

"I was reading one of coach John Wooden's books. Of course I knew his story about UCLA, the great basketball program, and all that stuff, but I was reading it to confirm—well, I don't know why exactly I was reading it. Let's face it, I'd just been fired. I had plenty of time on my hands.

"I got to the point in the book where he said that he was in his sixteenth year at UCLA before he won his first national championship. He'd coached other places before; he'd won Pac-10 championships, he had a great winning record. But as soon as I saw that, I smacked the book closed." He clapped his hands together; the loud sound had a startling effect on the rapt crowd. "Shit. It hit me just like I got punched right in the forehead!

"Once he got it, he just nailed it. Once he figured out what was right for him, how to engineer his program in the way that best exemplified his philosophy, nobody could touch him. He wins ten of the next twelve championships, and then he retires, just goes off into basketball heaven. How beautiful is that?

"*And then I thought, Oh, crap, it took him sixteen years. And I don't even have a job. I better get my act together.* I started working that moment. I got a notebook out and started writing. I asked myself: *What is my philosophy, what is my approach?* And I came up with the thought that if I was going to describe me, the first thing I'd say is I'm a competitor. Just one simple line. I'm a competitor. That's my whole life since I was three, four years old. I tried to beat my big brother in every game we played. All of his friends would just laugh at how hard I'd try. I'd be fighting and scratching and crying and whatever it took, from the time I was a little kid. Reading Wooden, I realized: If I'm gonna be a competitor, if I'm ever going to do great things, I'm going to have to carry a message that's strong and clear and nobody's going to miss the point ever about what I'm all about.

"From there, the next thought that came to mind was Jerry Garcia of the Grateful Dead."

Carroll stopped pacing, looked up and surveyed the crowd, expecting some acknowledgement....

But all he saw was a sea of blank faces. In fact, in Carroll's private writings—some of which he shared with the understanding they would remain off the record—he mentions a wide range of influences, including psychologist Abraham Maslow (self-actualization), author Tim Gallwey (Inner Tennis), countercultural Swiss psychologist Carl Jung, Tibetan Buddhist monk and meditation master Chogyam Trungpa, and Zen master D.T. Suzuki. Not exactly the normal philosophical territory of a football coach.

"Jerry Garcia said that he didn't want his band to be the best ones doing something," Carroll explained slowly, wanting the words to sink in. "He wanted them to be the only ones doing it. To be all by yourself out there doing something that nobody else can touch—that's the thought that guides me, that guides this program:

"We're going to do things better than it's ever been done before in everything we do, and we're going to compete our ass off. And we're gonna see how far that takes us."

A few minutes before seven on a Saturday morning the queues were already forming outside Heritage Hall. It was time for yet another football camp, this one for actual players. High school kids wearing colorful Under Armour and shower sandals, their cleats strung over their shoulders, were packed butts to nuts, like so many skewers of multi-culti shish kebab, their accompanying family members settling in for the day's long haul—most will picnic along the sidelines of the Howard Jones practice field, one of the few in the college ranks with an open policy during the season. (That the neighborhood around the university is historically dicey would keep most of the families on campus until 4:30 p.m., when the camp ended with the fastest-man contest.) By the time the doors opened, more than 350 had registered, at a reasonable sixty-five dollars a pop, some clutching highlight DVDs, others just out for the thrill of being coached by Carroll and his staff. A dozen of high school juniors and seniors in attendance were actually scholarship worthy—the staff knew well who they were.

Upstairs, in coach's country, a game day atmosphere prevailed. In the common area are display cases with the NFL uniforms of former Trojan greats—Frank Gifford, Pat Hayden, Junior Seau, Marcus Allen... an awesome list, all the way through Steeler All-Pro Troy Polamalu. The opposite wall is dominated by reproductions of every *Sports Illustrated* cover that has ever featured USC. There is an illustrated timeline of team highlights, dates of all eleven national championships and trophies everywhere, one or two of them noticeably off-kilter, like maybe they'd been dropped.

The staff meets in the War Room. (In a culture so steeped in tradition, everything has a fancy name.) Around the rectangular wood table are fourteen high-backed leather swivel chairs; each of the assistant coaches takes their same chair every time, with Carroll at the head. Behind them, a hodgepodge of stools and folding chairs for the GAs—some of them former players, some manager types who never played a down. Two walls are dominated by double white boards; panels slide to reveal depth charts of players and recruits; another whiteboard lists the name of every offensive play and the number of yards the play averaged last season. With desks occupying two corners and video-projection equipment in a third, the room is close and tight. There is much scathing humor and shit-giving, bro love in its highest form. Coming and going entails stepping over legs and is often accompanied by brotherly shoulder-squeezing and back patting, the occasional mischievous tittie tweak. Deep into a session you will find some of the larger guys reclining so far back they were practically in the lap of a GA.

At one minute before seven, one of the GAs walked in with two giant sacks of Egg McMuffins.

"All right!" somebody screamed. "The hockey pucks are here!"

"*Pucks!*"

"Go Pens!" hollered Brennan Carroll, in honor of his favorite hockey team, the Pittsburgh Penguins, who had just won the Stanley Cup.

A feeding frenzy ensued. Large men reached and grabbed for bottles of hot sauce and mini containers of jelly that live permanently at the center of the table.

"It's time to get ready for some football around this muthafucka," yelled Ken Norton Jr. The son of the former world-champion boxer, he was himself an All-Pro linebacker who retired after thirteen seasons. He never set out to be a coach. He happened to meet Carroll, things between the two men just clicked. Now he's going into his fifth year at USC. Nobody gives him shit for being a UCLA alum, particularly at the regular noontime pickup basketball games, where Norton is known to let out the monster, playing Shaq to Carroll's Kobe. Since the last NFL draft, when three USC linebackers were scooped up in the first round, people have begun joking that USC, once known as Tailback U, needs to be renamed. Norton's Egg McMuffin appeared tiny in his giant paw. His rock like mandible made quick work of it. He helped himself to another.

Carroll entered from his office across the hall, McMuffin in hand. His mouth was full, he was chewing, he was wearing the silly/happy expression of a guy who just came to work after his morning surf. "What's happenin' boys?"

"A little camp today!" hollered the defensive coordinator, Haruki Rocky Seto, "Rock" to his friends, a first-generation Japanese American legally named for the boxer Marciano (His brothers are named for Sonny Jurgensen and Johnny Bench). An undersized junior-college fullback who made the Trojans as a walk-on, Seto entered the coaching ranks as a video assistant, filming practices. When Carroll first came to town for his USC press conference nine years ago, Rocky was the kid who picked him up at the airport. Now he's in charge of Carroll's first love: defense.

"That's what I'm talkin' about!" hollered offensive-line coach Golden Pat Ruel (his actual full name). He's known Carroll since 1977, when they were both graduate assistant coaches making $172 a month at Arkansas. Like most of the veterans in the room, he's coached in the NFL, but chooses to work for Carroll for less money. "How many people do you know who enjoy driving to work every morning?" he'd testified at the fantasy camp.

Carroll talks a lot about his coaches "growing up in the program." He likes grooming his own people instead of bringing in established stars. He is proud of the fact that former assistant coaches, like Lane Kiffin and Steve Sarkisian, who recently departed for Pac-10 rival Washington, have gone on to head-coaching jobs themselves. "I want guys to come to the program knowing that I'll do everything in my power to get them the job of their dreams at some other place," he says.

In his off-the-record writings, it is clear that Carroll sees himself as a mentor; his mission is helping each person under his command make himself into the best he can be. The same goes for players or coaches. "You watch guys like Rocky Seto and my son, Brennan," Carroll says. "They had no coaching background, but they had energy, they had smarts, they had passion, they had tremendous competitiveness about them. In time, these guys started becoming our philosophy. Going in, it doesn't matter what they know, it's who they are that's important. What do they bring as people? I look for a guy who brings excitement to the game because they love being around it, a guy who can translate that love and teach it to the kids."

Gulping down the last of his sandwich, Carroll took his chair; the GA in charge of statistics fired up his iPod and the classic rock flowed. The coach ran the meeting briskly—calling on guys, fine tuning, getting annoyed here and there, speeding things along, singing a line or two of a random song—controlled chaos. And then a few final words:

"I want us to come out of our shoes on these kids today, man," he told his staff. "Let's just coach the shit out of these guys. I want lots of enthusiasm. I want you frickin' screamin' and yellin' and makin' 'em feel it. Make it memorable—but don't abuse anybody. "

Everyone laughed.

"Dude! You suck! Get the fuck out of here," bellowed offensive coordinator Johnny "Mo" Morton, who arrived a few years ago from the New Orleans Saints.

"Get off my field!" hollered special-teams coach Brian Schneider, a new hire, fresh from the Oakland Raiders

"You fuckin' suck!" hollered BC, never to be outdone in loudness by anyone.

"Let's not do that," Carroll said, playing along, aghast, his tone recalling a guy with a secondary teaching credential, which he has, along with his master's degree in physical education. "But make sure they feel us. Get 'em fired up, hustling their ass off. And have your phones in your pocket. If you see somebody great, call me and say, 'Hey, come over and see this kid.' And remember: if somebody gets hurt, don't throw a fuckin' fit, hollerin' for the trainer. Do it cool and calm like we been there before, so we don't freak anybody out."

"Unless there's a fuckin' bone stickin' out," Johnny Mo offered.

"If there's a bone sticking out, you can frickin' go crazy!" Carroll hollered, standing to leave.

"*Aaaaaiiiiiii,*" somebody cried in agony.

"*Ohhhhhhhhhaaahhhh,*" groaned somebody else.

"*Trainerrrrrrrr!*"

"Go Pens!" hollered BC.

And then they all piled out the door.

I was sitting in the tan leather overstuffed chair in Carroll's cardinal-and-gold-carpeted office, studying for the umpteenth time the oil painting of Reggie Bush slicing between Oklahoma defenders in the 2005 Orange Bowl, which the Trojans won 55–19 to capture the Bowl Championship Series title.

Carroll was doing his best to ignore me. By this point, I'd been around nearly a week; he'd taken to spending a lot of his time visiting his assistants in their various offices, creating a little competitive shell game—find the coach. It didn't help that he trotted everywhere. He is a slippery booger, to be sure. On day one of our time together, I'd mentioned to the Carroll that besides riding his hip, if he didn't mind, I'd need at least two, one-hour sit-down interviews for this story. In depth stuff, I told him, to better take stock of his soul.

He'd looked at me briefly, as if deciding what to say. Then he changed the subject. Then he got up and left the room.

Now he was sitting behind his desk, facing away from me, kicked back deep in his swivel chair, listening to music, alternating between e-mail on his Mac and texts on his iPhone. (He uses the stopwatch app to clock forties.) Photos of his family and his dog face outward on his desktop; there is one of his first grandchild, BC's son. Like his mom, BC's wife was a volleyball player.

At last Carroll swiveled around to face me. He looked over the top of his reading glasses, which hang around his neck when not in use. A tone of resignation: "What do you got for me?"

Tell me about your parents, I said.

Carroll frowned. "Nobody really gets into too much of that. We're pretty private."

Did your dad like sports?

"My dad was a great fan."

Was he an athlete?

"A little bit. He was a good golfer and stuff like that. But he was real competitive. And really smart. It was hard to beat him in anything, you know, he was really tough. He was kind of brash and all that. A good man, though, a really good man. A good average guy."

How about your mom?

"My mom was really cool. She's the one that gave me the mentality about believing in myself and trusting it, that I was always gonna be okay and that I could do things in a special way. She just pumped me up, you know?"

Were you always a good athlete?

"I was the best guy, you know, all through little league and Pop Warner and that kind of stuff. But when I went to high school, I was undersized. I didn't grow. I was behind in the whole puberty cycle. I didn't like high school. I was always pissed because I wasn't who I wanted to be—the person I knew myself to be just wasn't happening. At one time I was the best. And then in high school—shit. I looked like the mascot in the frickin' team picture.

"When I went to junior college, it started happening for me. And when I finally got to Pacific, my first year I made the all-conference team, I was captain, all that shit. It was like I had a chip on my shoulder. I had something to prove; I was gonna prove it to everybody. I've lived that way ever since."

Deep into Sunday afternoon, another camp; June is the month of camps—there is one nearly every weekend... for rising stars, for grown men, for kickers, for under-privileged children. This one was for interior linemen. The sun was hot but the air was cool; the sky was a cloudless blue. There were 260 big guys on the field, high school beef on the hoof, sweaty and red-faced, grunting and straining through an afternoon of drills—a description of the air quality in Heritage Auditorium during the post-lunch film session defies attempt. Carroll and his coaches have one more scholarship available for a lineman next year; they're keeping their eyes peeled.

Big Balls Pete strolled the field. He was again wearing the shorts with the quarter-sized butt stain; from behind his sunglasses he was watching the Category I players go through a pass-rushing drill—senior standouts, a couple of promising juniors. Starting in a down stance, each man had to explode off the line, throw a forearm at a large tackling dummy—man-sized with a weighted bottom to make it self-righting— then run around another dummy, then sprint to a orange traffic cone. Carroll's arms were crossed. The only part of him that was moving was his jaw, furiously working a piece of pink bubble gum. For once, he seemed utterly still.

What are you seeing? I asked.

"When you run around a corner, some guys just naturally plant their toe and swivel—it's called turning the toe." He pointed to the kid going through. "That guy can't do it."

He watched another. "That guy's trying to go sideways. He can't do it either."

The next kid lost his footing, fell piteously to his knees, a sweaty heap. "See how that one wanted to pick up his foot to turn? You gotta turn the toe to get around a guy," Carroll said. He planted his toe and swiveled, demonstrating.

Can you teach it?

"Certainly you can teach it. But some guys are naturally better than others. It's a certain flexibility in your ankle."

The devil's in the details, I said.

"From the discipline and repetition comes the ability to improvise and be creative," he said matter-of-factly. "If you try to be creative and improvise without the discipline, you have chaos. But once you have the discipline, once you take care of all the details, you can play with it. You gain the ability to add accent, to improvise with trust and confidence, to make it into jazz."

All around us, huge guys were hollering and grunting. Bodies collided. Whistles twittered. Large metal sleds bounced violently down the field. Carroll crossed his arms, satisfied, and returned to watching, as if from a mountaintop—a crooked, blue-eyed guru behind rose-colored Maui Jim sunglasses.

Just then, somewhere across the field, Carroll spotted something he liked. "Wow!" he exclaimed. "Did you see that? That's a nice move over there."

And off he went at a trot.

(2009)

The Demographic Man

Kenyatte Nelson is thirty-one years old—six foot two, two hundred pounds, with high cheekbones and a chiseled jaw that tapers into a sexy cleft chin. He is all of us and he is nobody at all—like the guys in the advertisements he inspects so carefully, he is a picture of who we're supposed to be, the iconic upscale consumer. Take a stroll in sensible designer shoes with the winner of Esquire's Best Dressed Real Man contest.

The Demographic Man lifts a forkful of omelet and chews thoughtfully, savoring a healthy combination of chicken and veggies, part of a dietary redirection that has left him, after six months of supreme willpower and about a trillion crunches, nearly twenty pounds lighter with six-pack abs—a boon to his self-esteem, his love life, and, most directly his tailor, who has had to alter all of his clothes.

He carries two BlackBerrys, one for work and one for personal use. The latter is a red Pearl, his favorite color, a Mother's Day special he bought himself cheap. The ringtone sounds like an old rotary telephone—deep down, beneath the need for currency, he is a nostalgic sort. For a wallet he prefers a Kenneth Cole cardholder; four cards and a folded-up twenty dollar bill for emergencies. He used to go with the money clip, but he never had enough cash to fill the damn thing. Until recently he was dating the ex-wife of a pro athlete. They first met on a Saturday night, when her girlfriend pulled him over on the highway after spotting him earlier in a club. At a bar his go-to drink is Grey Goose and tonic; at home he likes Mike's Hard Lemonade. He knows his way around the dance floor but is more comfortable in the DJ booth. Though he is not particularly religious, he eats no pork; he prays silently before every meal. He watches CNN and ESPN every morning, reads *USA Today* about three times a week, the local paper every Sunday with brunch. He also reads *The Onion* and the *Drudge Report* online and watches *Real Time with Bill Maher* and *The Colbert Report* as often as he can. "Brilliant shows," he says of the political lampoons.

He received his M.B.A. from Florida A&M University, an historically black institution. Now he's with Procter & Gamble—after eight years, he has risen to the position of brand manager for global hair color. If it involves Clairol's Nice 'n Easy hair dye, you've got to talk to him. "I own the world," he likes to say with the appropriate amounts of pride and irony. He makes about $150,000 a year. He picked the most expensive health plan offered by the company; he'd rather pay a little more to get the best. He drives a previously owned 2004 Lincoln Navigator, bought in '05 with twenty-nine thousand miles for under thirty grand—because buying a new car just seems stupid, losing value the way a new car does just driving off the lot. He doesn't care that his Navigator is maroon.

His name is Kenyatte Nelson, pronounced Ken-*yat*-tah, more on which later. He is six foot two, two hundred pounds, a Leo (August 1), thirty-one years old. He has high cheekbones and a chiseled jaw that tapers into a sexy cleft chin. His large black eyes are set against luminescent whites. His ebony face and skull have been shaved clean with a Wahl clipper, an Andis trimer, and a Gillette Fusion razor— a ritual he performs about once a week. His more intimate body hair is similarly maintained. He is all of us and he is nobody at all, he is uniquely himself. Like the guys in the advertisements, he is a picture of who we're supposed to be, the iconic upscale consumer, the Demographic Man. Lucky for him, he has spent within his means. Many have not been so fortunate. They have busted the economy trying to buy a life like his on credit.

Almost every weekend, usually both days, Kenyatte eats brunch here at the Daybreak diner. It is a large, uncomplicated space in a strip mall in Hyde Park, the hippest and most overpriced part of Cincinnati, Ohio. His own neighborhood, one exit south on I-71, is slowly up-and-coming. Nearby Xavier University is in the midst of a growth spurt, but you still see a lot of locals in long white T-shirts on the corners. We're waiting at the moment for his friend Stefan, another A&M alum. He also works at P&G, as a "consumer-knowledge market manager" in the "home sector" of products. They are the type of friends where you can go ahead and order when the other one is late.

Kenyatte's dieting campaign came about after this woman he knows pointed out a tiny pot belly he seemed to have developed. Once a nerdy, picked-on kid "built like a fuckin' stick figure, with a big head and skinny everything else," he was beginning to look a little overfed—nearly a decade of unfettered social life had begun to take its toll. Thanks to his membership at Bally Fitness (only a mile from his office) and also to the $700 Fitness Gear Ultimate Smith Machine in his home office/gym (which he uses on weekends because Ballys is twenty minutes from home and gas is expensive), he's had to have the waists of all his pants taken in nearly three inches. A lot of his jackets needed reshaping, too. He has four closets filled with suits and sport coats. The closet in the home office/gym holds seventeen winter-weight blazers: an orange corduroy Kenneth Cole, a blue velvet Dragonfly, a green velvet Hugo Boss, a camouflage number from Express, a red cotton from Boss, a couple more from Boss—Boss is his guy. The guest-room closet is crammed with summer sport coats, among them a madras and a floral print, both from Ralph Lauren. There is also a coat closet in the foyer, in which he keeps three dozen outercoats: a peak-lapel dress coat, a couple of car coats, several raincoats, a black Kenneth Cole motorcycle jacket, a Tom Cruise-style bomber jacket with a sheepskin collar that he always wears with his aviator sunglasses, and an army-green snorkel jacket with a fur-trimmed hood that he used to wear with sagging jeans and Timberland boots. (Upstairs, in the master walk-in closet, there are boxes of vintage Jordans he no longer wears but can't quite allow himself to donate.)

Luckily he has a great tailor, his tailor, a wonderful Old World craftsman named Paul who was more likely born Pablo. Since his weight loss, Kenyatte has spent more than $1,000 on alterations—obviously he couldn't fix everything, just the wardrobe staples. We won't mention the cost of the new stuff, one size smaller, 42L. Everyone who has ever lost weight knows that smaller-sized clothes are among the sweetest of all purchases. Each time he puts on his brand-new Givenchy suit—gray with a black pinstripe, cut narrow and *Mad Men*-esque—his chin juts forward and his back straightens; he feels a surge of power and confidence, a palpable psychic tumescence that says, I'm the man.

"Emily Dickinson once wrote that what makes life so grand is it will never come again," he says, blotting his lips with a napkin. "You're given this incredible blessing of life, but at the same time it's a curse, because the second it starts, it begins to end. So you have to take full advantage of it. In every aspect of my life, I try to take full advantage. If people would have the mind-set to live life with a little bit of urgency, if they just have the mind-set to try a little harder in everything they do, who knows what may happen? That's the way I try to live."

Despite the diet, Kenyatte eats out almost every night. He's at P.F. Chang's at least twice a week, usually by himself at the bar; they don't even bring him a menu anymore. He loves sushi, especially half-price Wednesday nights at Beluga, where all the pretty girls and models gather. He likes places where the owners know his name. He's likely to order the fruity vodka special. He "tends to like wines that are probably in the middle of the palate, chardonnays and pinot noirs." In his effort to become more educated about oenology, he has purchased, from World Market, a set of glasses that includes vessels for every type of wine. There are glasses for Riesling, for champagne, for zinfandel, etc. There is also a decanter. The whole set is stored in his kitchen, in a rolling wine rack/bar, also from World Market, which he likes because it's sort of like "Pier 1 taken to the next level."

He'll occasionally smoke a Macanudo cigar. He has no respect for the Cincinnati Bengals. He doesn't even think about the Reds. He once sprained his ankle real bad playing hoops—there is a heroic play-by-play if you ask to hear it. He is often in situations where there are few (if any) other black people in the room. He likes being well liked. He is eager to please. He has a lot of friends; wherever he goes he seems to run into one or more of them. He believes in loyalty. Of his two best friends from college he says: "I would die for them and they would die for me." He works until seven or later most nights and then drives to the gym. There is never a time he is not on the move. He wishes occasionally he could just go to bed at 8:00 pm. Last night, a Saturday, he stayed home alone because he was sick. It was the first time in adult memory he had stayed home alone on a Saturday night. He watched *The Real Housewives of Atlanta*. He was appalled.

His house has five bedrooms and four full baths, a circa-1910 brick Victorian he bought for $245,000 with no money down. He honestly doesn't know the square footage. The mortgage is $1,600 a month. His five-year ARM expires this year. He found the house halfway through a spec renovation, so he was able to have a lot of input on the finished product—which of course became like having another full-time job. He picked out every fixture, appliance, floor covering, and color; he recommends joining a buyer's club like DirectBuy. You pay a pretty significant fee to join, like four grand, but it's a three-year membership. You get everything they sell wholesale: furniture, electronics, appliances, outdoor-living stuff. He priced out his kitchen at Home Depot—forty-two-inch cherry-wood cabinets, granite counter, all the trimmings: It was $15K for the cabinetry alone. At DirectBuy, he paid like five grand for everything, including the appliances; he chose Amana, made by Whirlpool, because he knew the name. While he was away on a weeklong business trip to Switzerland, the refrigerator died. There is a new motor in a box in his foyer. The repairman is coming next week. In the meantime, unspeakably noxious organisms have taken up residence inside the fridge. He's kind of hoping that if he doesn't pay attention, the rancid food will clean up itself.

He owns two Hunter Ceiling Fans, one in the home office/gym, one in the guest room. The home office/gym is painted Rich Red. The kitchen is Slate Green but looks avocado. The dining room is Honey Pot Yellow. The downstairs bathroom is lavender and features the original claw-footed tub, which has been refurbished—it looks brand-new but still old. The moldings and crown moldings and window frames throughout the house are all painted Natural Light White. The master bedroom is Mocha, though Kenyatte likes to call it "paper-bag brown." His dad used to tell him stories about restaurants black folk could eat in only if their skin was lighter than a brown paper bag. The guest room is painted with alternating light-and-dark yellow stripes. He got the idea from a decor magazine. It seemed like a good idea. It took him an entire week. Every night he'd come home after work and mark off the lines with tape and a laser level and paint until well after midnight. It's incredible how tired your wrist and arm can get from painting. It takes a lot of scrubbing to get those rubbery little dots of latex-based paint to come off your skin. Because his new bedroom suite hadn't yet arrived from Rooms to Go, he had to sleep in the guest room as he was painting it. The fumes were overwhelming. His dreams were narcotic. He will never do that again. When you turn on the Hunter ceiling fan using the wall-mounted switch in the guest room, the one in the home office/gym also turns on, and vice versa. He knows there's a way to fix this, but he has lived here more than four years and hasn't yet bothered to figure it out. Likewise, he never turns on the huge chandelier in the dramatic atrium stairwell. Should the bulb blow, he has no clue how he'd ever get up there to change it.

The third floor is a rental unit, a cool space, all eaves and angles. The tenant is *hot*. She has her own entrance but likes to come through the house. She went to a pricey eastern boarding school on scholarship and then graduated from Stanford. Now she works for P&G, in research and development in the homecare sector. Until recently, in her off-hours, she participated in something called "figure fitness competitions." Let your imagination wander. YouTube if you must. She and Kenyatte are just friends. "Never shit where you eat," Kenyatte says. The same goes for "fishing off the company pier."

He is the runt of his family. A "mistake" born ten years after his brother, a preemie who lived his first several months in an incubator. The doctors were worried he might be brain damaged. As it is, there are some weird splotches on his skin, places he didn't develop properly—like somebody spilled bleach. His dad, Ellis Nelson, wanted another kid, but his mom was considering a try at modeling—everyone at church always said she was so statuesque. Ellis is six foot seven; everyone calls him Big E. He spent his entire working career as a chemical compounder on an assembly line at a tire factory. He is the definition of dapper; Kenyatte got his clothing sense from him. Kenyatte's brother got all the height and athletic ability. He is now a truck driver who lives in Charlotte, North Carolina, where they grew up. As a child Kenyatte collected comics. His favorite character was Wolverine. He'd buy two copies of each issue, one to read, one kept in the original cellophane for collecting, all of them stored under his bed. He was early into graphic novels. He used to draw a lot. "It's a talent I probably squandered," he says today.

At his mostly black middle school, "I was the kid who, if I was running down the hall, someone would trip me." At his mostly white high school, he gained renown as a rapper and was elected president of the student government. He attended A & M on an academic scholarship, a combined B.A./M.B.A. program. It was there that he first encountered wealthy African-American kids. Prior to that, he'd never even heard of Prada. To earn spending money in college, he spun records at private parties and clubs. He was known as DJ Diamond. If anybody calls him that today, he visibly winces. He never took a drink of alcohol until well after college graduation.

If you wanted to spell his name phonetically, you would put an A on the end: K - E - N - Y - A - T - T - A. That's the real spelling, actually. How it should have been spelled. There's a story behind the name, of course. When Kenyatte's mom was pregnant, his parents were looking through a book of African names, a trend during the late seventies among church-going middle-class black families like theirs. Jomo Kenyatta was a lion of a man who led Kenya to independence from Great Britain and became its first president. Literally translated, the name means musician. There was only one problem. His mother felt the A at the end made the name feminine in appearance. She changed it to an E.

"My name was always murdered," Kenyatte says. "People would call me Ken-yah-tay. Or Ken-yat. Or Koonta-ken-yat"—lampooning the character from the classic mini-series *Roots*, which traces the African American experience. "Nobody could pronounce it; it made me feel so different. And when you're young, when you're a kid, you don't want to be different. You don't understand the value of differentiation. That's one of the things in branding—in branding you learn that differentiation is fantastic. You need it, you want it, you desire it, you *strive* for it. But when you're a child, you don't understand that concept. Sameness is...paramount. I mean, you want to blend in, you want to be with the mass, right? When I was a kid, I was left-handed, my name was Kenyatte, I was a stick figure with a balloon head. And I was black. And I was living in the South. It was like strike 1,2,3,4, and 5."

There is a warm timbre to his voice, like a radio announcer's. When he speaks in paragraphs, a slight stutter or hesitation becomes evident, as if he's trying very hard to enunciate properly, to pronounce everything just so, to say exactly what he means. He was the first in his family to earn a four-year degree. He wouldn't bring this up if he weren't asked, but Kenyatte is wealthier than any of his relations have ever been; it's something he always considers. Kenyatte is a discriminating consumer, a healthy consumer, a loyal consumer, a fashion forward consumer...but he is not a crass consumer. Unless asked, he does not generally talk about all the things he has bought or wants to buy. He does not talk all the time about money and the cost of things the way some people do, people who make it seem anymore that money is a god and that spending money on things is a religion, a belief system that requires them to always stay focused on the next thing they are going to buy, some important piece of clothing or electronics, some vehicle or house or vacation to a life-altering place, something they just have to have to make themselves feel more complete... until they set their minds on the next thing.

"It kinda makes you want to barf," Kenyatte says. "How much shit do you need?"

As a reflection of his perspective, Kenyatte signs his e-mails—and his new blog, TweedandVelvet.blogspot.com—with the slogan *Make it an outstanding day*! He appropriated it from a Ford company recruiter who had it on his voice mail. This was back when Kenyatte was in grad school; a lot of the big companies go to A&M to recruit executives. (The other night he went clubbing with some of his closest friends—in a coed group of seven, there were five A&M alums and one from Howard University; five of them are management types for P&G. When I joked that P&G must have pulled a truck up to the back door at the A&M and onloaded an entire class of future minority executives, Kenyatte deadpanned. "It was a private jet.")

"My father was really big on attitude," Kenyatte says. "The thing that I would get in trouble for the most was having a bad attitude, being disrespectful. My dad's thing was 'Your attitude shapes the outcome.' If someone asks me, 'How are you doing?' I say, 'Phenomenal.' And when I say that, it's amazing how many people will stop and look at me, as if I've found the secret to life. They're like, 'How is it you are doing phenomenal? I need to understand that. Because I do not feel phenomenal. I want a piece of what you've got.' When I meet people or leave a message on the phone, that's what I'm trying to convey. Here's a trick. Try it. When you're on the phone, smile as you talk. You will sound different. And people are able to tell. I guarantee it. You will get results."

When Kenyatte smiles, his teeth gleam with the evidence of his twice-daily use of an Oral-B Sonic Complete electric toothbrush. He always uses Crest toothpaste. Period. It doesn't matter what flavor so long as it's Crest, which he buys because P&G makes it and because he is a loyal company man and because every single month he maxes out his contribution to his 401(k)—half of which he puts in P&G stock. He also uses Old Spice deodorant, Gillette body wash, Tide laundry detergent, Downy fabric softener, a Swiffer for his wood floors, Dawn dishwashing liquid—all of it from P&G. When you visit him, it doesn't really look like he uses the Swiffer too often, or any of the cleaning products, really. Random observation: the bathrooms of single heterosexual men younger than age 35, no matter what their economic station, are nearly always a disaster area. Kenyatte has a gardener—his father used to make him mow and pull weeds— but no maid. He just doesn't seem to notice the rust inside the toilets or the smell of mildew in the fancy slate bathroom with the rainforest showerhead. Maid service: a marker of a certain stage of adulthood that Kenyatte has yet to reach. His grandma was a hotel maid, but that doesn't really figure into it the equation. After a raucous party some time back, three of his female friends returned to his place the next day to tidy up. They ended up scrubbing the baseboards and the toilets, leaving it far cleaner than it was before the party. A half-full bottle of Pellegrino water remains on the dining-room mantel piece as a souvenir of the evening, integrated into the sticks/rocks/vase arrangement he purchased as separates at Pier 1. To Kenyatte's eye, the exotic-looking label on the Pellegrino bottle complements the large, colorful Leonetto Cappiello posters that dominate the dining room and kitchen. He collects the posters because he likes the way they look, but also because they were commissioned in the 1920s and the 1930s to advertise products. Kenyatte himself oversees multimillion-dollar art budgets and commissions famous photographers for Nice 'n Easy. He's always admired people who have skills in crafts or arts, people who express themselves through imagery, form, pictures, sound, what have you. If Cappiello's adverts are hanging on his walls, is it too much to think that someday maybe his Nice 'n Easy box covers... okay, maybe that's going a bit too far. But you get the point. For him, living and and decorating and eating and dressing well is also an art form; it's the way he expresses the aesthetics of his soul.

Kenyatte tears out pages of men's magazines and saves them on an unusual shelving system comprised of L-shaped wooden boxes, along with other keepsake magazines and books. He scoffs at people who buy the exact outfits off the mannequins in stores. He's always looking for interesting ways to maximize his wardrobe, to recombine or recycle different items, and also for new fashion ideas, marriages of styles he would have never considered, like wearing a tartan plaid tuxedo jacket with two tone bucks or a brown tweed vest with a blue velvet blazer. He is a jeans man. The entire bottom rack in his spacious bedroom closet is taken up with jeans—thirty-two pairs, about a third of which are now too large. Baggy, slim, boot cut. A dark pair fitted at the ankle he likes to wear with a tuxedo jacket. A red pair, a white pair, a gray pair. The other night, out clubbing, he wore skinny Sliq jeans from H&M with black combat boots from Zara, strings untied and tongues dangling, and a black canvas bomber jacket with a black faux-fur collar from Armani Exchange. As a scarf he wore an authentic black-and-white-checked Arab kaffiyeh that he bought from a street vendor in New York. Most of the jeans were pretty expensive, something like $250 a pop; he hasn't had the heart to give them away, even though so many of the pairs no longer fit. Eventually, they will go to Goodwill. There is a pile of old and too-big suits growing on the banister on the second-floor landing. They will be delivered to a group he works with called Career Gear, which offers career counseling, interview coaching, and recycled business clothing to down-on-their-luck men actively seeking employment.

Kenyatte smells pleasantly of Prada D'Homme. On top of his dresser—which was purchased as a set along with the dark-stained sleigh bed, the bedside tables, two lamps, and the TV cabinet/ armoire—he keeps his portfolio of fragrances. Tom Ford and Dolce & Gabbana's the One are his current favorites. Next to the bottles are his jewelry box, his watches (an admitted weakness—seven Invictas, a gold Donald J. Trump, and an IWC), and a wedding picture of his parents. Clearly he inherited his mom's wide nose. Her name is Rose, short for Rosalee, but her brothers and sisters call her Annamae. She grew up in Charleston, South Carolina, speaking Gullah, a dialect particular to descendants of West African and Caribbean slaves. She met Kenyatte's dad when they were both students at Denmark Technical College in Denmark, South Carolina. Ellis studied interior design. (After retiring from Continental Tire, he returned to that interest for a time, painting home interiors.) Rose took a secretarial degree. Over the years, she worked her way up to the position of executive assistant to the head of a large manufacturing firm; she was forced to retire only when it became painfully apparent that she was suffering from the early stages of Alzheimer's. She was only fifty-three.

Rose Nelson still lives at home in a state of twilight. Kenyatte drives the seven hours about four times a year. He frets that the disease has "robbed my parents of their golden years." On his father's sixtieth birthday, five years ago, Kenyatte walked into the restaurant where the family was celebrating and "my mother looked at me and she had no idea who I was," he recalls. "Today she's about as nonresponsive as she could be. No facial expressions, no talking, nothing. She can't get out of the bed or a chair without someone's help." His dad bathes her, brushes her teeth, does her hair, feeds her, clothes her—24/7, 365. He has never visited Kenyatte in Cincinnati because there's nobody else who can take care of Mom. "My dad is the most amazing man I have ever known," Kenyatte says. "He is a perfect example of what devotion looks like. Which is probably one of the reasons why I hold people to such high standards."

Kenyatte's favorite piece of footwear is a pair of light-tan cowboy boots appropriated from his father, one size too large. His shoe collection is copious, everything still in the orginal box. Aldo, Saks, Madden Dior, Vittorio Russo, Kenneth Cole, checkerboard Vans, classic white Chuck Taylors. Even so, when Kenyatte won *Esquire's* Best Dressed Real Man contest and appeared on television's *Today Show*, he wore his dad's cowboy boots as a tribute.

Kenyatte does not want to get married. Yet. But he's starting to get a little tired of "talking to multiple women" at one time. "I love women and women love me," he says matter-of-factly. "I'm not perfect, I've done some dumb shit and I've hurt people I care about, but I'm a pretty good person, and I truly think people can sense it. I know how to make a woman feel safe, appreciated, and sexy. A woman who feels that way will do anything with you sexually because she is comfortable. Sometimes the women I've dated find themselves comfortable doing things they haven't done before or enjoying things that they hated doing with the previous guy." He's been offered a threesome on multiple occasions but has never thought the offer was genuine. "In every case I felt like I would be taking advantage of one girl or the other, or both, and I couldn't go through with it." Several times he has been approached by middle-aged couples. "Usually the husband is asking me to sleep with his wife. I've never done it because I tend to believe karma is a motherfucker. I want to get married one day."

Like many of us, Kenyatte is a little bit afraid of the future; he tries not to think about it very much, except in the vaguest of terms. He likes to salute people when he passes them in the hallways at work. He got it from his brother, who served in the military, who once lifted him over head and then dropped him face first on the concrete because he'd ridden his bike out of the neighborhood when he wasn't supposed to. The salute is a sign of something he calls "servant leadership," a sign of respect. "Whether you work for me or with me or above me, it's a symbol in my mind that I'm serving you. It's a way of saying, 'Hey, I know we're on the same team, we're in this together.'" In answer to the eternal question: He used to wear boxers. Then he liked boxer briefs. Lately he's been wearing 2(x)ist briefs. The fit is just a lot cleaner, less bunched up in the legs and crotch.

From his father he learned to "dress like the cover of a *New York Times* best seller." From his grandma he learned that it is never too late to do the right thing. From his college roommate he learned that if you buy cheap, you're going to pay more, and also that you can't wear the cordovan shoes without the cordovan belt, even if you just bought them both and you're dying to take them out for a spin. From a former manger he learned how to make sure you're always working in the "high-importance/low-urgency quadrant of priorities." From his aunt on his father's side he learned how to cook soul food. From his Williams-Sonoma cookbook, *Savoring Italy*, he learned to cook his signature dish, shrimp-and-crabmeat risotto. From his contractor he learned that "people who do anything involved in house

construction are paid way more fuckin' money than they should be."
From his trainer, with whom he worked for only a few sessions in
order to get a program started—"I can count the reps myself, thanks"—
he learned to use low weight and high reps, even if the other guys in
the gym think he looks like a pussy.

He's realized that it's an unfortunate irony of life that you don't
appreciate your parents until they're old. He loves meeting people
and having conversations and chatting with folks on a plane or on
the street or wherever. Regarding Marc Jacobs' skirts, he believes that
"there's a difference between a fashion trend and just being fucking
ridiculous. I'm not following him out the window on that one." He
is determined to make the best of every situation. "When I go out
with my friends, I'm going to have a good time. I could have fun in a
closet." His philosophy has always been "Money can buy you fashion,
but it can't buy you style." Neither can it buy you talent or class. He
believes that having something that screams "I paid a ton of money
for this" pales in comparison to someone saying, "Wow, I never
thought of putting those pieces together that way." He just wants to
look good for himself. It helps when women notice, too.

"Honestly, I feel like my life is a dream," he says. "A wife and
kids would be nice. I always liked the idea of having the big family
dinner on Sundays, looking at my wife and thinking, *We did a pretty
good job*. That'll happen one day. For right now, I'm living the dream
as they say. Anything else would just be icing. I do kind of like icing,
though."

After brunch, the Best Dressed Real Man in America needs to
do some shopping. He has a bad cold; he might have picked it up
from his friend Sy, also from A&M, also a P&G employee, a senior
purchasing manager.

His infirmity notwithstanding, Kenyatte looks smashing as
he strides down the sidewalk of the strip mall on a bright and chilly
football Sunday afternoon. He is wearing a herringbone car coat from
Express, a black cashmere sweater from Saks Fifth Avenue, a black-on-
white polka-dot dress shirt from Banana Republic, a white tank-top
undershirt from 2(x)ist. The jeans are Rock & Republic stone wash
(over 2(x)ist boxer briefs.) Gucci belt, black leather with a faux-gold G.

Kenneth Cole black leather ankle boots, size 11. The socks are striped numbers from Banana Republic. "I'm a big sock guy," he says. "I think socks are one of those forgotten accessories for men."

Entering the store, he finds the proper aisle, sets about perusing the seemingly infinite choices that modern life offers, in this case, for the quelling of flulike symptoms. So much of living is about choice these days. Which plan? Which product? Which strategy? Which philosophy? Which road to take? We research and fret and ask our friends and fret some more. Who to believe?

The shelves are crowded with different cold, flu, sinus, and allergy remedies. A girl he knows has suggested Advil Cold & Sinus. Now all he has to do is find it. He searches high and low. At last, he comes to a small plastic holder containing cards with an *image* of a box of Advil Cold & Sinus. The wording directs him to present the card to the pharmacist.

Because he keeps up with the news, Kenyatte is aware that one of the ways the government is fighting the drug war is by making it more difficult to buy products like Advil Cold & Sinus, which contains small amounts of a legal drug that people need in huge quantities to cook up a batch of illegal methamphetamine. Because he's delving into the subject of illegal drugs... and because he's an upstanding citizen—a dutiful son, a former scholarship student, an executive at a huge international conglomerate that makes family-oriented household products—a slightly uncomfortable feeling begins to overtake him, a prickly sort of heightened awareness. That he is the only black person he's seen (besides the waitress) in this little strip mall may be adding to his discomfort. The outfit he's wearing, perfectly suited outside in the brisk air a few moments ago, starts to feel heavy and constraining in the store. Moisture begins to gather in the places that men feel moist in these circumstances.

Reaching the pharmacy, Kenyatte finds the area behind the register empty. There are two employees over to the right, behind the customary high counter. One of them is a woman. She is youngish, not unpleasant-looking at all. She is busy counting pills. The other worker, a man, steps to the register. "How can I help you?" he asks.

Kenyatte hands him the Advil card. Soberly, the man asks to see an ID. As Kenyatte opens his Kenneth Cole cardholder and hands over his driver's license, he happens to glance up to his right, toward the woman.

She's staring at him.

Kenyatte is used to having women look at him. But there's something about the way she's looking at him. It seems not right somehow, not the kind of look you give when you're impressed by someone. To Kenyatte, it seems more of a confused look. Like she doesn't know what to think. Really weird. Maybe it's his flu, but something doesn't seem right to him. First they're asking him to show an ID in order to buy a supposedly over-the-counter product. Now this female pharmacist is looking at him all cockeyed. *What the hell is this about?* he wonders.

He returns his focus to the register, takes back his ID from the man, thanks him very politely. The man disappears into the cool white bowels of the pharmacy. After an interval, Kenyatte cuts his eyes again to the right.

She's still looking!

A wave of heat and nausea washes over his head. He feels clammy and faint. *What the hell is he doing back there?*

At last she breaks the silence. "You look really nice," she says.

"I th-thought I was doing something wrong," he stutters.

"Oh, no no no!" she says musically. She cocks her head to one side and removes her glasses. "I was probably just staring at you."

(2009)

The Porn Identity

When his wife decamps from the household, leaving his life and his bank account in tatters, our hero takes a much needed assignment traveling the country in search of... retired porn starlets. From Nina Hartley's toy-filled dungeon, to Kay Taylor Parker's spirit-filled studio, to Asia Carrera's split-level hideaway in the mountains north of Las Vegas... How one man got his mojo back.

I am somewhere around Barstow on the edge of the desert when the Motrin finally kicks in—the electric pain scorching down the back of my leg begins to subside; once again I can feel my foot on the gas pedal. The ache in my heart is another matter. I remind myself to breathe.

Three hours down, four to go, the best car my money can lease. The sky is big, blue and cloudless. The atmosphere is fragrant. My tunes are cranked, an inspiring anthem by the artist Milez called "We Have Hope." I've played it six or seven times already, or maybe 10, I don't know. It might have something to do with the message of the song. Or it might have to do with the fact that Milez is my son—it's something he recorded at the conclusion of a long holiday weekend in the house that used to belong to him and his family but now just belongs to him and his dad. I have 450 miles of highway to cover, spanning four states, hopefully before nightfall. The last stretch, through Arizona and into southern Utah, is said to be treacherous; I've been advised to get through the soaring, weathered canyons before the temperature drops and the road freezes. As I will learn, fatalities happen—lives torn asunder. There are all kinds of ways.

That I've left this particular part of my mission for last now seems prophetic. But then again, everything about this assignment has been weirdly synchronistic. There I was, suffering through the latter stages of a swift and painful divorce, a middle-aged man facing single life after 20 years with the same woman— a recovering cuckold, damaged goods, the male animal at his lowest.

A tornado of anger and resentment and powerlessness swirled through my inner space, turning everything gritty and gray, and all these motherfuckers with their hands in my pants, massaging my misery, waiting for their gusher to come in. Just yesterday I was signing over my assets, three decades worth of pension and gifts and savings. That the Notary Public was a kind lady who worked in the local branch of Mailbox, Etc seemed somehow fitting, more irony to stoke the clichéd satire that had become my reality.

For months I've felt as if I've been operating on safe mode— you can give me commands and make me function, but everything seems dull and slow and monochromatic. I wander through my house, going from room to room. I don't know what the hell I'm doing. Putting the scissors away. Emptying the trash. Folding laundry. Shopping for groceries. Making lunch. Changing passwords. Worrying about the future—college for my son, retirement for me. Retirement! I always imagined I'd grow old with her—in some ways, to be honest, it was a scenario that didn't thrill me. At least now I get to sleep in the bed by myself. She used to take up three quarters of the damn thing, which was kind of metaphorical for my life with her—me sleeping on the itty-bitty edge of the big antique bed that had been in my family for 90 years.

And then, serendipitously, an e-mail arrives from the venerable Rabbit. They want me to hit the road. They want to give me money. They want me to track down...

Retired porn stars.

You're fucking kidding me, right?

At high noon the Mojave Desert shimmers in all directions. My speedometer is holding steady at 80; cars are passing on my left like I'm standing still. Twisted Joshua trees stand here and there like prickly, gawking townsfolk, stooped and wringing their hands, bearing silent witness to my tortured thoughts. There is snow on the mountaintops; sculpted ridges and balancing rocks landscape the middle distance; a palette of rich reds, strong browns, wan tans —a tribute to nature's powerful and uncluttered sense of color and design. The intro to "We Have Hope" starts up again. I sing along with the chorus. Maybe I *do* have hope, after all.

As you might imagine, finding retired porn starlets turned out to be... not so easy. I left emails on websites, texted blind cell numbers, sent out Facebook messages. Nothing. And then one afternoon, sitting stuporous in my chair, fretting, wondering what the hell I'd gotten myself into, I got an idea.

I went up to the garage and dug into some boxes, found some old paper files, pulled up a few names of ancient contacts. Perhaps in no other arena would my decades-old status as a biographer of the seminal porn star John Holmes serve as a helpful distinction. Every world has its own constellation of reality, its own pantheon of gods. Most of the people I was trying to find didn't particularly want to be found. I was willing to leverage whatever I had.

Luckily, it turned out that my old contacts were still my contacts—not always a sure thing in my business. As it happens, it does matter how you comport yourself. It matters how you treat people. It matters how you leave things, how you choose to word your sentences. People remember—even after twenty years.

And so it was that I found myself one evening at the historic Sportsman's Lodge in Studio City, CA, at a memorial wake for John Leslie, one of the great founding fathers of the porn industry, which is what the pornographers like to call the business of X-rated movies. Everyone you could imagine was there, from Ron Jeremy to Holly Hollywood, a room full of Triple-X history, past and present. As the evening wore on, as testimonials were given (even Rocco Siffredi via Skype from Italy), as the liquor flowed from the cash bar and prescription vials of medical marijuana were produced, introductions were made and conversation flowed. Numbers were exchanged. In short order I found myself transported once again into the netherworld of professional sex workers and its vast network of loveable odd fellows.

Over the next three months I drove nearly 2,000 miles. I met Kay Taylor Parker at her little cottage by the sea. For a small fee (I insisted) she performed something called a Body Talk session; the previous day, we dined in a tony restaurant—Maria Shriver, the wife of the former Governor of California, was seated a only a muffin-throw away.

Nina Hartley and her second hubby, Ira, a writer and a director of bondage films, occupy a loft space/dungeon happily overlooking a lake. If you go to a dinner party at their house, Nina might be wearing this apparatus called a pony head harness. You will probably have your group sex first, and then eat after, since nobody likes to fuck on a full stomach, she'd explain.

Amber Lynn turned up at the luxe, ground floor restaurant at the Viceroy Hotel in a blue designer frock that complimented beautifully her fetching blue eyes. For three hours, over a delicious seared-tuna salad, she held forth on her life and the lessons learned, the tricky job of navigating between her porn self and the real woman inside, the girl who had her fun and her issues, the woman who wants legitimacy and a normal life. Sure she made fuck films and danced naked at the best strip clubs across the country. Sure she had a nasty penchant for alcohol and smoking cocaine. But now she's been sober for eleven years. Why can't she get a date?

The asphalt highway ribbons out before me. I pass through an Indian reservation, clusters of shacks and old busses and motor homes baking on the hillsides. I push my thoughts ahead, to the woman at the end of the Interstate. I never even thought I'd be making this part of the trip.

From the beginning it was clear that the golden ticket in this X-rated lottery was Asia Carrera, one of porno's first Asian goddesses. Half German, half Japanese, she was a child prodigy who played piano at Carnegie Hall twice before the age of 15—and then ran screaming to the dark side to escape the expectations of her overbearing parents. (Tiger moms, take note: This is what can happen when you push too hard.)

In her films Carrera is forever captured as she was in her prime: five feet eight inches tall, with geisha girl eyes, six-pack abs, a cheerleader's well-muscled ass—which, incidentally, she never gave away on film until she co-produced, co-directed, wrote the script and owned the rights. She appears to orgasm easily and often; in the throes of passion she is often moved to laugh. There is an aw-shucks quality to her afterglow. I'm not sure I've ever witnessed a porn princess—or anyone—who appears to enjoy fucking more than Carrera.

No wonder she'd been number one on my editor's wish list of potential interviewees.

There was only one problem.

Nobody in the industry had seen or spoken to her in years. She was said to be living in seclusion in southern Utah.

Eventually, working my rejuvenated contacts, I found an e-mail address. We struck up a halting correspondence. She was friendly, but I couldn't get her to commit. This went on for several weeks.

Finally, one week out from the date I'd first mentioned for our interview, still unconfirmed, I forced the issue: "Looking forward to seeing you next week!" I typed.

"I love how you're reminding me all nonchalantly, like I haven't been terrified about the date since the moment you told me," she wrote back.

"I'll be gentle, I promise."

"You sure we can't do this by e-mail?"

"In person is better—more accurate."

"C'mon," she chided. "Nobody ever won a Pulitzer for talking to porn stars."

"I'm just a guy whose wife cheated and left. I'm sure I'm more scared of you than you are of me. I'll be gentle if you will."

And then—nothing.

No reply.

Shit!

Had I played my cards wrong? A good journalist knows: It's not about you, it's about your subject. Maybe in my state of emotional disarray I was slipping a little bit. Maybe I'd revealed too much of myself, too soon.

The next day, an email appeared in my box. With a sense of dread, I clicked and opened.

"Wow. I had a dream that we hooked up, NOT kidding. Then I woke up and asked myself, 'Where the heck did THAT come from? The guy's married!' And now you tell me your wife has left you? Oh no! LOL!"

LOL, indeed.

In the off-kilter afterglow of my Body Touch session, I lingered on a comfortable divan chatting with Kay Taylor Parker. A busty red-head wearing an aquamarine sweater to match her sparkling eyes, she best remembered for her highly charged incest scenes in the 1980 porno classic *Taboo.*

Parker was known in her day as the Prude of Porn. With her British accent and air of innocence, she seemed a little too proper to be in fuck films, despite her 38DDs. She was 33 years old when she entered the biz, a well-traveled British Navy brat who'd arrived in San Francisco during the Summer of Love. Workshop trained as a thespian, she embarked on a porn career in the interest of acting.

Parker came to prominence at a time when X-rated movies were as much political statement as erotic entertainment—actors took care to leave their clothes in a convenient pile lest the cops raid the set. (The first priority before dashing was always to make sure to gather up the *film*, which was subject to confiscation.) During this era of near-mainstream offerings like *Behind the Green Door* and *Deep Throat*— a time of bushy pubes and long, stilted dialogues between sex scenes—Parker's films (with male co-stars like John Leslie, Mike Ranger, and Tom Byron) were shown mostly in old theaters in city centers around the nation, ornate places frequented by adventurous couples and the proverbial men in overcoats, everyone well spaced among the seats.

In all, Parker starred in fewer than 100 movies in this lifetime, which has thus far spanned 67 years. She is aware, she says, of having lived at least 182 other incarnations since her first arrival on Earth, as a female scientist in ancient Atlantis, a Star Being sent to this planet to "help usher in the God-ing through Fourth Dimensional Ascension." For this latter distinction she has been called the Shirley MacLaine of porn. Today she earns her living as a spiritual practioner; she may be contacted through her euphonious website.

We sat together in her parlor, decorated with geodes and crystals and potted plants, attended by a number of vocal cats. Through the open, sun-filled window came the scent of flowers and sea air, a soundtrack of chirping birds. It was the second day of my visit; our lunch and interview yesterday had gone swimmingly, we seemed to be well matched. There was a nurturing vibe about her; I think she felt okay about me, too. Yesterday, within a few minutes of our first hellos, Parker experienced a ringing sensation in her right ear. She paused a moment and raised her eyes to the heavens to confer with a force above—I believe it was the spirit of her mentor, Aaron. "You're being given the thumbs up," she said.

For my Body Touch session, Parker asked me to recline on my back on a massage table, covered by a sheet, one arm exposed. She spoke out loud, though not to me, asking questions of— and getting answers from—a higher source... possibly Aaron? As she muttered, she pushed and poked at the meat of my exposed forearm as if working a keyboard or a set of switches—I got the sense she was toggling through a sort of table of contents in my life.

From there she asked a series of leading questions that prompted answers and more questions. There was something about my leaving my girlfriend to go to college at 18, she said. There was something about my choosing, as a young journalist, to work nights instead of days to advance my career—further confounding the same tortured relationship. There was something about my bedroom—specifically about the bed. It had belonged to my grandparents on my mother's side. They'd slept in it together for more than 60 years of marriage. Having inherited the piece, I'd had it lovingly enlarged by a craftsman when my wife had become pregnant.

And then one morning, without notable provocation, my wife had opened her eyes and proceeded to launch into a tirade about the bed. She hated it. She always hated it. Etc. Etc. Not yet aware of the true cause of her sudden misplaced mania—the *denouemont* was still some weeks away— I'd followed her wishes *posthaste*. With the help of my son and an electric drill, the bed was dismantled and garaged.

Working the keyboard of my forearm, mumbling to her higher source, Parker focused on the bed and its role in my personal history. At last she found what she was looking for.

I had a missing piece.

There'd been a rape six generations ago on my mother's side, apparently, back in the old country, Eastern Europe. A splinter of my soul had detached and crossed over. Meaning that I was born incomplete.

I'd never even suspected.

Maybe that's why I always need to love the wrong girl?

She tapped my forehead with her fingertips, a maneuver of healing, she explained. Tap, tap, tap... It felt like being in the rain.

Now we were sitting together on the couch. I was drinking water as prescribed. Parker was paging through a volume called *Love Cards*, by Robert Lee Camp.

She asked my birth date, looked me up.

"You're a nine of clubs," she announced brightly. She handed me the book. "Read out loud," she ordered.

"Humanitarianism, higher law, universal love, selfishness...." I looked at her questioningly. "What does dissipation mean in this context?"

Perplexed, she consulted an alternate guide, a stapled set of papers. "Always dramatic and dynamic in approach. Leaders in their own field. Very successful as writers. Maybe subject to hampering home conditions but never fail in duty and devotion."

"Hampering home conditions," I repeated. I could feel my face forming itself into a rueful expression. "What about my love life?"

She consulted the pages, regarded me mournfully. "Perhaps you have some other things to do first."

At this point my dry spell had reached a personal record. Was it my destiny to be alone? "How big a part has sex played in your life?" I asked.

She smiled beatifically. "I haven't had sex in six years. Even longer before that."

I looked surprised, I suppose. She is still attractive for a woman in her seventh decade. There are still legions of fans on the Internet.

"I've come to the realization that sex isn't all it's made out to be," she said. Like everything, it's the spirit that's important. Whether we're self-pleasuring or interfacing with somebody else, at a core level it's really about a union with God. Or the divine. Or the creator. Or Fred—whatever we want to call that energy.

"Sex has become so hollow today—especially since porno is so huge on the Internet," she continued. "It leads me to believe that more people are sitting at home masturbating than engaging in intimate relationships."

Guilty as charged, I told myself.

She looked at me gravely. "If we could all have sex in the spirit of communion with God, we'd immediately eradicate war on the planet. To me that's what the fourth dimension is all about. It's about union, about communion, about—"

She was interrupted by the sound of wind chimes. Then the cats started up, meowing like crazy.

The door to the outside patio swung open.

"Come in, come in, come in..." Parker sang.

But nobody was there.

I followed Nina Hartley down a dark hallway on an upper floor of a spooky-cool converted loft building. Her celebrated bubble butt, high and round and sheathed in black leggings, was doing its work ahead of me. Back in the 1980s, Hartley's was known as the Best Ass in Porn. From where I was walking, it showed no signs of decline.

It was our second day together. We'd started with a long drive along surface streets—she prefers to avoid the freeway in her black on black T-Bird convertible— and spent the afternoon at a chic beauty salon on ritzy Montana Avenue—her colorist splits time between Los Angeles and Tel Aviv. After that, she'd appeared on an Internet chat show, "Porn Star Pundits," where heavyweights from the X industry hold forth on news topics of the day. "We are more than just the sum of our genitals, people!" Hartley was compelled to quip. She was joined on the panel by the younger male star Jack Lawrence; besides sharing a reputation for expertise in cunnilingus, it turned out, they are both fallen-away Jews. Off air, they decided their particular talent set had something to do with their culture's strong link between love and eating.

Hartley is one of the more outspoken porn stars, past and present. Her longevity and her status as one of the Erotic Eleven—she was arrested on obscenity charges in 1993 after a benefit performance for the Free Speech Coalition—have conveyed upon her a sort of queenly status. She has the upbeat, ironic, rat-a-tat delivery of a café society intellectual, distinguished by a slight lateral lisp. Throughout our time together, Hartley rarely took a breath, filling the air with genial patter, bright commentary and unconventional opinions—a lot of which make good sense. She described herself, variously, as "a sex-positive feminist," "a heterosexual butch dyke," "a gay man with female parts," "a bisexual exhibitionistic polyamorous person who is by nature emotionally monogramous."

Truly, her verbal skills rival her oral ones.

In some ways, you could say Hartley is an embodiment of the industry's own story arc. Curious about sex from an early age, the bookish girl took herself to see her first X-rated movie at 17 at an art house in San Francisco. The film was an adaptation of one of her favorite erotic novels, first published anonymously in 1887, *The Autobiography of a Flea*. The film version starred early porn gods Jean Jennings, Paul Thomas and John Holmes. In time, Hartley would meet or work with all of them.

Hartley is the daughter of a blacklisted local radio personality and his attractive brunette wife, whom Hartley credits for her ass. Hartley's ice-blue eyes are the heritage of her German Swiss dad, who went into free fall after being outed as a communist. The story is complicated; he ended up at one point finding employment as a short-order cook before her mom became the breadwinner. Her parents were together for 64 years; they worked hard on their marriage. Over time, Hartley explained, the couple investigated all manner of therapeutic options, including primal scream therapy, group therapy, biofeedback, bioenergetics and naked tai chi. At last they found their peace within the teachings of Zen Buddhism. They lived with others in a religious cooperative until recently, when her father died peacefully in a hospice with his family at his bedside. Hartley has eight nieces and nephews, upon whom she dotes. Uterine fibroid tumors and a lack of interest have precluded her own career as a parent.

Born in 1959, Marie Hartman (in everyday life, to maintain her anonymity, she uses at least two more different names), was the fourth and last child of her parents progeny, a "semi-feral child" raised with "benign neglect." Looking back, the business seems an almost obvious choice for a lonely young girl who grew up in the dark time after her father's fall from grace.

At 24 she entered her first amateur strip contest; she wore satin slippers and used a cream-colored vibrator as a prop—penetration was legal onstage in San Francisco in those wild, pre-AIDS days. She won $200 and a job... in a live peep show. During each shift she had sex with a different woman on a rotating bed in a round room. Along the circumference of the room were booths. Each had a window, a chair, a wastebasket and paper towels. If the guy wished to be visible to the entertainers, he could turn on a light in his booth.

Hartley started doing porn movies in the early 1980s, just as theatrical distribution was giving way to an amazing new home movie device called a VCR. Previously, only the wealthy could watch movies at home. (The poor went to peep shows. You fed a machine with quarters and watched black-and-white film on a tiny screen— just as the action got heavy, it would shut down and you'd need to insert another quarter.) The first porno I ever saw was played on an expensively-rented movie projector in the rec room of my college fraternity house. The year was 1975. I remember the film being fuzzy and breaking several times; the actor wore black socks; the girl was doughy and hairy and nondescript.

The first straight-to-video films still boasted decent pay, large budgets and discernible story lines. As video drove the X industry more mainstream—with revenue in the billions over two golden decades—Hartley crossed over as well. A nurse by education (dancing and adult-film work paid her nursing school tuition), she frequently lectures on sex and politics, has appeared on *The Oprah Winfrey Show*, has written a sex guidebook and produced a handful of instructional videos. In 1997 Hartley won a part in the mainstream movie in *Boogie Nights*. She was critically lauded for her turn as William H. Macy's unfaithful wife. (He finds her getting fucked missionary style on a sun-bleached and dusty driveway, surrounded by a crowd of onlookers. Between thrusts, she chides him for embarrassing her by interrupting.)

At 52, Hartley still does several scenes a month to make ends meet—MILF stuff and girl-on-girl. Enthusiast sites on the web credit Hartley with appearances in more than 850 different titles.

Making her... the George Blanda of porn?

For nearly 20 years, as she became more well-known, making movies and touring the country as a featured stripper, Hartley lived in a three-way union—two women and a man named Dave, a father figure she met at 19 who'd helped her get into film. Dave came with a girlfriend named Bobby. Since Nina was bisexual ("I got into porno because that's where the naked women were," she likes to say), this arrangement seemed perfect.

And for a time it was—or at least it seemed like it was, the blue smoke and mirrors of love's twisted heart.

"Some people blow their money on a bad drug habit," she said, unlocking the door to her apartment. "I blew mine on a bad marriage."

She led me into the great room. A bank of windows overlooked the city skyline. Nearby was an expansive green park, at the center of which was a lake with a fountain. To one side of the loft space was an eclectic kitchen—the funky, lived in, makeshift variety typical to loft conversions. The walls opposite the windows were lined with books; the top shelf was chokablock with martial-style caps—the type worn by police chiefs and military dictators with lots of do-dads and crosses and shiny gold trim. Nina's pony head harness was resting on an antique wig form, awaiting its next call to action.

"When I first got divorced, I said I would probably end up alone with cats and fuck buddies," Hartley said. "I never thought I'd be married again. Ever."

"I kind of feel like that now," I told her. "Except for the cats and the fuck buddies."

Hartley regarded me piteously through her chunky square-framed glasses—magnified, her eyes are like twin sapphires. "It's tough in our society," she said soothingly. "We're supposed to marry for love. Your partner is supposed to be your best friend and your soul mate and the best lover you ever had. And that's supposed to last your entire life."

She gestured as any proud homeowner would, bidding me to follow her on a tour of the long rectangular space she occupies with her husband, Ira, also known as Ernest Greene, a porn pundit and director of bondage films. "I guess I was lucky," she continued. "I met my husband during a threesome, so we had non-monogamy as the starting point. We love threesomes together. In that way we are so compatible."

Down the hallway, there are partitioning walls but no doors, except on the two bathrooms, so every room has a view out the large windows. She showed me a bedroom, another bedroom, and then... the office/playroom.

On one side is a desk, a phone, files.

The rest of the room features, in no particular order: A stainless-steel stand-up cage (three feet square by six feet high), an X frame for flogging, a spanking horse, a bondage bed, a custom-rigged suspension pulley, countersunk floor rings for restraint purposes and a "bounce wall"—a thickly padded section of wall against which to throw people, also known as a vertical trampoline. There is also a wall of tools arranged neatly on a home-workshop-type pegboard: whips, chains, paddles, riding gear (some by very high-end European luxury-goods houses), leather cuffs, padlocks. And of course a cabinet of safer-sex supplies: condoms, gloves, lube, an assortment of Hitachi Magic Wands—Hartley has never come easily... she has a high threshold, she says.

Entering the space, I nearly tripped over a knee-high leather boot, one of a number of pairs scattered around the rubber floor (for easy cleanup). Apologizing in the manner of a housewife entertaining an unexpected guest, Hartley made quick work of lining up and straightening the boots.

"Ira is much kinkier than I am. *Much kinkier*. He's 100% kinky," Hartley said, not missing a beat as she policed the floor, picking up a riding crop, some wadded tissues, a tube of lube. "I'm kinky, sure. I like a little power exchange, a little orgy, some girl on girl—I can even go for some bi-boy action. I'm a universal adapter. If it involves naked adults, count me in. I'll watch, I'll help, I'll hold your foot, I'll hold your coat. Whatever.

"But with Ira, if it's not BDSM, he ain't interested. Period. He'll keep his clothes on, thank you very much. That's why he supports me having a lover, my boyfriend, whatever you wanna call him—I've known him since high school and he's pure vanilla. And I do the same for Ira—he has this partner with whom he completely shares his sexual nature. She is one hundred percent masochistic-submissive. I know it's good for him; I want him to have it. It makes it easier for both of us to return to the other at the end of every day. I have to tell you: the idea that I still want to make love to the same man after ten years blows my mind."

I looked around the playroom, wanting to take it in, but not wanting to seem like a tourist. "You're lucky," I managed. I meant it.

"It took me a long time, but now I understand what it means to create your own reality," she said. "For so many years I didn't understand anything about being in a healthy relationship. Things spiraled out of control. It got to the point where I was lying, withholding and cheating. If I had been raised to be more honest and ethical and not a liar, I would have been able to go home and face my ex sooner and say, 'You know what? I've met somebody. The relationship we have doesn't work for me.' But I didn't know how to have that difficult conversation. I didn't know how to stand up for myself. I didn't know how to operate from a position of strength. Instead, I lied."

Her words resonated. There'd been a lot of lying in my own deceased marriage. I've had trouble trying to figure out how my "best friend" could do me like that.

Sensing my grief, Hartley took a step closer and put her hand on my shoulder. We looked out the window, past the cage and the bondage rack. The sun was setting over a green park; the sky was pink and orange.

"What are you doing for dinner?" she asked.

I looked up from my booth in the restaurant at the Viceroy Hotel and caught sight of Amber Lynn, striding toward me across the high-gloss oak plank flooring like a super model plying a long runway, wearing a pair of gold Michael Kors pumps with four-inch heels and a short, stunning Alice + Olivia dress, the electric blue of which harmonized beautifully with the Caribbean blue of her eyes. Her silken blonde hair, expensively cut, floated back and away from her sculpted face. It seemed as though a spotlight was following her as she moved, setting her aglow; I was reminded of one of those slow-motion dream sequences you see sometimes in movies. Time stops—for the horny teenager... the 40-year-old virgin... the hapless divorcee—as the lust object enters the room.

Lynn was known in her day, along with her friends Ginger Lynn and Traci Lords, as one of the Golden Goddesses of Porn. If you add up the numbers, Lynn probably started in the industry when she was underage, just as Lords did so notoriously before becoming a legitimate actress. Lynn was an original Vivid Video girl, though not a contract player. With her mid-1980s nimbus of blonde curls, this petite Melanie Griffith look-alike reigned over video's glam years of glossy box covers, high salaries and rock-star perks—limos, makeup artists, hotel suites, Peruvian cocaine... all of it at a time when the

Reagan and Bush administrations were spending billions on wars against drugs and immorality.

On-screen, Amber Lynn was as tough as nails, a no-nonsense dirty girl known for her snarl; she seemed as likely to bite off a dick as to suck on it. The bulk of her films were made between the mid-1980s and the mid-1990s. She has 373 titles to her credit, according to the web. Early on, she had a reputation for being particular: it was said she wouldn't do anal or bi-racial scenes. Later, during her darker years, there seemed to be fewer rules. After quitting film, Lynn worked for more than a decade as a featured dancer in strip clubs all over the United States and Canada, making as much as $25,000 a week, some of it in the form of $1 bills, hauled out each night in garbage bags.

After a run-in with the law, Lynn hit rock bottom and began the long process of turning her life around. Now 47 (48, according to Wikipedia and other sources), she's been sober for 11 years. She is a real estate agent specializing in luxury properties. She also works as a personal recovery assistant, known as a sober companion, counseling detoxing drug users—some of them young porn starlets.

As she sat over a lunch of seared-tuna salad and bubbly water, Lynn's story unfolded—porn's cautionary tale. One of her mentors, the critic and historian Bill Margold, another member of the Erotic Eleven, has always called the business "The Playpen of the Damned." Looking back over her life, Lynn's path seems almost predestined.

Laura Lynn Allen grew up in Orange County, California, the daughter of a retired Air Force officer and his brittle wife. The couple had two boys and then a girl who died, at the age of two, of a previously undetected heart defect. Lynn was conceived as a "replacement child," she explained, picking at her salad. "My brothers and my family were very overprotective."

The sadness of the little girl's death cast a deep shadow over the household. When Lynn was three, her father was discovered to have a second brood with another woman. There was a divorce. Lynn's mother had a nervous breakdown and was institutionalized. Lynn was sent to foster care. There was physical abuse.

When she was seven, Lynn reunited with her mother. Shortly thereafter, they were driving on the interstate after a holiday vacation when high winds caused a cement mixer to jackknife in front of their car. Lynn was thrown clear of the wreckage. Her mother was nearly decapitated; she died at the scene. The young girl witnessed all. "At that moment, part of me split," she said. "That's what children do. They kind of split emotionally so they don't suffer the trauma."

Lynn's father moved into his old house with his new family—by now he had four boys with the stepmom. In total, there were eight boys and Lynn. When she was 11, her father died from alcoholism and heart failure. Her stepmother carried on, seemingly as best she could.

Entering her teens, Lynn was "a pudgy, bucktoothed" tomboy, by necessity one of the guys. It was a small town. Everybody knew the misfortunate Allen clan; several of the boys were in car clubs, popular at the time. "I started going to the gym with my brother (who would go on to become the porn actor and director Buck Adams; a hard partier, Adams died from heart and liver failure at age 53).

As she approached her teenage years, "I guess I kind of blossomed," Lynn said. "I was maturing, losing my baby fat. I developed this rocking little body. I started doing fitness modeling and bikini modeling—I would be in a bathing suit down at the Orange County Raceway, that kind of thing, or I would do hot body contests. I had a fake ID, and my brother was the doorman at this club where they held the contests, and it was his job to check the IDs. So he would let me into the club and I would enter. I had, like, no breasts—anybody who knows my original stuff knows I had very little up there. But these contests were all about the lower body. I had these great abs, great legs, the great ass, the whole package. The purse was like $350 to $500 dollars, which was a ton of money to us. I would cut everybody in on the deal, and we would party for the weekend. That's how we got our money.

"At one point, I remember, the first g-strings came out," she continued. "Nobody had ever worn g-strings on the beach in Newport. They hired me, I think I was 16, to skate up and down the boardwalk in a g-string. And I remember when I did it, it was like, WOW. It was such a rush! I mean, people stopped and stared. Heads were turning. After that, I kind of became addicted. I remember getting off on the attention. Really, really getting off. This was my first taste of, like, 'Wow, this is making me feel....really hot.'"

She took a bite of her tuna and chewed, reflecting. "See, I grew up being known as little Lynnie. I always felt small and unsexy in this name, always overprotected by my brothers, the replacement child trying to live up to the perfect memory of my dead sister. As I started to feel the power of being noticed by men, oh my God, I just wanted to shed this whole image of the broken little girl."

She laughed wickedly, the insight of age. "The funny thing was, I thought I was so wild, but I was not very sexually daring at all. I was strutting my stuff but I wasnot a slut by any means. I was an inno-cent—we did like backseat petting and, and you know, rode on our boyfriends' motorcycles and did all these things, but it wasn't like I was having intercourse with boys. There was a lot of stuff I didn't know anything about. We weren't even giving blowjobs."

Lynn embraced this new, empowered self and started pushing her boundaries. Venturing an hour north to Hollywood, she became a regular at rock clubs on the Sunset Strip like the Rainbow Room and the Starwood. She partied hard. She lost her virginity. She got an agent. She posed for *Penthouse* magazine and was paid a healthy sum. She met the wife of *Hustler* founder Larry Flynt, the star-crossed Althea, and became her pal, riding around town in the Flynt's white stretch limo, a naked woman airbrushed on the side. Years later, Lynn's affinity for the rock scene would come full circle when she'd dance on tour with Motley Crue and Guns n Roses—before a crowd of 50,000 at Wembly Stadium in the UK. For a time she was romanti-cally involved with Arrowsmith sideman Tom Gimble.

When she was 17, Lynn was sent by her agent to a "go-see" for a movie. She knew it was not a Hollywood film; the director was a well-known porn veteran. In those days there was a difference between being a naked pinup model and being a porn actress. There was legitimate work for girls who did nude/no sex, even in X rated films. That's what Lynn was there to audition for.

Sitting down with the director in the opening moments of their conversation, Lynn recalled, the director said: "You seem nervous. Do you want a hit?"

Even though she was young, Lynn (and Lynnie, too) had plenty of experience partying. "We drank whatever booze we could steal off our parents. We used to buy kegs and put them in the back of my brother's mini truck and go out to the desert. We did LSD. We did mushrooms. We smoked a lot of grass. It was home grown. My brother grew it. We had pipes all over the house. That's how we rolled."

Now the director handed her a glass bong. She took it without hesitation, assuming it was a marijuana pipe.

"I remember as I was taking the hit, I looked down into the bowl —and I'll never forget this: there was a white rock on top that was melting into the weed as it burned. And I thought, "What the hell is that?"

A dark look crossed her face, which shows ample evidence of a plastic surgeon's work. "I'll never forget the way it hit me the first time. It was like, Oh. My. God.

"Anybody who has ever freebased knows the feeling, especially if you've been an addict. It's as if the birds are singing. The light is brighter. All of a sudden I'm no longer this gangly nervous teenager. I'm sitting there going, 'Oh wow!'

"They say you can't rape the willing, and I was completely willing...I was completely open. Because I came from a dysfunctional family, I didn't have really good boundaries. I'm the kind of person, If I'm standing on a cliff and I'm looking down, I might be thinking, you know, 'Wow, it looks like it could really be good fun to just jump off the fucking cliff with no parachute.' That's always been sort of innate in me my whole life—I will do things that are complete insanity."

The next day, still high on freebase cocaine, Lynn filmed her first movie.

The day after that, while preparing to film her second, she walked into a house and met porn legend Jamie Gillis, who would become her longtime partner and the love of her life.

A week later, she met Ginger Lynn—who promptly took her hand, led her to a chaise longue by a pool and made passionate love to her. It was her first experience with another woman. The two would remain close for years.

And thus Amber Lynn was born—the amber for the sun-kissed color of her fresh and supple skin. The drugs and alcohol would continue for nearly two decades. Little Lynnie was successfully eradicated.

"Cut to a few years later," Lynn said, using her fork to separate the waxed beans and pickled red onions from the warm white new potatoes. "Me, Ginger Lynn and Traci Lords were all on a set together. We're partying in our dressing room. And we started, like, competing over who was going to do what in the film—who was going to do more than the others. We were all sort of friends, but at the same time, we were all competitive. We're all like, *How am I going to outdo these other girls?* Cause we all thought, you know, *I'm the girl who's number one.*"

Lynn shook her head abashedly, an old vet telling war stories. "We all outdid ourselves that day. We all did stuff we'd never done. I shot a DP, a double penetration, and Ginger shot a DP, and then I think Traci shot...no, I didn't do a DP. Ginger did a DP, and I did...."

She threw up her hands; her Donna Karan bracelets jingle-jangled.

Who can remember?

"I started out drinking Ketel One and slicing off crystals of Peruvian rock," Lynn said. "I wound up broken down, drinking Kamchatka out of a half-pint stashed in the bottom of my purse, with my crack pipe stuffed in the lining of my jacket. By the time it was done I was a can't-get-myself-out-of-my-closet type of drug addict."

And I thought I had problems.

We talked for hours. She spoke about her charity efforts, her work with addicts, her desire to be seen as a legitimate player in entertainment history rather than as a closeted embarrassment. "It's just sex," she said. "Everybody does it, people! And everybody watches it? So what's the problem?"

The sun moved across the sky. The light softened. The longer we spoke, the more beautiful she seemed, the more human, the more real. At last the restaurant was empty. I paid the check and walked her out to the valet to get her car.

"Amber Lynn was all the things Lynnie never was," she said as we waited in the portico. "For a while, that's all I cared about; killing off Lynnie. But now I've come full circle. I don't want to be Lynnie, but I don't want to be Amber anymore, either. I just want to be myself."

She paused for a moment, considering what she was about to say next. "Not so long ago, I was living with somebody. We had this huge blowout, and he became abusive and I had to call the cops. And after I put down the phone, you know, he yelled at me, he was like:

'Nobody's going to believe you. You were in fuck films.' He was really trying to belittle me.

"But when I look back on my time in porn, I'm proud of what I did, especially the charity stuff I did for the Youth AIDS Foundation. You can say what you want about porn, but back then we were rock stars; the rock star and the porn-star image began to kind of look alike. We were no longer a seedy little underground business. We were in everybody's living room. Anybody who was hip, it was like *the* thing to have a porn collection. And if you collected anything, you had to have the top three women in porn—Traci Lords, Ginger Lynn and Amber Lynn."

"There should be a Mount Rushmore of Porn," I joked. "You'd be right up there."

She smiled wickedly. "When the cops came to take that abusive roommate of mine away in handcuffs, I thought to myself, *What are they going to remember you for in twenty years, shit bird?*"

Her car appeared. I tipped the valet and opened the door myself. Lynn's dress was short. Her amber-colored, perfectly toned thighs scissored open and closed.

She caught me staring.

I felt myself blush.

"Give me a call if you have any follow-up questions," she said coquettishly.

And then she was gone down the long driveway.

Standing before the limited offerings in my motel room closet, I consider the options for my big night out with Asia Carrera. If you can believe it, my date tonight, this beautiful hapa cyborg and multi-orgasmic member of Mesa, a veteran of more than 350 X-rated titles, hasn't been out to dinner with a man in five years. I'm determined to pull out all the stops.

It is late in the afternoon of my second full day in southern Utah. I feel like I've driven through a time warp, a small town from the past—big families, low crime, everyone smiling, everything closed on Sundays, the sharp white spires of the Mormon temple gleaming against the awesome red rocks. The fact that porn is illegal here and that I'm visiting a porn star has not been left unconsidered.

Neither has the fact that certain of my medical prescriptions aren't valid across state lines. I have dressed thus far to suit my surroundings—sometimes it's best to blend in.

From the moment she picked me up yesterday in her aging SUV, her hair frizzy and pulled back, her mismatched workout suit stained with food, her figure quite a big fuller than in the movies, we'd sort of clicked. If it were true that deep intellectual communion could be included on the list of the fun activities that dwell under the rubric of sexual congress—if intense, revelatory sharing of intimate personal details by two consenting adults were considered a type of sex—you could say that Asia Carrera and I had been going at it like a pair of college kids: nonstop, all over town, all over her house, sitting, standing, eating, walking, driving.

We talked and brunched at Cracker Barrel and Denny's. We sat together for hours in her great room and talked and shared tears. She talked as she autographed naked pictures for me and my son. (What I really wanted was a ceramic Asia figurine, but I was too embarrassed to ask.) We talked and ate dinner with her two children at IHOP—that was me completing the Rockwell-esqe family picture, holding the hand of her blond-mulleted four-year-old son as we crossed the parking lot together. The older child, six-year-old Catty (short for Catalina, the island where her parents became engaged), is a miniature Asia. She held her own in the conversation, chattering away on diverse topics, including the subject of her second-grade class, which she attends with kids who are two and three years older. (The school's principal wanted to skip her yet another grade, but Carrera worried about the social effects. It's bad enough it's a Christian school and Catty is an avowed atheist.)

A brilliant and somewhat manic personality, with an IQ over 150, Carrera owns six cats. They come and go, meowing and spatting among themselves like the female cast of a low-budget porno, through a little cat door in the great room of her overlarge investment property in a semi-rural housing development, where some of the neighbors keep horses. The cats bring in dead birds, bunnies, lizards, chipmunks, scorpions, the occasional snake. Sometimes the birds come back to life. There is a high ceiling. Carrera has to drag a ladder from the garage and climb up there to catch them.

There is seemingly nothing she can't teach herself to do. She is the woman you'd like to be paired with when the end-times come—a glance through her bookshelves reveals a survivalist's bent for self-sufficiency. She riffs on the geology of the surrounding area. The use of a weed whacker. The market for renovating and flipping houses. The several fortunes won and lost investing in Latin American stocks, the high-tech bubble and online gambling. The curious phenomenon of something called a pink sock, an unintended result of anal sex. And the fascinating clinical details of her easy-to-reach G-spot.

Born a Jessica and raised on the Jersey Shore, Carrera was the eldest of four kids. Her mom is German; her dad is Japanese—"a perfect storm of iron will and overachievement," Carrera said. There were dance lessons, piano lessons, spelling championships, math Olympiads, the two appearances at Carnegie Hall before 15. Carrera wanted to be a pianist but her parents wanted her to go to Harvard; they made her quit piano to concentrate on her studies.

"My father is the brilliant one," Asia said. "He's practically autistic. He's definitely Asperger's. And he would come home and go into his computer room and close the door. He never said more than two sentences to me or expressed any emotion or had any input as a parent. My mother was not as smart as me—she didn't know what to do with me. By the time I was in fourth or fifth grade, my mother couldn't do the math anymore. She thought she could make me perform better by punishing me more or beating me harder. That was all she knew how to do.

"To her, an A-minus wasn't good enough. If I came in second place in the school spelling bee, my mom would be like, 'Why didn't you come in first? Who came in first? Why aren't you like them?' I won more awards than anybody in my school. I still have them all in a freaking book in the garage. And I never got a word of praise from her. Nothing was never ever ever good enough. I was always feeling like a turd. I tried to kill myself so often that it was just a joke. My friends were like, 'Ha ha she tried to kill herself again.' I was in hell. I took up cutting as a hobby because I was always trying to vent pain and anger and frustration. I had slashes all up and down my arm. I was always having my stomach pumped in the hospital. It was just miserable."

At 17, she ran away from home. "I was sleeping with people for a place to stay. I was seriously hungry. I'd ask my friends to bring me some Doritos. But I wouldn't go home. I was stubborn."

She was saved from the streets by a full scholarship to Rutgers University, which included room and board. For spending money she worked as a shot girl in a bar. One night the boss asked her to do a private party. She poured drinks, danced on the bar and came home with $350. Of course it didn't take her long to do the math. She dropped out of college, got a nose job (they called her Big Nose all through high school) and started dancing and modeling. Eventually she flew out to Los Angeles and found her way into porn.

"The things I was doing on the streets made porn seem like paradise. At least in porn I could take my pick of the hot guys and get paid a lot of money to do it and call all the shots and stuff. Porn was a step up for me after leaving home, believe me."

The business proved a perfect fit for Carrera's rare type of genius. "I like being a workaholic. I like being a perfectionist. I like being an overachiever—as long as I'm doing what I want to do. I was able to write all my own scripts, star in my movies, design my box covers and do my own makeup and hair—I even cut my own hair. I did freaking everything. And I would show up with my script memorized. I knew everybody else's lines, too, so I could cue everybody if they forgot their lines without screwing up a take.

"I would even bring wardrobe enough for everybody. It's like, if they said, 'We need a watch this scene, I had three watches in my makeup case. If I ripped my outfit, I was like, 'Hold on! I've got a sewing kit!' I was not the prettiest girl in porn by a long shot but I was easily the most perfectionist. The directors loved me. I would always get a call after every shoot with the director kissing my ass and saying thank you for working so hard, because I did. That's why I got hired so much. They knew when they called me I would show up on time and I would be prepared and I would have everything done and then some."

After working for a year as a Vivid girl, Carrera started making her own films with her first husband, the porn director Bud Lee, who was some twenty years her senior. But even as she enjoyed her success, the demands of fame were crippling. One of the few big porn stars who did not elect to go out on the strip circuit, Carrera harbored a terrible secret: "I was terrified of people."

The more popular she became, the more her public recognition grew... the more difficulty Carrera had being in public places. Making pornos was fine. It was the world that scared her. Just the thought of signing autographs at the annual Consumer Electronics show in Las Vegas would leave her "absolutely terrified. I'd curl up in the shower and just cry. See, I'm a perfectionist. And how can you be perfect in front of all of those people with their cameras for hours on end? Nobody can be perfect for that long. The pressure is unbelievable. I've got lipstick on my teeth, there's a booger coming out of my nose. What if I have to sneeze? Is there toilet paper on my shoe? Is somebody looking up my dress? Is there, is, is there like deodorant coming out of my armpit.

"This is how I am. I have a high IQ. My brain goes very fast. I'm able to extrapolate one million things that can go wrong in the space of just walking out there. It's like bzzzz, my brain short circuits with thoughts of all the things that can go wrong. And I'm trying to prepare for every possible thing that could go wrong. I bring like 10,000 outfits and backup outfits and shoes and backup shoes. It's three days and I've got like 15 outfits and 10 pairs of shoes lined up. And *oh my god*. And like backup jewelry and backup makeup and, and I take like two hours to get ready."

Carrera vowed to leave porn by the age of 30 with a wad of cash. She followed her plan—for the most part. Bad luck with investments and an addiction to online gambling took her fortune. But at the age of 29 she met Don Lemmon, a fitness guru and nutritionist. Lemmon had approached her about being a spokesmodel for his male-enhancement product. With his long flowing hair and muscles, he was just her type.

Lemmon moved in with Carrera after three days. The pair was engaged after three weeks, married after three months. A few months later Carrera became pregnant with Catty. "It was such a storybook romance. It was just head-over-heels love. It was so amazing."

After Catty was born, the couple moved to southern Utah, a quiet place with good schools and low housing prices. Lemmon and Carrera figured nobody would recognize her in a place where porn was essentially outlawed. And it turned out to be true, mostly—the few people who did recognize her were thrilled to find a kindred spirit in their midst. They bought a house and settled into an idyllic co-dependent, semirural existence. The family was rarely apart. Carrera became pregnant with their second child. Everything was perfect.

And then, in the early morning hours of June 10, 2006, driving home from a business dinner in Las Vegas, Lemmon lost control of his Jeep. His blood alcohol level was found to be almost triple the legal limit.

"The last entry I'd made on my blog was all about how freaking great my life was and how it was like a Cinderella story. I wrote, literally, 'My life is a fairy tale.' And then my next update was, 'Well, the fairy tale is over.'"

Carrera was 32 years old. And eight months pregnant.

"Every day I would wake up as though I'd been kicked in the gut, thinking, *Oh my God, the nightmare is still real; he's still not here.* I would take his urn down and just lie on it and cry and go, 'Daddy, please come home, please come home, please come home.' Catty would come over and she would cry and she would push me off the urn. I didn't want to upset her; she was only 15 months old. And I knew it wasn't good for me to be lying on the floor screaming in hysterics with a baby in my belly. I wasn't in a good place. I was completely co-dependent on Don. I hadn't driven a car in two years. I didn't even go to the store without him. I was scared of the whole world. I'm socially phobic. It was so hard on me."

Then she found out that Lemmon was broke.

"Don had told me he was doing really well and business was great. I wasn't working except for my website; he was paying all the bills, I was just using my money for play. Everything was cool. Or so I thought. It turned out that he was like robbing Peter to pay Paul, and he was juggling all these debts because he wanted to keep me in the lifestyle that I was accustomed to. It turned out we had $2,000 in the bank, which was like enough to pay one mortgage payment, and that was it. And then all these debts, including like $30,000 owed to the IRS and then all his product makers are calling me up and saying, 'Well, he owes me for this and he owes me for that.' I was like, 'I don't have any money to give you people, and I'm grieving my husband

and I'm freaking pregnant and my world just freaking fell apart.' Oh god, it was such a nightmare."

Carrera went through the paperwork necessary to give up her unborn son for adoption. "I didn't think I could handle it. I was just such a mess. I was like, 'I've got a 15 month old, no husband, no money. I'm probably going to lose my house. How am I going to take care of another kid? So I found somebody who was going to adopt him. She was half Asian and had a white husband and had a son who looked just like Catty. I was like 'Okay, this is going to be perfect.'"

As it happened, Carrera went into labor two weeks early. For months, even before Lemmon's death, she'd been planning to deliver her child at home. She decided to proceed.

"I set Catty up with her sippy cup, watching a *Wiggles* video in the next room. And then I got the shower curtain down on the floor and all the tools and stuff laid out. I tried to do a water birth in the backyard, but the water was fucking freezing. I'm sitting there thinking, *This is not relaxing.* Then Catty climbs into the pool with all her clothes on, so then I have to take Catty and change her into warm dry clothes—meanwhile I'm having contractions. I called the midwife, and I was like, 'You know what? I guess it's time to go to the hospital.' But then I got on my knees over the birthing pad, and this little head pops out of me. I'm like, *Oh my God! There's a baby down there.* So I just delivered him.

"And there he was. He was lying on the shower curtain and the towel, and I'm taking pictures of him—he's still connected to me by the umbilical cord and I'm taking pictures. And I've got these great pictures of Catty looking at him, like, *What is that thing?* It was so cute. She was so small, looking at the baby, and there's little Devin, and he's like covered in ketchup and mustard.

Then I carried Devin into the bathroom and took pictures of us together in the mirror, and he's still connected to me by the cord and I'm taking pictures in the mirror of us. And by the time I got him cleaned up and swaddled, the doorbell rang. It's the midwife: 'I'm here!' And I said, 'Well you can go now, I'm all done." And I open the door and I have the baby in my arms. And she's like, 'Oh my god!'

"The funny thing is: Had Devin come on time, he would have been adopted. It was just a freak of fate that he came two weeks early. But everything happens for a reason, right? It's weird, but the whole ordeal of the birth was exactly what I needed to make me feel strong enough to be able to handle raising two kids by myself. I thought, If I can birth a baby by myself, I can do this without Don. I was like, I am Superwoman; I can do this. It was an incredible high."

Then another twist:

About a year after Devin's birth, a statement came for a life insurance policy premium. She'd been bugging Lemmon to get one. Turns out he actually had. Due to the circumstances of his death, the policy paid double.

"Right now, my life is my kids, period," she said, standing by the fish tank at her house, feeding a giant one-eyed pacu named Pacu. "I don't have the time and energy to dedicate to a relationship. My kids don't have another parent. They don't have other family here. They don't have anybody but me, and I'm a perfectionist workaholic. If that means putting my own needs aside, that's absolutely fine. I'm totally cool with that. It's as though Catty is the Asia that could have been if she hadn't been abused by her parents. And Devin is such a special little dude. I'll be Mommy until they're 18. That's fine with me."

The elevator dings open and I cross the lobby of my motel, which doubles in the morning as the site of an all-you-can-eat breakfast buffet. I decide to damn the local sensibilities and go with Full Writer Drag: black dress shirt, black jeans, black leather car coat, high top Dr. Martens. Asia hasn't been on a dinner date with a man in over five years. She deserves the full treatment, does she not?

I wave to the clerk behind the front desk; he's been so nice, this towering, apple cheeked Mormon lad with a friendly smile.

Only right now he's not smiling.

He looks as though he's just seen the devil.

Before I can react, someone links my arm. Asia Carrera towers over me in four-inch fuck-me pumps. She is wearing a long blue floral dress with a plunging neckline; her cinematic 36Cs are on full display. Her hair has been carefully coiffed; her eyes are vividly awash in her trademark blue eye shadow and thick China-doll mascara—just like in all her old photos.

Dumbstruck, I'm led through the automatic doors. I recover my wits enough to remember to walk her around to the driver's side.

"Just because I'm all dressed up doesn't mean anybody's getting lucky," she purrs.

"I feel like I'm already lucky," I tell her, buckling my seat belt. It sounds like a good line. But I think I really mean it.

Sure, I have some big-time hurt to get over. I have to find a way to finance the future for myself and my son—and to pay "equalizing payments" for the next five years and alimony for the next seven. And I have to find a way to move on, to heal the wounds—presumably I'll be able to trust someone again; presumably I'll want to share my life with another human being. I still find myself crying at times; I still find myself spiriting around the house like a ghost, moving from place to place, trying to figure out where the fuck I'm trying to go.

But you know what? I think I'll be okay. Fuck my ex for fucking me over like that—she'll be sorry someday, I'm sure of it. I'll make more money. I'll love my son; already our bond is much stronger than it ever was. I'll turn the hurt I've suffered into wisdom; it will make me a better writer and a better human being. If Asia, Nina, Amber and Kay can transcend their various trials and miseries, certainly I can too.

"Did you see the face on the kid behind the front desk?" I ask Carrera.

"It's nice to know I still have my secret powers," she said.

And off we went, in the direction of the setting sun—two grown-ups with lots of hurt and history to put behind us, doing the best we can to move along.

(2011)

Also By Mike Sager

NONFICTION

Scary Monsters and Super Freaks:
Stories of Sex, Drugs, Rock 'n' Roll, and Murder

Revenge of the Donut Boys:
True Stories of Lust, Fame, Survival, and Multiple Personality

Wounded Warriors
Those for Whom the War Never Ends

Tattoos & Tequila:
To Hell and Back with One of Rock's Most Notorious Frontmen

Next Wave
America's New Generation of Great Literary Journalists

FICTION

Deviant Behavior
A Novel of Sex, Drugs, Fatherhood, and Crystal Skulls.

High Tolerance
A Novel of Sex, Celebrity, Murder, Miscegenation... and Marijuana.

Acknowledgments

Marvin M. Sager (rip), Beverly Sager, Wendy Sager, William "Buddy" Sager and family, the Culpeper Cousins.

David Granger, Peter Griffin, Lisa Hintelmann, Ryan D'Agostino, Tyler Cabot, Josh Schollmeyer. Helene F. Rubinstein, Mark Warren, Ross McCammon, Richard Dorment, Peter Martin, Mark Mikin, Robert Scheffler, Kevin McDonnell, Lydia Woolever, Elizabeth Sile, Aimee E. Bartol, Michael Norsing, Alison Unterrelner, David Curcurito.

Gloria Hwang, Ziad Damanhoury, Sara Adams, Phil Adams, Tanya Huang, Sohrob Nikzad, Emily Stanford, Andrew Mayer, Bruce Kluger, Jeremy Spencer, Arthur Jay Harris, Heather and Bill Kenney at La Jolla Photo, Yvonne Negron, Josh Cohen, Steve and Sheri Cohen, Walt Harrington, Andrew Greenstein and SF Appworks, Siori Kitajima, Darius Zagrean, Edwin Lap, Martjin Lap, Milan Ajdinovic, Rod Jemison, Peter Bogue, Malik Rasheed.

Permissions

The following story was first published as a shorter excerpt in *Esquire*:
"The Man Who Never Was", May 2009.

The following stories were first published in the same or different form in *Esquire*:
"Ugly", May 2012; "A Girl in Love", May 2012; "The Someone You're Not", March 2011; "Bobby Jindal, All American", February 2009; "The Boss", January 2012; "Vetville", July 2011; "If Someone Shot You In The Face And Left You For Dead, Would You Try To Save His Life?" December 2011; "The Zen of Big Balls Pete", December 2009.

"The Demographic Man" was originally published in a different form under the title "The Secret Life of a Well Dressed Man" in *Esquire*, March 2009

The following story was first published as a shorter excerpt in *Playboy*:
"The Porn Identity", September 2011.

About the Author

MIKE SAGER is a best-selling author and award-winning reporter. A former *Washington Post* staff writer under Watergate investigator Bob Woodward, he worked closely with gonzo journalist Hunter S. Thompson during his years as a contributing editor to *Rolling Stone*. Sager is the author of four collections of non-fiction, two novels, and one biography. He has served for more than fifteen years as a writer at large for *Esquire*. In 2010 he won the American Society of Magazine Editors' National Magazine Award for profile writing for his article "The Man Who Never Was." Many of his stories have been optioned for film. For more information, please see www.mikesager.com.

About the Publisher

The Sager Group was founded in 1984. In 2012 it was chartered as a multi-media artists' and writers' consortium, with the intent of empowering those who make art—an umbrella beneath which artists can pursue, and profit from, their craft directly, without gatekeepers. TSG publishes eBooks; manages musical acts and produces live shows; ministers to artists and provides modest grants; and produces documentary, feature and web-based films. By harnessing the means of production, The Sager Group helps artists help themselves, *artifex te adiuva*. For more information, please see www.thesagergroup.net.

Made in the USA
San Bernardino, CA
15 February 2018